Architectural Rendering

Architectural Rendering

The Techniques of Contemporary Presentation

Third Edition

Albert O. Halse

Edited by
Spencer L. George
Helen A. Halse

McGraw-Hill Book Company

New York St. Louis San Francisco Auckland Bogotá
Hamburg London Madrid Mexico Milan Montreal
New Delhi Panama Paris São Paulo Singapore Sydney
Tokyo Toronto

Library of Congress Cataloging-in-Publication Data

Halse, Albert O.
    Architectural rendering.

    Bibliography: p.
    Includes index.
    1. Architectural rendering.   2. Architectural
drawing.   3. Architecture — Designs and plans —
Presentation drawings.   I. George, Spencer L.
II. Halse, Helen A.   III. Title.
NA2780.H3   1988   720′.28′4   87-21365
ISBN 0-07-025629-2

1234567890   HAL/HAL   8983210987

ISBN 0-07-025629-2

The editors for this book were Nadine M. Post and Georgia Kornbluth, the designer
was Naomi Auerbach, and the production manager was Thomas G. Kowalczyk. It was
set in Auriga by Progressive Typographers.
Printed and bound by Halliday Lithographic.

In memory of
ALBERT O. HALSE,
architect, renderer, and teacher

Contents

Color Plates

Foreword

This book is devoted to an analysis of the pictorial method of design study used by the architect. Called "rendering," or "delineation," this pictorial study makes it possible to visualize structures while they are still in the design stage. It is an indispensable tool for the architect.

Albert O. Halse

The editors of this third edition of *Architectural Rendering* are committed to the above opening statement from the foreword to the second edition. Those who wish to learn the art of rendering should understand that dedication, practice, and experimentation are more important than simply talent. This edition broadens the scope of *Architectural Rendering* by including computer graphics, reprographics, and photographic techniques as tools for rendering. It is important to present a general overview of the field of delineation as a valued tool for architects, designers, professional delineators, and teachers of architecture or design.

Albert Halse attempted to provide a simple approach to the study of rendering; in this edition, some of his methods have been combined, altered, or expanded. The principles which apply to all media have been emphasized and illustrated where necessary. Chapters devoted to composition, color theory, light, and entourage have been reinforced with discussions of mixed media and the importance of value and color studies, along with descriptions of methods for experimental testing of various media. Most chapters contain examples of both student and professional renderings, and the last chapter contains an expanded gallery of professional work.

The editors would like to stress that this book covers numerous methods of rendering. What is important is the general approach to rendering rather than how to do rendering in any specific style. The first chapter gives a brief overview of the changing history of architectural drawing and rendering throughout recorded time. Without a doubt, new materials, media, and techniques will continue to be developed in the future of rendering, as in every other art form. The reader who studies this new edition and applies the information provided should be able to acquire skill and to experience success and confidence in experimenting with new technologies as they arise.

It is the author's thesis that all readers of this book will be inspired and encouraged by the information provided. The principles presented should be practiced and applied as many times as necessary to develop skill in their use. The skills required in rendering are developed in direct proportion to the frequency of their use.

Spencer L. George
Helen A. Halse

Professor Halse hoped that the information in the original 1960 edition of *Architectural Rendering* would be a source of inspiration and encouragement to architects, designers, professional delineators, and teachers of architecture and design. Over the years these hopes have been realized. It is, therefore, a source of deep satisfaction to me that the publishers selected Spencer L. George, architect, to revise and update the book and that I have had the opportunity of working with him. It is my hope that this new edition will continue to teach and inspire young architects and also be a useful reference work in schools and offices.

Experience has shown that the architectural "picture" or rendering is the most effective means of communicating to the client not only the architect's design for the proposed building but also the use of materials and color, and the building's relation to adjoining buildings.

In 1960, professional ethics precluded the use of Professor Halse's own renderings in the book. In this edition, however, as a matter of historical record, we are pleased to include a rendering that he did between 1943 and 1948 (see Figure 1.33). This rendering not only illustrates his technique but also serves as an example of a commercial building of the time.

Helen A. Halse

Acknowledgments

The editors of the third edition of *Architectural Rendering* would like to take this opportunity on behalf of Albert O. Halse to pay tribute to those who have been involved in this effort.

This volume has been made possible by the support, encouragement, and faith of some special individuals. I thank, first, Helen A. Halse for sharing in the organizing, assembling, and refining of each chapter; second, my wife Jane and our son Ian for their daily inspiration; and third, my mother for making it all possible. Special thanks are extended to the architectural firm of Swanke Hayden Connell Ltd. and to the firm's entire staff of fellow employees and friends, who have my respect and admiration. In addition, there are some rare individuals who must be mentioned because of their friendship over the years: William Rosecrans, William C. Wilkinson, George Hahl, Lou DiPaolo, Jeremy Robinson, Robert Kenyon, Warren Pope, and Robert Zaccone.

Like previous editions, this edition is based on the effort of the students, professional delineators, and architects whose work is reproduced in the book, as well as on the cooperation and enthusiasm of friends too numerous to mention, who have made this effort a sincere pleasure.

Spencer L. George

Sincere apologies are extended to architects who may still recognize some of their uncredited designs in student work; if such omissions are called to the author's attention, he will be glad to make amends in future editions.

The author also thanks the professional delineators and architects whose work is represented for their sincere interest and cooperation.

Finally he wishes to acknowledge his debt to sources of many of the illustrations for Chapter 1, The Development of Rendering. These sources are indicated below; fuller information will be found in the Bibliography at the end of the book.

Figure	Source
1.1	Jean Capart: *Egyptian Art*
1.2	N. DeGaris Davies: "The Rock Tombs of El Amarna"
1.3	H. Carter and A. H. Gardiner: "The Tomb of Rameses IV and the Turin Plan of a Royal Tomb"
1.4, 1.7, 1.8, 1.22	James Burford: "The Historical Development of Architectural Drawing to the End of the Eighteenth Century"
1.5	George S. Goodspeed: *A History of the Babylonians and Assyrians*
1.6	Henricus Jordan: *Forma urbis Romae, regionum XIII*
1.9	Robert Willis: *Facsimile of the Sketchbook of Wilars de Honecort*
1.10	Georg Moller: *Bemerkuingen über die aufgefundene original-zeichnung des domes zu Koeln*
1.11, 1.16	Uffizi: *Desegni di architettura*
1.12	Dagobert Frey: *Bramante's St. Peter entwurf und seine appokryphen*
1.13	Valeria Mariani: *La Facciata Di San Pietro Secondo Michelangelo*
1.14	Giovanni Battista Falda: *Le chiesa di Roma*
1.15, 1.20	Hermann Schmitz: *Baumeisterzeichnungen des 17 und 18 jahrhunderts*
1.17	Giovanni Battista Piranesi: *Roman Architecture, Sculpture and Ornament*
1.18	Jacques Androuet du Cerceau: *Les plus excellents bastiments de France*
1.19	Anthoine le Pautre: *Les oeuvres d'architecture d'Anthoine le Pautre*
1.21	Reginald Blomfield: *Architectural Drawing and Draughtsmen*
1.23	James Malton: *An Essay on British Cottage Architecture*
1.24	Johannes Kip: *Brittania Illustrata*
1.25	Maurice Fouche: *Percier et Fontaine, biographie critique*
1.26	Eugene Emmanuel Viollet-le-Duc: "Compositions et dessins de Viollet-le-Duc"
1.27, 1.28	August Brisebach: *Carl Friedrich Schinkel*
1.29	"Techniques and Tradition in British Architecture." Courtesy of Alan G. Thomas, present owner, and Roger Senhouse, former owner, of original
1.30	Joseph Gandy: *Designs for Cottages, Cottage Farms and Other Rural Buildings, including Entrance Gates and Lodges*
1.31	Maurice B. Adams: "Architectural Drawing"

Albert O. Halse

Architectural Rendering

chapter 1

The Development of Rendering

Art has been practiced in various forms since Paleolithic times. First efforts were confined to achieving beauty and symmetry in tools. Later, artists found enjoyment in the use of color on their bodies and in their clothing, as well as in ornament. Evidence of the first expressions in painting and sculpture have been found in caverns in Spain and France, where, with the help of artificial light, artists painted numerous pictures in color, chiefly of animals. Paints were made by mixing red and yellow ochre with animal fat.

During the Mesolithic age people still roamed as hunters, and although artistic achievements were less impressive than formerly, both metal and writing were invented. The written word enabled people to communicate information, and by passing it along to those who lived after them, to pyramid it into what we call "civilization." As people settled in groups, clear communication of information became more important and both the picture and the written word were needed.

When people built simple structures they continued to use words, but when buildings became complicated it became necessary to explain the ideas to another person or to make a record of the building. Builders used a pictorial method which gave not only a briefer description, but a more accurate one.

The pictorial method seems to have received strong encouragement from the erection of the great monuments of ancient Egypt. There, in the Ancient Kingdom (4400–2466 B.C.), architectural hieroglyphs were invented (Figure 1.1).

During the Amarna period (1375–1350 B.C.), a style of drawing combining plan and elevation was developed and used not only for the guidance of builders, but also as part of the mortuary art on the walls of the tombs of kings (Figure 1.2).

This pictorial type of drawing may be considered a distant relative of present-day delineation. For actual construction, plans were drawn on papyrus (Figure

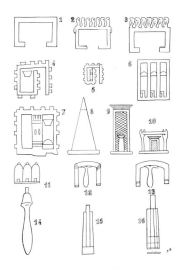

Fig. 1.1 Architectural Hieroglyphs.

Fig. 1.2 "The Palace," Painted on Stucco.

Fig. 1.3 Plan of the Tomb of Rameses IV,
Painted on Papyrus.

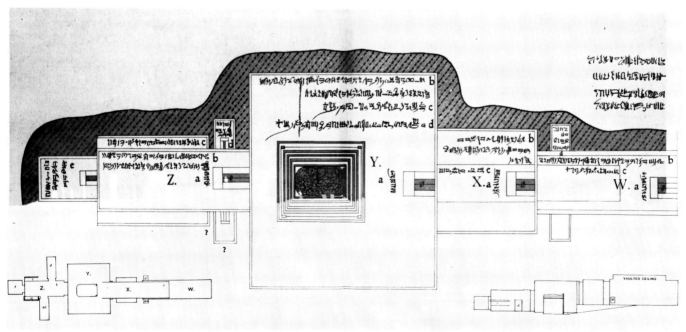

1.3) or on limestone (Figure 1.4). Both of the plans illustrated were drawn in several colors of ink to represent the various materials shown.

While this remarkable development was going on in Egypt, a similar development toward the pictorial was in progress in Babylonia and Assyria. There earth, landscape, fields, and buildings were drawn on clay tablets with a pointed stick. Curved lines were avoided because they were difficult to draw in soft clay (Figure 1.5).

Although there are many epigraphic and literary references to a developed system of architectural drawing in ancient Greece, none of these drawings has been found. This is probably because they were made using such perishable materials as whitened or waxed wood, lead or charcoal on wood, and pottery. Authorities who have studied the administration of the Greek temples explain that the choice of wood or marble depended on the importance of the document and the length of time it was to last. Architectural plans were evidently classified as temporary.

The early Roman works were built by Greeks. A Greek architect, for example, was imported for the construction of the temples of Jupiter and Juno, both of which were built in Rome in 146 B.C. But because the practical side of architecture appealed to the Romans, they soon undertook the work for themselves. Thermae, amphitheaters, basilicas, temples, aqueducts, bridges, tombs, palaces, and houses all testify to the ability the Romans eventually developed. There is little doubt that drawings must have been used in building these great works. Their very complexity and the perfection of parts are proof enough. Yet Rome, like Greece, left few drawings, and only record plans on marble, such as "The Marble Plan of Rome" (Figure 1.6) have survived.

Fig. 1.4   A Plan on Limestone of the Tomb of Rameses IX.

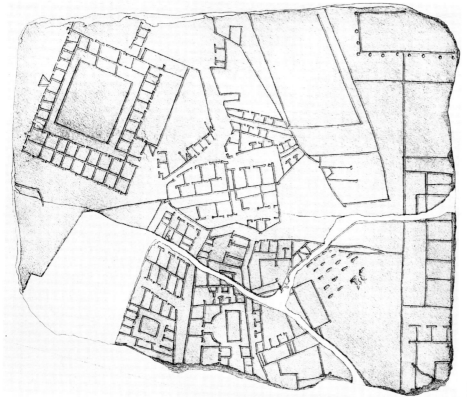

Fig. 1.5   Clay Tablet with Plan of Nippur.

Fig. 1.6   The Marble Plan of Rome, Fragment 184.

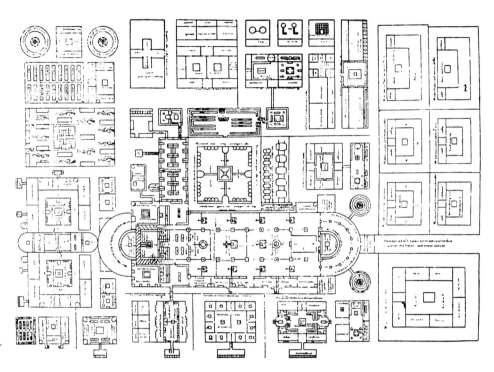

Fig. 1.7 The Plan of the Cloister of St. Gallen.

Drawing in the Monasteries

The lack of pictorial architectural drawing (other than the plan drawings mentioned) extends to the period between the fall of Rome and the year 1000. What little drawing was done then was probably executed in monasteries, where the feeble flame of civilization was kept alive. The plan of the Cloister of St. Gallen (A.D. 820) shown in Figure 1.7, a building on the shores of Lake Constance, in what is now Switzerland, is typical of this simple type of drawing.

A later plan (Figure 1.8), this one quite pictorial, was produced some time in the twelfth century by the monk Eadwin. In this drawing the elevations are given a false perspective to help explain the form of the building.

Unfortunately, the period during which the monks built the great abbeys was marked by many construction failures because the monks were unskilled in engineering calculations. As the abbeys grew richer, however, they began to employ lay architects, or master masons. These men, with their groups of masons, rarely settled in communities, but usually wandered from job to job. The bonds of fellowship between the members of the masons' guild seem to have been strong, and gradually, building returned to lay hands.

Master Masons

Of the many names of architect-craftsmen that have come down to us, one stands out — that of a Frenchman named Villard de Honnecourt, who lived about 1250. Like most cultured men of his time, de Honnecourt traveled through France, from north to east, and across the entire German Empire. During these travels he recorded details of French cathedrals, making ink sketches in a vellum sketchbook that he kept for his own use and for the instruction of his pupils. Here we find plans, elevations, and even pseudoperspectives (Figure 1.9).

The tireless work of de Honnecourt and men like him eventually produced the great cathedrals of Europe. These were built from plan and elevation drawings, supplemented by details which were made on the site as the job progressed.

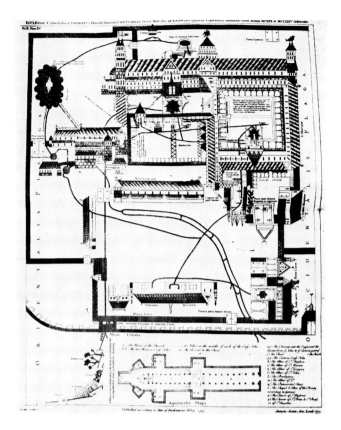

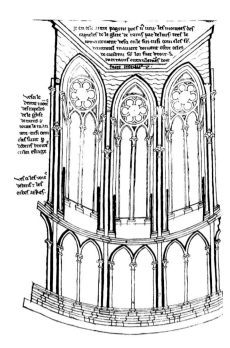

Fig. 1.9 The Cathedral at Rheims: Inside View of Choir Chapel.

Fig. 1.8 A Twelfth-Century Plan of the Cathedral and Monastery of Canterbury.

During this period draftsmanship reached a high peak of perfection (Figure 1.10). True, because the principles of descriptive geometry were not yet known (they were to be developed in 1794 by Monge) such oddities occur as the lack of foreshortening in circular windows in the splayed corners of towers, but in spite of these shortcomings the Gothic draftsman produced some beautiful drawings.

Fig. 1.10 Cologne Cathedral: Partial Elevation of Tower.

Because master masons lived on the job for its duration (and sometimes the lives of three master masons were consumed in the building of one cathedral), they were able to visualize the end results of their conception without the help of renderings. They, therefore, needed to make only working drawings, supplementing these with an occasional model. The beauty of the Gothic cathedrals of France and Germany testifies to the success of this system.

Renaissance Rendering

Rendering as we know it was born during the Italian Renaissance. The discovery and publication in the fifteenth century of the *Vitruvius Treatise on Architecture* (written during the reign of Caesar Augustus) stimulated a new interest in classical antiquity and an upsurge in the activity of building. In Italy, where the Reformation did not take hold, and where comparatively few churches had been built during the Middle Ages, there was a revival on a grand scale of church as well as domestic architecture. It was in the building of these churches that architects developed the principles of perspective and rendering.

Whereas the Gothic churches were constructed far from the influence of the Church of Rome, the architects of Italy had to work in constant consultation with the popes. As the heads of the church were vitally interested in the appearance of the new buildings, it was necessary to make as many "pictures" of the proposed structures as possible. The stage had been set for the invention of scientific perspective by the painters of architectural subjects, who, although they had no rules, used "perspective by eye." Paolo Uccello, a Florentine, and Andrea Mantegna of Padua were among the first writers on the rules of perspective. Others, such as Leonardo da Vinci, Michelangelo, Raphael, Titian, and Giulio Romano, followed. During the sixteenth century more elaborate books were written on the subject by Serlio and Vignola, and still later, in the seventeenth century, a thorough treatise on perspective was published by Pozzo.

Perspective, Paper, and Printing

The late-fifteenth-century Italian architects Bramante and Peruzzi (Figures 1.11 and 1.12) were the first to design in perspective.

Fig. 1.11 Sectional Perspective of St. Peter's, Rome. (Draftsman: Donato Bramante.)

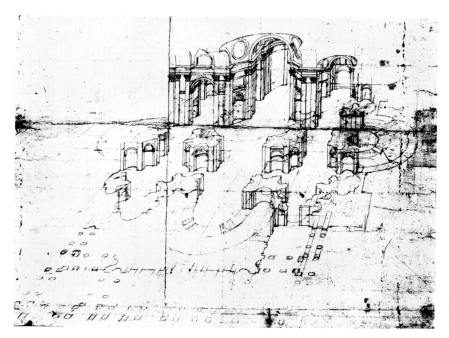

Fig. 1.12 Sectional Perspective of St. Peter's, Rome. (Draftsman: Baldassare Peruzzi.)

Another great stimulus to the drawing of the Renaissance was the invention of paper. When Egyptian papyrus was brought to Europe it quickly became popular because it cost less than the animal skins then in use and because it could be rolled. It continued to be used occasionally in Italy until the eleventh century, when parchment and cotton paper were introduced.

The Chinese are given credit for developing the art of making paper from fibrous materials[1] converted to pulp in water, and the earliest clearly dated paper shows the year A.D. 264.

The Arabians introduced the art of paper making into Europe through Spain, and linen and hemp fiber came into use, as well as cotton. By the seventeenth century, France was the center of the industry, shipping paper to Russia, Sweden, Denmark, Holland, Germany, and England. Both Holland and England perfected the process by the beginning of the nineteenth century.

While the fifteenth-century Italian architects found paper still expensive and scarce, it was more abundant and easier to draw on than any of the materials previously available; this fact encouraged experimentation and, therefore, progress.

The printing press, together with the invention of paper and the development of an understanding of perspective, made possible the exchange of architectural ideas through books. It was only a step from the linear perspectives of Bramante and Peruzzi to the development of the full picture, or the expression of form in perspective by the use of light and shade (Figure 1.13).

At first the buildings were rendered either in perspective or in a false-perspective type of elevation. There was no attempt to add the surrounding environment to the rendering. Later, however, the buildings were represented in actual settings (Figure 1.14). Here the values and scale of the surroundings not only located the church in its actual setting, but also complemented the main building in the picture.

Fig. 1.13 A Design for the Facade of St. Peter's, Rome. (Draftsman: Michelangelo Buonarotti.)

---

[1]Joel Munsell, *Chronology of the Origin and Progress of Paper and Paper Making*, 5th ed., J. Munsell, Albany, New York, 1876, p. 5.

Fig. 1.14 Church Dedicated to St. Luke Evangelist.

Fig. 1.15 Stage Design for Il Ciro. (Draftsman: Filipo Juvara.)

Other Italian Renderings

While the architects of Italy had the church as an important client, they were also commissioned to execute stage designs. These were, for the most part, drawn in perspective and shaded with watercolor washes (Figure 1.15). Baldassare Peruzzi (1481–1537) was another architect who used a combination of perspective and shading with watercolor wash (Figure 1.16). In addition, he sometimes worked in pen and ink over a preliminary red, brown, red and brown, or black charcoal sketch. Often he used brown or gray washes, and occasionally he employed bistre, a dark-brown watercolor.

Another source of income for the architect in Italy lay in the great interest of the public in pictures of Roman ruins in imaginary compositions. The most skilled and prolific delineator of this type of rendering was Piranesi (1720–

Fig. 1.16 Stage Design with Roman Buildings of Ancient Times. (Draftsman: Baldassare Peruzzi.)

1778), whose works are still regarded as masterpieces of draftsmanship and composition. Figure 1.17, Tempico Antico, illustrates his ability to "lead" the eye of the spectator to the vital portions of the drawing.

Early Delineation in France and Germany

Although delineation had developed in Italy during the fifteenth century, it was not until a century later that the architects of France became aware of these new developments. At first the French were timid in their efforts to use the newfound skills, but eventually they not only employed the rendered ground-level perspective, but also began to experiment with aerial perspectives. These were first drawn without surrounding land beyond the borders of the immediate plot of land (Figure 1.18), but later were shown with complete surroundings. The French later began to study their buildings by the use of the rendered sectional perspective (Figure 1.19).

Germany, where building was dominated by the master mason for several centuries, was slow to adopt the rendered perspective. For the most part, archi-

Fig. 1.17 Tempico Antico. (Draftsman: Piranesi.)

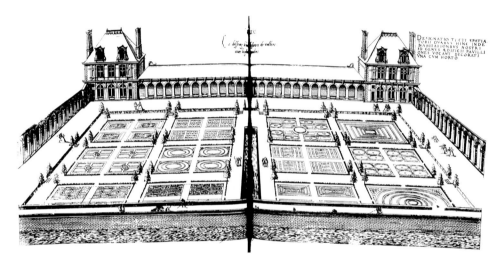

Fig. 1.18 An Aerial View. (Draftsman: DuCerceau.)

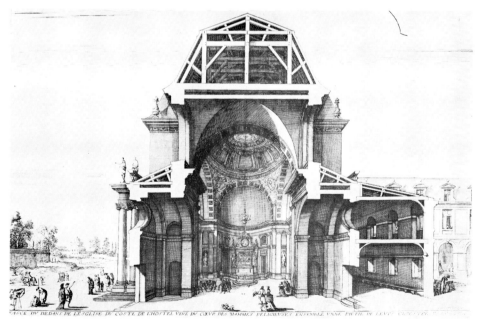

Fig. 1.19 L'Eglise Du Monastere du Port Royal. (Draftsman: Le Pautre.)

Fig. 1.20 Entwurf für ein Warenlager. (Draftsman: Andreas Gaertner.)

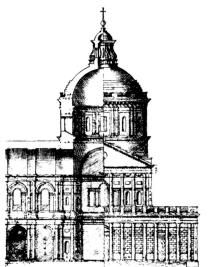

tects still used plan and elevation to study their buildings. Architects' training emphasized engineering, and the pictorial approach of the rendered perspective had no place. A few of the German Renaissance architects traveling in other countries, however, began to render elevations of their projects (Figure 1.20).

Early Delineation in England

Because England was so far away from Rome, it was the last country to be stimulated by the new movement, and English Renaissance drawings were linear in quality. Inigo Jones (1573–1652), who traveled in Italy and modeled his work after the Italian architects of the fifteenth and sixteenth centuries, rendered first in pen and line (Figure 1.21) and later in line and pale wash. When the ''grand tour'' became popular among the wealthy, travelers' stories of the new type of Italian architectural delineation influenced spread of the style.

The rendered elevation and the fully rendered ground perspective were soon added to the architect's presentation of plan, section, and elevation (Figure 1.22). During this period, James Malton published *An Essay on British Cottage Architecture*, complete with rendered elevations. Figure 1.23 shows two of the simpler designs, both rendered in watercolor. Other media used were pen and ink; wash used alone or with pen and ink; or watercolor used alone, with pencil, or with pen and ink.

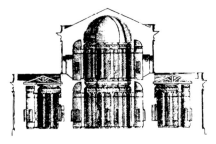

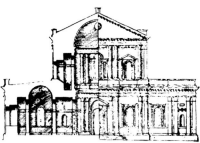

Fig. 1.21 Studies for a Church. (Draftsman: Inigo Jones.)

Fig. 1.22 St. Paul's, Covent Garden. (Draftsman: Thomas Malton.)

Fig. 1.23 Two Cottage Designs. (Draftsman: James Malton.)

Additional stimulation to the art of architectural rendering was provided by a number of foreigners who came to England and were commissioned to make "views" of English buildings and landscapes. These were, for the most part, aerial perspectives (similar to those done in France) of such subjects as the king's palace, seats of the nobility and gentry, cathedrals, and public buildings (Figure 1.24).

Nineteenth-Century France

The end of the eighteenth century in Europe was a period of revolution, and also one of invention. The migration of architectural thought was hastened by improvements in travel and communication. In France, architectural education became formalized and delineation was influenced accordingly. The Ecole des Beaux Arts stressed beauty of delineation in the study of designs, while the Ecole

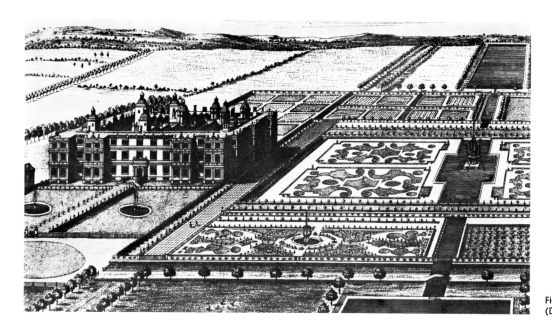

Fig. 1.24 Longleat House in Wiltshire. (Draftsman: Jan Kip.)

Fig. 1.25 Vue de l'Intérieur de L'Eglise Notre Dame. (Draftsman: Charles Percier.)

Polytechnique emphasized the simple engineering technique for architects primarily interested in construction. It was the Ecole des Beaux Arts which influenced rendering most strongly and created the climate for the development of many of the advances in delineation in France.

The work of Charles Percier (1764–1838), one of the architects to Napoleon, provides an excellent cross section of delineation as it existed in France at the beginning of the nineteenth century. An examination of his drawings shows the use of most of the techniques and media known in his day, including the modern graphite pencil, which was invented in 1795 and soon replaced sticks made from pulverized graphite, metallic lead, or metallic silver. Many of Percier's drawings were made in pencil washed with bistre. He also combined pencil with Chinese ink and used Chinese ink alone. Occasionally on the same drawing he combined pen and ink, Chinese ink, and watercolor. An example of his use of pen and ink is shown in Figure 1.25.

Even more prolific, and certainly the greatest draftsman of nineteenth-century France, was Eugene Emmanuel Viollet-le-Duc (1814–1879), who consolidated and combined the various techniques of those who lived before him. One of his most realistic perspectives was the "Projet Academia Impériale du Musique" (Figure 1.26), which was made in a combination of pencil and watercolor. By careful manipulation of his brush so as to obtain a certain amount of tonal variation and texture, the accurate plotting of shades and shadows, the selection of an excellent viewpoint, and the use of dark values in the foreground and light values in the distance, he obtained an almost photographic quality. Since his renderings were made a short time after the invention of the photographic camera (sometime between 1816 and 1829), it seems obvious that his realistic style was an attempt to simulate the accuracy of the new instrument.

Nineteenth-Century Germany and England

The same kind of photographic quality was obtained by Carl Friedrich Schinkel in Germany (1781–1841) in his "Dekoration zur 'Zauberflote'" ("Design for 'The Magic Flute'," Figure 1.27). While the watercolor rendering illustrates his ability to simulate reality when he wished to do so, his pencil presentation "Packhofgebaude, Berlin" (Figure 1.28) shows that he could also, when he wished, present a much more simplified study. This simplification may have been a frank recognition of the simplicity of "modern" architecture, which was beginning to appear.

Fig. 1.26 Projet Academia Imperiale du Musique. (Draftsman: Viollet le Duc.)

Fig. 1.27 Dekoration zur Zauberflote. (Draftsman: Carl Friedrich Schinkel.)

This versatility is also evident in the renderings of nineteenth-century England. James Wyatt (1746–1813) in his "Preliminary Design of Fonthill Abbey" (Figure 1.29), shows the building standing starkly in the late afternoon sunlight against the beautiful English countryside. Instead of describing the building in detail, this treatment emphasized the mood it was to have. During the same period, numerous small cottage designs were done in a similar manner (Figure 1.30).

A number of architects also began to explore the possibilities of the newly invented pencil. Sir Charles Barry, in his "Design for Dunrobbin Castle" (Figure 1.31), seems to have understood the new medium better than most of his contemporaries, many of whom merely covered the paper with graphite in their effort to show detail.

Twentieth-Century Delineation

The beginning of the twentieth century brought overwhelming changes to architecture and the methods used to illustrate buildings from conception through

Fig. 1.28 Packhofgebaude, Berlin. (Draftsman: Carl Friedrich Schinkel.)

Fig. 1.29 Preliminary Design of Fonthill Abbey. (Draftsman: James Wyatt.)

final design. All human endeavor was to be challenged by the refined technology of the tools used in the industrial revolution; hence political, social, and economic changes occurred with each passing decade of the new century. Depressions, world wars, atomic power, and space travel are only a few factors which have affected and shifted world power.

Traditionally, a student of architectural design studied at the Ecole des Beaux Arts Institute in Paris, which was founded in 1671. "Ecole students," as they were known, studied according to a system established at the Institute. The established method of teaching ecole students involved several elements: first, the students worked as members of a studio (atelier); second, older students helped to give instruction to younger students; third, a jury process was organized under the direction of the master architect; and fourth, the students learned from critiques of their *esquisses* (sketches). The ecole educational system was adopted worldwide and, among other things, all students were required to know the classical orders of architecture. Upon completion of study, the ecole student was well versed in architectural history and was also a creator of form and a trained delineator of form.

The Ecole des Beaux Arts educational system went unchallenged until 1919, when the Bauhaus was founded in Germany under the direction of Walter Gropius. The ideas of the Bauhaus influenced teaching concepts by merging design, building, and craftsmanship into one overall study. Unfortunately, Gropius's Bauhaus school was forced to close in 1933 for political reasons and never reopened. Many of the famous Bauhaus faculty migrated to England and the United States, where international recognition came to some of its artisans — Gropius, Ludwig Miës van der Rohe, Laszlo Moholy-Nagy, and Lyonel Feininger, to mention a few.

In just 14 years of existence the Bauhaus and its founders paved the way for architects and designers to cast off the bonds of the Ecole des Beaux Arts classical education. What later emerged was modern architecture known as the "international style."

Fig. 1.30 Design of a Cottage for a Single Laborer. (Draftsman: Joseph Gandy.)

Fig. 1.31 Design for Dunrobbin Castle.
(Draftsman: Sir Charles Barry.)

Delineation in the United States

It is understandable that the European tradition has had a strong effect upon delineation in the United States. The numerous European architects who migrated to America brought with them the methods and techniques they had learned and practiced in their homelands. The architects who practiced in the United States were either educated in Europe or trained in the United States under the European pupilage system. Group architectural training was first given in American schools of technology, and as early as 1860 was taught as part of the science of building. However, the Society of Beaux Arts Architects, formed in New York in 1894, helped to encourage a less mathematical approach to rendering. Gradually, as the American schools of architecture matured, they took the burden of education upon themselves. Today great numbers of students from various countries of the world come to the United States to study architecture.

Rendering Today

As previously illustrated, the importance of delineation at the Ecole des Beaux Arts was almost an entity within itself, and design was a separate but equal entity. On the other hand, the Bauhaus used delineation as a tool to the more important aspect of the design concept.

Not only are the traditional materials, such as watercolor or pen and ink, used in present-day rendering, but new materials and media are constantly being invented, and the traditional media are constantly being improved. New kinds of pencils, inks, and papers are being offered, and they are relatively available and relatively inexpensive. Looking back, it may be seen that the forces that affected the development of architectural rendering have been interwoven with the major developments that helped shape the civilization of the world. The skills and techniques developed by architects since people first became interested in the pictorial aspects of architecture have been nurtured, then passed down to each succeeding generation. The line of development from the architectural hieroglyphs of the Ancient Kingdom of Egypt to today's renderings is a straight one, varying now and then, but always growing and developing toward a more versatile presentation.

This line of growth was made possible by many forces, some of them architectural, some not. Chief among them was the desire of all architects to bridge the gap between their own imaginations and those of other people who were not architects, to explain complicated thoughts in an uncomplicated manner. Today any subject matter may be pictured if the basic tools and a knowledge of techniques are at hand.

Perspective, shades and shadows, and other techniques could be discovered only when someone provided paper and drawing media. The ability to render may have lain dormant, incapable of expression, for centuries before paper appeared at the time of the Renaissance. To this one invention alone we owe eternal gratitude. If the landscape painter gave the stimulus to the quest for reality, so did the inventor of the camera, but neither could have produced rendering as we know it. It took the endless patience of many architects to experiment and to push into the unknown, as well as to try new media.

The Architect as Delineator

This brief outline of the history of delineation and the forces acting upon architectural rendering in the twentieth century points up the fact that, historically,

Fig. 1.32 Residence. (Architect and Renderer: William C. Wilkinson.)

Fig. 1.33 Office Building for Colgate Palmolive. (Architect: The Austin Company, Architects & Engineers. Renderer: Albert O. Halse.)

most architects have rendered their own designs to present to their clients, as in Figure 1.32, for example. The complexity of the modern architectural office does not afford the major present-day architect the luxury of time to deal with the mechanics of presentation and rendering. Thus presentation is delegated to the most talented designers in the studio. This new responsibility has given great prestige to that individual in the modern office (Figure 1.33). Even in small studios where the major architect is totally involved with all aspects of a project, often the delineator is a staff member who does all the office renderings.

Frequently, professional delineators who are known for their talents will be hired as consultants. The most noted independent delineator and architect was Hugh Ferriss, who established and inspired contemporary renderers. The dramatic style of Ferriss is shown in the aerial perspective of Rockefeller Center in Figure 1.34. Another outstanding renderer commissioned by architects was Schell Lewis. Again, Lewis's style, composition, and renderings are good examples for students and professional renderers (Figures 1.35 and 1.36).

Today professional delineators are commissioned for their style (Figure 1.37), use of composition (Figure 1.38), specific technique (Figure 1.39), and

Fig. 1.34 Impression of the RCA, French, and British Buildings, Rockefeller Center, New York. (Architect: Reinhard & Hofmeister, Corbett, Harrison & MacMurray, Hood & Fouilhoux. Renderer: Hugh Ferriss.)

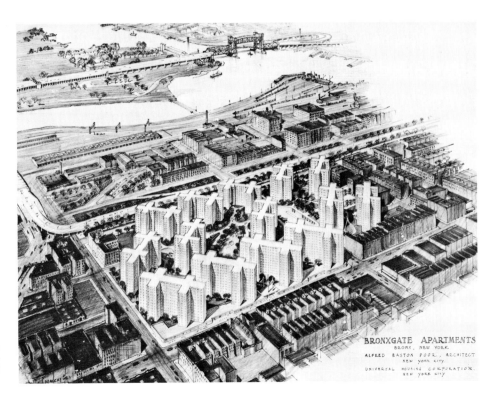

Fig. 1.35 Bronxgate Apartments. (Renderer: Schell Lewis. Architect: Alfred Easton Poor. From the private collection of William C. Wilkinson.)

skill with media (Figure 1.40). A renderer may provide services not only to architects, but to advertising agencies, industrial designers, and large corporations.

No doubt all architects have at times felt the desire to know enough about delineation to be able to show clients conceptions of their prospective buildings. Many architects have not had sufficient specialized training in rendering and hesitate to sketch because they lack information about materials and techniques. With the directions found in this book, an architect will have to expend

Fig. 1.36 Housing Project. (Architect: Unknown. Renderer: Schell Lewis. From the private collection of William C. Wilkinson.)

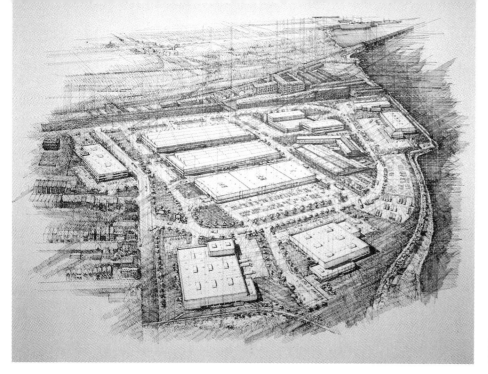

Fig. 1.37 Proposed Singer Industrial Complex. (Renderer: Robert M. Zaccone, A.I.A. Real Estate Developer: Jerry Novak.)

only a little effort and persistence to master the various techniques. Proficiency will come with practice.

The Importance of Rendering in Architecture

Modern construction is complex, but what would it be like if instructions were by words alone? The answer is, of course, that a large building such as a sky-

Fig. 1.38 Copley Place Project. (Architect: The Architects Collaborative, Inc. Renderer: Howard Associates.)

Fig. 1.39 The Westin Hotel, Seattle, Washington. (Architect: John Graham and Company, Architects, Planners, Engineers. Renderer: Earl Duff.)

Fig. 1.40 Parker Building, Lobby. (Owner: Henry Horowitz. Renderer: Licht/Levine.)

scraper probably could not be built at all, while even the smallest building would require constant on-the-job direction by a resident architect. Since with this system an architect could build only a few buildings in a lifetime, there simply would not be enough architects to go around. All available practitioners would be hired by the wealthy, and other people would literally be out in the cold.

Drawing as Communication

Drawing, then, is of great value, not only to the architect, but to everyone in this complex society. But if our society has become complex, so too has architectural drawing, and today few lay people can understand or read working drawings. Because of this, the architectural picture, or rendering, has become an important and indispensable part of today's practice. The picture is a bridge between the intellects of the client and the architect — a common meeting ground without hard-to-understand technicalities. Both of the two possible substitutes have proved inadequate: the model because it completely lacks human scale, the unrendered linear perspective because it neither describes materials and textures nor tells which areas are voids and which solids.

If rendering is important as a means of communication between architect and client, it is doubly important to architects themselves, inasmuch as it is their means of visualizing the building and thereby eliminating flaws in the design.

Owners, Architects, and Sketches

The owner's basic program may be in written form or developed as a sketch. The finished sketch usually represents an amalgam as well as a refinement of the ideas of both owner and architect. The owner, when first interviewed, usually

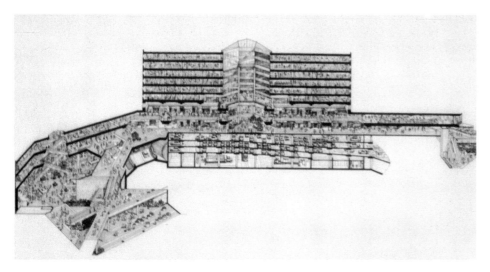

Fig. 1.41 Ink Sketch of Copley Place Project. (Architect: The Architects Collaborative, Inc. Renderer: Howard Associates, Inc.)

describes many ideas to the architect verbally, or possibly by a rough sketch. Using knowledge and skills, the architect tries to utilize the owner's ideas and, if possible, to improve upon them. This is done by sketching (Figure 1.41). The pencil or ink sketch is of mutual value to architect and owner because it can help to settle at an early stage any possible disagreements and misunderstandings about the design of the building. The architect, to "prove out" the design that has grown from the meeting of minds with the owner, usually makes numerous freehand perspective sketches of the building from various points of view. These quick sketches enable the architect to eliminate flaws before they become part of the working drawings and are built. As a final guarantee that the design is acceptable to the owner, a finished rendering (Figure 1.42) — the degree of finish will depend upon the size of the project — is made and shown to the owner before working drawings and specifications are begun.

Fig. 1.42 Final Rendering of Copley Place Project. (Architect: The Architects Collaborative, Inc., Architects. Renderer: Howard Associates, Inc.)

Renderings for Study

The rendering accomplishes a number of other things for the architect. It permits, in one of the few approved ways, "selling" the project to a client. Many a project has been abandoned in the sketch stage because the client was simply not inspired by a good rendering to want to build. The rendering also offers an early opportunity for determining textures and colors of materials. If these look well in the rendering, which is a finished building study, they stand a good chance of being handsome in the finished building. The rendering is more than a pretty picture; it is a guide for actual construction.

Some clients suggest colors and textures of materials, but if clients do not volunteer suggestions, the architect can ask for their ideas and try to find out if there are colors and textures that the client dislikes, since these must be assiduously avoided. Finally, the architect must be sure to show accurately and honestly how the building will look in its actual surroundings, being particularly careful to show existing trees and bushes if they are to remain; the owner usually admires foliage on the property, as illustrated in Figure 1.43.

If the rendering is important in communicating with an individual client, it is doubly helpful in dealing with building committees, boards, or design juries. An adequate picture often serves as a strong point of agreement between groups (architects as well as lay people), since it provides an equal opportunity for each individual to see what the final building will look like. It quickly evokes an approval and eliminates hours of haggling. On the other hand, if the design is poor or if the rendering is too sketchy, "stunty," or badly drawn, a group, like an individual, will quickly react unfavorably. In the school of architecture, a poorly rendered design, or one presented in the graphic linear manner, gives the jury the impression that the student does not understand the design, or is afraid of bringing out its bad points. There are exceptions to this, and rightly so, but for the most part an adequately rendered design problem will always compete favorably with others.

Renderings and Financial Backing

Once the rendering has been made and the design accepted, the rendering becomes a useful tool to the owner. Together with sketch plans, it is a tangible aid in applying for a mortgage or other financial backing. Few lending institutions will advance money without a proper description of the project.

If the structure is being planned for a large organization, it is usually necessary

Fig. 1.43 Freehold Township Justice Complex. (Architect: The Grad Partnership. Renderer: Licht/Levine.)

Fig. 1.44 School Addition and Rectory for the Church of the Assumption, Emerson, New Jersey. (Renderer: Allen Davoll. From the Private Collection of William C. Wilkinson.)

for those in charge of the building program to obtain final approval from the president and board of the company before proceeding to the construction stage. Once such approval is obtained, they can turn the rendering over to an advertising department or agency, which will in turn stimulate public interest and justify the expenditure to the stockholders. Such a picture has definite prestige and advertising value to the company itself. Charitable institutions and churches can use such a drawing to raise funds for the proposed addition or new building (Figure 1.44).

There are times also when a rendering is needed to obtain approval by zoning boards, planning commissions, and other governmental bodies. Sometimes, if acceptance of a building depends upon public vote, thousands of copies of the rendering are made and distributed directly to the voters before election.

Renderings and Prestige

The rendering, then, is an indispensable, practical item for both architect and owner. But it must be recognized that it also gives a great emotional satisfaction to the client, who usually has saved or planned for years before being able to proceed with the project. The rendering is visual evidence of success, and it also helps the architect to carry the owner's dreams toward reality.

chapter 2

The Magic of Imagery

The Natural Setting

The world of nature supplies an inexhaustible storehouse of inspiration to the delineator, who may be required at any time to portray in its natural setting a mountaintop ski lodge, a tropical house, or anything in between. The delineator, who must have the ability to visualize scenes in brilliant sunlight or dull gray mist, according to the location and mood of the project at hand, should be familiar with all kinds of trees and shrubbery, from the twisted, gnarled limber pine of the heights to the graceful spruce, fir, pine, elm, maple, and oak of the fertile hills and valleys. Skies are an important concern too, whether light blue and cheerful, or dark, gray, and forbidding.

Many projects are built near bodies of water. The renderer must be able to simulate them, whether as small and placid as a street puddle, as peaceful as a lagoon, or as wild as the bubbling, rushing mountain stream, and must also be able to borrow from the wild fragrant beauties of the deep wood, the quiet dignity of the well-mannered countryside, or the bustling excitement of the smoky city.

These raw materials of nature provide inspiration and vocabulary for pictorial expression. Selected according to need and combined as desired, they provide colorful settings for the endless varieties of buildings to be rendered.

It would be helpful indeed if this great vocabulary could be memorized, but few of us can manage such feats. Instead, the average renderer studies the basic qualities and proportions of elements, such as trees, that are used most often, and if possible, takes pictures of each site and renders from those, adding or removing foliage as required. Finally, the renderer draws upon the work of the photographer and usually keeps a file of pictures nearby for inspiration.

Selection of Elements

A great part of the success of any rendering depends upon the proper selection of natural elements for the project at hand. A public building must, above all, appear dignified, and therefore should be rendered with a quiet, cloudless sky and quiet surroundings. If color is used, it should be subtle.

A mausoleum might be rendered in much the same way, but with the introduction of weeping willow trees, whose bowed branches and trailing foliage suggest sorrow. A church is often pictured best in the oblique rays of morning light, since it is usually used at that time. On the other hand, many buildings, by their very nature, should be rendered in a gay, bustling mood. Theaters, restaurants, motion picture houses, and bowling alleys are in this category. Here the spectator can be made to "feel" the excitement of the building by the use of fleecy clouds, large groups of scale figures, automobiles, and bright spots of color. Natural elements should be carefully selected for each project, with suitability ever in mind.

Skills for Rendering Buildings

The world of nature supplies ideas for the setting of the rendered building, but what about the building itself? Illustrating it requires knowledge of a combination of sciences: perspective, shades and shadows, and the workings of light. If it is to be rendered in color, the principles of color theory must be observed, since they provide the renderer with certain simple rules not only for the sophisticated use of color, but for the actual mixing of the pigments themselves. The subtle colors in a fine rendering are not accidental: they are the result of much study and experience. Most people (that is, all who are not color-blind) can attain excellent results by the use of a few simple rules. Color-blind delineators — and there are a few — usually work in one color, or in black and white.

Finally, facility in composition is vital to the renderer. Unless the various forms in a picture are composed properly, chaos will result. Frequently, beginning renderers develop an active repertoire of rendering styles which may be filed by media — watercolor, pencil, pen and ink, etc. Another method of filing is by categories such as entourage, people, objects, and media experimentation.

Achieving Reality plus Beauty

Use of all the above sciences will provide a perspective in line and a color scheme, if color is to be used. From this point forward, the skills required are those of the renderer. While the modern artist often works for abstract beauty alone, the architectural delineator seeks abstract beauty plus the illusion of reality.

Abstract beauty in an architectural picture is the result of conscious arrangement of the representational elements in the picture (such as building, foreground, background, trees, sky, and scale figures), so that they form a surface design that is pleasant to look at even if interest in the subject matter is disregarded for the moment. Abstract beauty is obtained by organizing the various components of the picture, such as lines, planes, lights, darks, movement, and color, into a pleasing and unified geometric pattern. This is done by making a number of preliminary charcoal or pencil sketches of the composition before the final rendering is begun. These preliminary studies are known as "value studies" or "color studies."

Choices of Medium

The technique — that is, the method used in the execution of a rendering — depends upon the medium to be used, the subject matter, and the desired mood of the picture. Pointed media, such as the graphite pencil and pen and ink, lend themselves to the rendering of buildings with a lot of texture and small elements. The carbon pencil, smudge charcoal, pastels, watercolor, tempera, and the airbrush, all of which are "area" media (with the possible exception of the carbon pencil, which can be used as either a pointed or an area medium), are most suitable to rendering buildings with large, plain wall areas. Sometimes watercolor is combined with graphite pencil or pen and ink.

It is interesting that the average delineator specializes in one or two media. This limitation is sometimes due to the shortage of time available for rendering, or lack of time for experimentation. More often it is because of a lack of training in the use of other media. While few people attain equal proficiency in all media, it is a good idea at least to try them all. This frequently leads renderers not only to discover that they like a new medium better than ones they had been using, but that their degree of success is greater. Part of the enjoyment of teaching rendering lies in helping students discover the medium to which they are psychologically best suited. After finding their best media, renderers become more self-assured and the renderings begin to assume a professional appearance.

Refinement and Style

At times a quick sketch is sufficient, and at others a finished rendering is called for. The time element will always be with us. In all the chapters on technique, the author has endeavored to describe both methods. It is earnestly hoped that the reader will not only try the methods described in this book but will experiment with new media and techniques. Each technique illustrated in this book is excellent for experimentation with new media. All experienced renderers test new media, but those who are successful with new media have taken time to experiment in several media. This will be illustrated in Chapter 15, Mixed Media and Unique Media.

Finally, a word about developing a style. Everyone in an elementary school class is taught to write the same way. Before long, however, each individual's writing begins to look different from anyone else's. Each adult's writing has characteristics all its own, and even the average bank teller can distinguish one signature from hundreds of thousands of others. It is the same with style in drawing or rendering. If a delineator admires and copies the style of a professional renderer, little growth will manifest itself until the model is put aside. After looking at the work of many, analyzing it, and learning from it, the delineator must then try to use that knowledge in developing a personal style. Competence comes with much patience, practice, and experience.

chapter 3

A Quick Look at Perspective

Artists, Architects, and Perspective

The development of perspective drawing by the painters and architects of the fifteenth century gave them and all who lived after them a means of combining in one drawing width, depth, and height. Drawings made before that time were distorted and flat. For about four centuries the three-dimensional perspective was used by artist and architect alike, and many painters produced pictures of existing buildings and also worked along with architects to render in perspective buildings still on the drawing board. When the camera was invented early in the nineteenth century, the photographer quickly took the place of the artist in painting existing architecture. Artists began to seek new means of expression that the camera could not duplicate and found such expression in the cubists' use of a fourth dimension and in abstraction, dadaism, expressionism, fantasy, fauvism, and the like. Many artists, shunning realism, followed the new movement and no longer worked with architects. Cubists, for instance, combined in one picture a number of different views of the same object from a number of stations, as if they were walking around the object. Architectural rendering, however, requires clarity and simplicity and could not utilize this concept. As no better method than the rendered scenic perspective has yet been invented for studying or illustrating architectural design, it is still universally used by architects, some of whom have become specialists in architectural rendering.

Rules plus Experience

Most beginners do not realize the importance of making a proper perspective before they actually begin to render. There is no substitute for a thorough knowledge of all aspects of perspective, which it is assumed the reader already has. Most students of perspective, however, are appalled, not only by its complexity, but also by the fact that very little is said by many authors to bridge the gap between the rules for constructing a linear perspective and the magical finished mental image which the students intend to put on paper. Anyone who has studied perspective as a science can draw a finished perspective, but there is a difference between a soulless mechanical drawing of this kind and one which takes advantage of a few rules discovered by the professionals. One can learn about the rules of baseball by reading a book; playing it is another matter. So can renderers learn the basic rules of perspective, and apply them in an unintelligent way. Later, however, experience teaches them that the selection of a viewpoint, for instance, must be made with great skill if they are to get the most out of rendering. Most renderers have had the sad experience of laboriously plotting the various required points for a perspective, only to discover after hours of work that the viewpoint selected did not show the building to its best advantage. If they were doing the job for themselves, they wasted several hours of precious time. If they were working for someone, it was hard to explain such an error to the employer.

Perspective as Indicator of Bad Design

What are the purposes of a linear perspective? Certainly to provide a good, clean drawing which describes the shape of the building and gives a complete guide for the rendering. But even more than that, and more basically, the linear perspective shows, before the renderer has spent a great deal of time on the rendering, what the building is going to look like from various angles. If the proportions of the design are bad, this shortcoming will quickly manifest itself, and it will be immediately apparent that the sections of the building that do not look well must be redesigned. Unscrupulous persons have sometimes purposely drawn their perspectives incorrectly so as to "improve" inferior designs. This approach is not only dishonest but dangerous, since the eventual disillusionment can have legal implications. The renderer should be totally familiar with a project and think in terms of plan, elevation, and section; thus, any possibility of error is greatly reduced. The final perspective of a structure should be from the most complimentary standpoint and should illustrate the materials and details accurately.

Selection of Viewpoint

There is no substitute for a correct and honest perspective. In addition to its truthfulness, a perspective should be marked by its ability to make the building seem to "live" — to look exactly as it will when it is constructed. The viewpoint chosen must be believable but need not necessarily be at the usual eye level. Sometimes it is better to take a viewpoint that is either higher or lower than eye level. The viewpoint should vary with the size and type of building.

The viewpoint, or "point of station," is the fundamental point of a perspective, since the position of every working point depends upon its selection. The point of station has a dual position; it appears in both plan and elevation. The position in plan decides the location of the vanishing points and measuring points. Its location in elevation determines the location of the horizon. A house designed for the top of a hill might be studied so that the spectator seems to be looking up at it from the bottom of the hill. This means that the renderer would select a viewpoint at the elevation of the bottom of the hill. On the other hand, if the house is perched on the edge of a cliff, a viewpoint at the bottom of the hill would show too much of the underside of the building. Here a bird's-eye view, with the eye level above the level of the house, would probably provide the best picture.

The viewpoint for a house with a body of water in the foreground must be chosen to show enough water for interesting reflections. The viewpoint for a tall building, such as a church or other towerlike structure, or perhaps a skyscraper, should be quite low so that the inspiring height of the building will manifest itself most clearly. On the other hand, if a bird's-eye view of such a building is required, the viewpoint should be high enough to show the whole building and all its interesting setbacks. Large trees, rocks, or other identifying landmarks should be carefully located in the pencil perspective to help the client visualize the actual site with the building in place.

Aerial Perspective

Sometimes, for large complexes of buildings such as industrial establishments, it is impossible to obtain a truly descriptive view without resorting to an aerial perspective, as well as one or more ground-level views. In selecting the viewpoint for aerial perspectives, several rules must be observed and then modified by experience. To begin with, too high an eye level will show too much of the roof area and too little of the wall areas. If the building complex is made up of groups of buildings which are located at various angles on the plot, the point of view must be one from which none of the buildings are shown in too foreshortened or oblique a manner. It is quite usual in selecting a point of view for such a project to include not only all the buildings but the driveways, walkways, parking areas, and surrounding areas such as farmland, forest, water, or adjoining buildings. Note also that, in aerial perspectives of low buildings, glazed areas are completely transparent and, therefore, floors, furniture, and other interior furnishings that can be seen must be completely and accurately constructed before the rendering is begun.

Details and Dominating Facades

The viewpoint may frequently be selected in order to show the approaches to a building and to point out the main entrance. It is well to indicate outstanding trees and bushes, and other important characteristics of the site, to enable spectators to orient themselves quickly. In a normal ground level view it is, of course, necessary to show these characteristics as well as other local color such as scale figures and sometimes automobiles, buses, or trucks. For industrial plants, railroad cars may be shown.

The most interesting ground-level perspective is the one that shows two sides of a building, with one side dominating. If the project at hand happens to be a city building with only one facade showing, the greatest interest can be obtained by taking the viewpoint to the left or right of the center of the building.

General Rules for Mechanical Perspectives

There are a few general guides which should be followed in making a perspective, and although most of them are mentioned in books specifically devoted to the subject, it is worthwhile repeating them here.

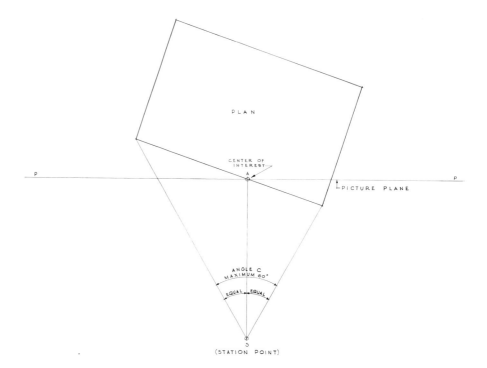

PLAN

CENTER OF
INTEREST

A

PICTURE PLANE

P ———————————————————————— P

ANGLE C
MAXIMUM 60°

EQUAL EQUAL

S
(STATION POINT)

Fig. 3.1 Locating the Station Point.

1. The location of the station point will determine the location of the vanishing points and measuring points. Angle C, created by projections between the point of station and the limits of the building, should not be more than 60 degrees. Some authorities even say that it should not be greater than 45 degrees, since a wider angle than this will distort the view of the building. In any case, the station point should be in the center of the visual cone (Figure 3.1).

2. A line between the point of station and the corner of the building which intersects the picture plan at A should bisect angle C. The picture plane should be perpendicular to the line of vision, SA.

3. The point of station in plan should be such that more of one side of the building, obviously the most important side, is shown. Foreshortening one side more perceptibly than the other gives a pleasing contrast to the perspective.

4. Avoid a dead-center vanishing point in a one-point perspective. A viewpoint either left or right of center will invariably give a better-looking perspective.

5. In ground-level perspectives, it is well to keep the horizon line low. This will enable you to limit the amount of foreground, at least on a flat site, and to concentrate attention on the building itself. It is difficult to arrive at a definite rule for the height of the foreground; however, an analysis of the work of successful renderers will show that this distance is usually limited to one-third the height of the sheet, at the very most. It may in fact be considerably less, and usually it varies from one-seventh to one-third the height of the sheet.

However, if the building is on a hill, or if there is something important to be shown in the foreground, such as a reflecting pool, the height of the foreground may be more than one-third the height of the picture.

6. If, after the rendering has been begun, the foreground appears to be massive in relation to the rest of the picture, it may be vignetted — that is, made smaller by stopping it at an irregular line before it reaches the mat line (Figure 3.2).

Fig. 3.2 Vignetting the Foreground.

7. When making a perspective of a long, low building, it is frequently desirable, instead of locating the picture plane at a corner of the building, to move it so that it bisects the elevation at a point approximately one-third the length of the building from the point closest to the point of view. This enlarges the perspective and keeps it from looking too long and low.

8. In order to locate the point of station properly, care should be taken not to place it too near the building, since this would place the vanishing and measuring points too close together and cause distortion. On the other hand, if the station point is located too far away from the building, considerable detail will be lost.

A good rule for locating the point of station in an aerial perspective is to limit the distance between the ground line and the point of station to one-half the distance between the station point and the nearest part of the building.

9. The backgrounds of aerial perspectives, particularly when they are very complicated and encompass vast areas, are not usually constructed, but are drawn by eye.

10. In the mechanical layout of circular forms, such as lighting fixtures or tables in interior perspectives, structures at the sides of the drawing usually acquire a distorted appearance. With these forms it is best to take liberties and draw the ellipses without distortion by using a horizontal axis as the center line of each ellipse.

11. To avoid distortion in the perspective of a circular building, lay out the perspective through the center of the circle.

Perspective Charts and Perspective Scales

For those who prefer a less mathematical method of constructing perspectives, there are perspective charts. These consist of perspective grids which have been laid out for different perspective conditions. A set of such charts consists of perspective grids for a number of desired types of perspectives. The architect simply fastens the desired chart to the board; lays a piece of tracing paper over it; and, using each grid section as a module related to the scale of the perspective, determines the horizontal and vertical dimensions over the grids below.

While the use of grid charts obviates the necessity for a large drawing board and certainly cuts down the amount of brainwork and patience required in the construction of a perspective, it should be recognized that perspective charts cannot be made for every desired condition. In addition, if the design of the building is slightly changed, it is much easier to go back to a constructed perspective to make the corrections than to try to make the corrections over a perspective chart. There are many cases when an architect will find both perspective charts and perspective scales useful.

Perspective by Approximation

Delineators are always looking for shortcuts, to reduce the amount of time required for making line perspectives. Some merely lay out the main lines of the building and then locate doors, windows, and other details by eye. Others, like Vincent Furno, use (on ground perspectives only) either of the two methods illustrated in Figure 3.3A and B, in which the main lines and a number of perspective guidelines are used as a basis for perspective by eye.

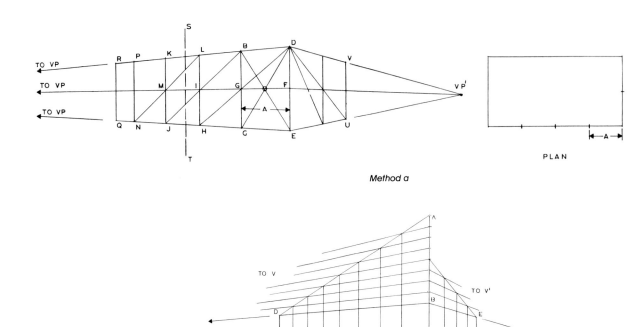

Method a

Method b

Fig. 3.3 Perspective by Approximation.

Method a

1. Draw a freehand sketch of the building as you want to see it.

2. Place another piece of tracing paper over the rough sketch and extend lines to obtain vanishing points VP and VP1.

3. Assuming the long facade has four equal divisions (this number will, of course, vary), lay out distance A in perspective by eye, and draw a vertical from B to C, thereby creating a square (or rectangle, as the case may be) in perspective.

4. Draw diagonals BE and CD.

5. Draw DE in halves.

6. Draw a line through FO, and extend it past the left end of the long facade.

7. Draw a line through DG, continuing it until it strikes the baseline of the building at H.

8. To create the second square or rectangle in the perspective, draw a perpendicular through H.

9. Draw a line through B1 to J.

10. Draw a vertical JK, thus creating a third square in perspective.

11. Draw line LMN.

12. Draw vertical NP, thus creating the fourth square or rectangle in the perspective.

13. Erase area PRQN, which is extra building length. The long facade represented by DENP is now in approximately correct perspective.

14. To complete the perspective, lay out all horizontal distances by eye in reference to the four equal squares or rectangles.

15. To lay out heights, slide your scale left and right, holding it vertically, until you find the point at which the height of the building scales correctly, say at ST. Scale all vertical dimensions on it, and vanish all heights left and right as required.

16. Depths of reveals, etc., are laid out along EU and projected to their proper locations in perspective.

17. Complete the perspective on the short facade by following the same method as described above.

Method b

1. Draw a freehand sketch of the building as you want to see it.

2. Place another piece of tracing paper over the rough sketch and extend the horizontal lines of the building to vanishing points V and V1.

3. Assuming you want to keep the length of your building as you have sketched it, refer to Figure 3.3b and proceed with steps 4 to 10.

4. Extend line CB vertically to A. (Length BA can be made equal to BC, or can be greater in length of ease of scaling.) If the long elevation of the building divides itself into, say, 30 equal parts, BA can be laid out in 30 equal increments at a convenient scale, such as ¼ inch to 1 foot.

5. Draw a line between A and D.

6. Draw a line from each point between A and B to V.

7. Draw vertical lines from the intersections of the vanishing lines drawn in step 6 and line AD.

8. You now have 30 equal spaces laid out in perspective, and horizontal distances can be laid out by eye in relation to them.

9. The same method can be used to lay out increments on side BEFC.

10. Heights and depths of reveals can be laid out as described for Figure 3.3a.

Transferring the Perspective to Rendering Paper

Great care must be exerted in transferring the perspective from the original construction — which is usually on tracing paper — to the paper upon which the rendering will be made. If the completed perspective itself turns out to be either too large or too small for the final picture, it can easily be increased or decreased in size by photographic technology. In fairness to your operator, however, you should note on the perspective the actual dimension — length or height — that you would like the print to be. The perspective may be enlarged or diminished by the use of a planograph, proportional divider, or other means.

There are a number of ways of "transferring" the perspective from either the original perspective drawing or the copy to the rendering paper. The best of these, and the one which will give you the cleanest line drawing, is done as follows:

Trace the perspective on a sheet of good rag-bond tracing paper, using an F or H pencil. After you finish the tracing from the original drawing, carefully roll and file the original in a safe place. It represents many hours of work, and you may need it again. To be safe, it is advisable to make a diazo record print or, even better, a diazo sepia reverse reading as a record drawing.

Turn the new tracing face down, and trace every line through on the back of the tracing paper. You are now ready to transfer the drawing to your rendering paper. Look at the charcoal or pencil study that you have made showing the location of the building in the picture, and, using this as a guide, locate the perspective in the proper place. Fasten the tracing down tightly with tape or thumbtacks, and then, with a sharp 2H or 3H pencil, trace every line so that the pressure of the pencil will transfer the graphite to the sheet below. If you press too hard, you will not only tear the tracing paper, but you will indent the rendering paper and damage it so that it may be useless for rendering.

After the transfer has been made, strengthen the drawing on your rendering paper so that you have a clear, clean, complete drawing to work with. This process may be used exactly for renderings in graphite pencil, pen and ink, watercolor, tempera, and airbrush.

However, the final transfer for carbon pencil, lithograph pencil, pastels, and smudge charcoal is best accomplished by inserting a large sheet of carbon paper, face down, between the tracing and the rendering paper. The process is then completed as before, and any strengthening of lines should be done with a carbon pencil. The use of carbon paper and carbon pencil is necessary in the above-mentioned media, as these media will not "take" over graphite pencil, which is a slippery medium.

Use of Colored Paper

If colored paper is being used for the rendering, it will be found that white carbon paper is desirable, allowing all the transferred lines to be easily seen.

A simple pencil (graphite or carbon) line drawing on the rendering paper will suffice for the various pencil media, pen and ink, smudge charcoal, watercolor, tempera, and pastels. For rendering in Chinese ink — in which much sponging is done — it is best to make a dilute ink line drawing on cold-pressed (CP) paper and then to erase all pencil lines.

When you have reached this point, if your schedule permits, it is well to put the drawing aside for a while, as the mechanical process of the work that you have just completed conflicts sharply with the more creative mental attitude required for the actual rendering.

chapter 4

Some Rules
of Composition

Rules, Practice, and Beauty

The beauty of a skillfully done, finished rendering frequently astounds the novice. Novices are likely to assume that the delineator is some sort of genius who can make beautiful pictures without any great effort, and they may sometimes be right. But most delineators (and even most geniuses) must learn the basic rules and methods when they first begin to study rendering. Not that some do not learn faster than others, but all must learn the basic rules and consciously practice them in the process of acquiring skill. Most of us must toddle before we walk, and walk before we run. Many architects, not understanding this and not realizing that renderings are executed by following a definite series of steps, have given up, believing that they have no talent for this art. The author can say unequivocally that *anyone* who has the patience and who *wants* to learn all the related arts, such as composition, can learn to render.

Arranging lines, masses, and color into a harmonious whole is an important phase of producing a satisfactory rendering. All the beauty of the building, as well as the beauties of nature, such as skies, trees, grass plots, and bushes, and the scale-giving elements, such as people and automobiles, can be incorporated into a homogeneous whole which is pleasant to look at, or they can be made into an inept, irritating collection of diverse elements which will not please the eye. Neither the architect nor the lay person may know why the rendering is not pleasant to look at — but both will know that it is not.

The three basic elements of composition may be called "unity," "emphasis," and "balance." Let us first examine the principle of unity.

Unity

The various parts of a picture must be united in a skillfully ordered arrangement. The whole picture should be composed around the building, which is the center

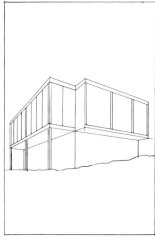
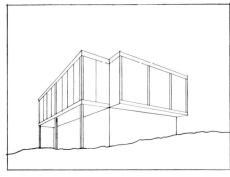

Fig. 4.1 Fitting the Problem to the Paper.   a. Wrong   b. Right

of interest. The building should occupy the greatest portion of the picture, so that it looks important and demands attention. Remember that the owner is interested first in the building, and second in the landscape and sky around it. The landscape around a building should be attractive, but only insofar as it complements the structure. The most magnificent sky, if it occupies too much of the picture or demands too much attention, will detract from the building, and the building will lose importance. If the building is more horizontal than vertical, the composition should be a horizontal one. If, on the other hand, it is more vertical, a vertical composition is called for. Following this simple principle will ensure that the shape of the building and the shape of the sheet of paper will complement each other and there will not be too much or too little sky area or entourage. See Figure 4.1.

When the size of the building and its proper relation to the shape of the paper have been decided, a number of charcoal or soft-pencil studies can be made on tracing paper, showing surrounding elements such as roadways, walkways, trees, bushes, scale figures, and automobiles in foreground, middle ground, and background.

If the view is from normal eye level, try locating the horizon line fairly low on the sheet so that the foreground is quite foreshortened. Remember that the distance between the bottom of the picture and the bottom of the building should never be the same as the height of the building itself, and that neither of these should be the same as the height of the sky. See Figure 4.2.

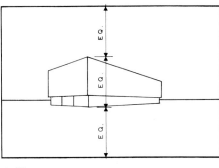
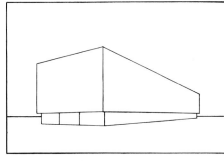

Fig. 4.2 Locating the Building in the Picture.   a. Wrong   b. Right

Fig. 4.3 The Perspective of Trees.

In these studies, try consciously to connect all the elements of the picture in a meaningful manner—perhaps by value, or color, or perspective movement. Keep the pattern simple, but also keep it from being monotonous. Eliminate all detail in these early studies; details will fall into their proper places if the main elements are first properly located. In placing trees, make one of them dominant—higher and more detailed than the rest. Make one side of your composition richer by the use of tree groupings, but not so much richer that the opposite side will appear flat. In showing trees, experiment by using them in groups: a single tree usually has a lonesome look and is not important in itself. If there are trees on the site which will be located between the point of vision and the building, draw them so that they will not obscure the building itself or parts thereof. Leave the lower branches bare.

The Illusion of Distance

One of the best ways to create the illusion of distance in a picture is to make the trees and bushes in the foreground tallest, those in the mid-distance slightly shorter, and those in the distance shortest. Trees in the foreground will be quite detailed; individual leaves and the tree structure will be seen very plainly, so these must be accurately detailed. Those in the mid-distance will be lighter in value and less detailed, while those in the distance will merely be shown in mass and may be quite light. See Figure 4.3. Remembering that a final effect of restfulness and repose is desired, avoid a perspective of landscape in which one or more of the elements (such as a row of trees) seems to run out of the picture. See Figure 4.4. If the site is such that this cannot be avoided, take the liberty of showing a dark tree of a type different from those on the site astride the row of trees that seem to run out of the picture. Make this tree higher so that it definitely "cuts" the perspective movement. See Figure 4.5.

Fig. 4.4 Tree Arrangements to Avoid.

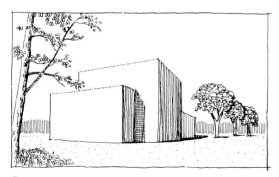

a

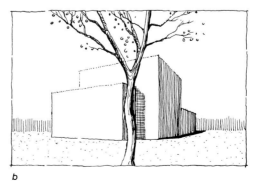

b

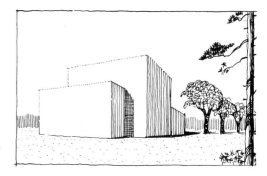

Fig. 4.5 Stopping Perspective Movement with a Different Type of Tree.

In rendering a building which is curved in plan or elevation, trees with straight trunks should be used in front of and near it (Figure 4.6A). If, on the other hand, the building is long and rectilinear, its appearance can be softened by using groups of bending trees — such as birches — to cut the harsh lines of the building and to keep it from seeming to "float." These trees should be located at a point which is roughly a third of the length of the building (Figure 4.6B). If trees such as these are not on the site, it is usually safe to show them and to suggest to the owner that they be included in the landscaping program.

Trees in a rendering may be arranged in numerous ways. A few of these are shown in Figure 4.6; analysis of the various illustrations throughout this book will reveal many others.

Bushes should be shown (and planted) in groups placed so that they soften the

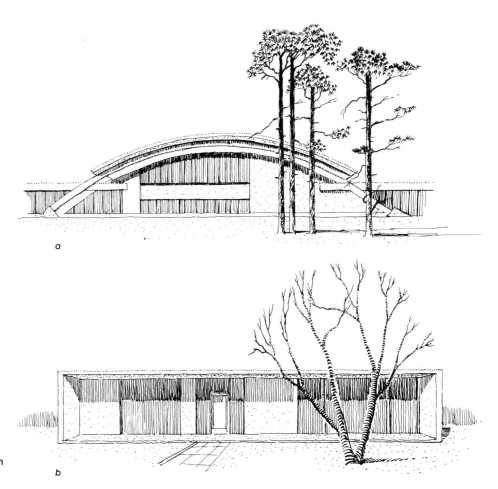

Fig. 4.6 Complementing the Design with Trees.

a

b

Fig. 4.7 Locating the Center of Interest with Bushes.

lines of the building and lead the eye to the center of interest, usually the entrance. See Figure 4.7. If there are hills or mountains in the background looming above the height of the building, centering one of them in the picture behind the building will make the rendering monotonous and uninteresting, and should be avoided. The highest peak can be located off to one side, and all the lower ranges placed so that they lead up to the highest mountain. Ranges of mountains should never be drawn parallel to each other; instead, the eye should be led from the low ranges in the foreground to the highest range in the background by the use of a zigzag arrangement of mountaintops.

Emphasis

As mentioned earlier in this chapter, the building must be the most important element in the composition. It must receive the greatest emphasis, not only by means of size, but also by value. When a rendering has been completed, it must be easily "read," or understood at a glance. This means that the building itself must be complemented by the use of value and color in the surroundings.

Having selected a source for the sunlight, the renderer already knows which side of the building will be in light and which in shade. Obviously, in order to make the building appear three-dimensional, the light side should have dark areas next to it for contrast. On the other hand, those parts of the building which are dark because they are in shade should have light values next to them so that they stand out to best advantage, as shown in Figure 4.8. A light sky, for instance, is often used behind the dark side of the building and a dark sky behind the light areas, so that the building does not seem to float in the sky. Using dark against light and light against dark is a safe rule to follow. The rendering is intended to express the forms of the architecture, and value comparisons should be arranged accordingly.

Fig. 4.8 Use of Contrast.

Value Studies

There are a number of basic approaches which are worth considering in developing value studies. The first of these, and probably the most usual, is (as described in the chapter on light) an arrangement showing elements in the foreground as darkest and those in the distance as lightest, with gradations between. As illustrated in Figure 4.9, Basic Value Arrangements, a number of variations on this scheme are possible:

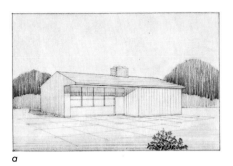

a

b

c

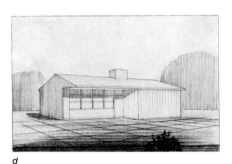

d

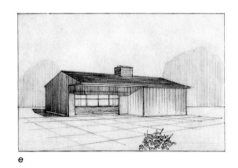

e

Fig. 4.9   Basic Value Arrangements.

a. Gray foreground, light building and mid-distance, and dark background.
b. Light foreground, dark building, and gray background.
c. Light foreground, gray building, and dark background.
d. Dark foreground, light building, and gray background.
e. Light foreground, dark building, and light background.

No matter which arrangement is used, it is well to throw a dark shadow on the ground in the foreground, whether from trees or from a building behind the spectator, so that the building will seem to recede into the distance. If, when the rough value study has been completed, the building or parts of it appear indistinct, putting some "gray" or dark trees immediately behind the structure will help it to stand out.

Emphasis within the Building

It has already been established that the building should occupy the major position in the rendering, and by so doing capture greatest emphasis. In addition, there should be emphasis within the building itself. This may be at an entrance, at a door, or at some other important part of the building. Emphasis on parts of the structure can be achieved by strong value comparison. For example, the wall area around an entrance may be quite light, while the entrance itself may have very dark shadows. A whole section of a building may be emphasized by rendering it light, with a dark background or with dark trees next to it. Once the part of the building to be emphasized has been decided, the rest of the building should be deliberately deemphasized, possibly by value comparisons less strong than those at the focal point, or by showing greatest detail near the center of interest and gradually reducing surrounding detail as its distance from the center increases. See Figure 4.10.

An entrance may be emphasized in other ways; a roadway, for instance, may curve from the foreground of the rendering to the entrance, thus leading the eye

Fig. 4.10 Locating the Center of Interest.

to it. Such a roadway may be lined with shrubbery or trees. Groups of figures may be located strategically so that the eye is led from a group in the foreground to others on the walkways, and still others near the entrance. Truck docks, carports, or garages may be pointed out by showing automobiles or trucks in or near them.

When color is used, vital parts of a building may be emphasized with bright colors, and less important parts of the building played down with more subdued colors.

To emphasize the height of a building, it is well to use a low point of view, i.e., near the ground, since this will diminish the height of the foreground and make the building seem high by comparison.

Compositional Balance

Once a dominant center of interest has been established, all other parts of the composition should be arranged around it so that each part receives its proper relative emphasis. The sections should be united by values which are neither too light nor too dark to hold them together. For instance, a dark foreground and a gray background will not hold together if a white streak of paper separates them. Such a situation may be remedied by joining them together with parallel ground areas which gradually diminish in value from the dark foreground to the light background. These areas may be tonal or color variations of earth, lawn, fields, shrubs, ground shadows, etc.

Tonal Balance

It is well to assess the value study as you work upon it. Pin it on a tackboard and analyze it critically from a distance. You must be your severest critic. You may discover during these analyses that one part of the rendering has become much darker than the rest, and the composition seems to be out of balance. Or a very dark shadow, or dark trees on one side of the rendering, may seem to weigh it down so that the other side seems to float. This situation can be remedied by lightening the side which is too dark; by drawing some darker objects, such as trees or shadows, on the opposite side of the sheet; or by doing both. Remember that a small dark area will balance a much larger "gray" area.

Occasionally you may find that no matter how hard you try, your composition contains too much sky. Showing a group of leafy tree branches which hang into the sky area from a tree located behind the spectator will improve the composition. In addition to correcting a sky that is too large, tree branches such as these usually help to provide a dark framework for the picture. See Figure 4.11, Framing the Picture with Tree Branches.

A good way to check the balance of a composition and make sure the building

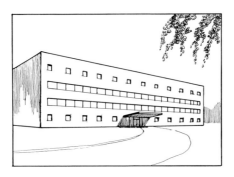

Fig. 4.11 Framing the Picture with Tree Branches.

is the most important item is to make sure that the area the building occupies is not equaled by either the area of the foreground or the area of the sky.

Abstracting the Composition

Beginners invariably try to show too much in a composition. They may indicate too much lawn, too many cars in a parking space, too much detail in the foliage, and so on. As they learn, they can profitably borrow from the approach of some modern artists, such as Matisse, who may begin by drawing or painting a detailed picture and gradually, in successive sketches, simplifying it, each time leaving out a detail which is not absolutely necessary for the purpose of identification. Architecturally this means that in the value-study stage we should deliberately leave out, or erase, parts of a lawn that has become too large, shrubbery which has become overpowering, parts of a stone indication that looks monotonous because there is too much of it, clouds that seem to detract from the building itself, and detail in general. Students sometimes consider this an ironical bit of advice because they believe that if a small amount of a thing is good, a large amount is better. However, as they become more proficient at rendering, they too eliminate unnecessary details.

chapter 5

A Study of Light

Light in Modern Architecture

Perhaps in no other era have buildings been glazed in so many different ways. Often glass is used in small openings; sometimes it is used in large areas. Occasionally glass is used as the major part of the facade. Many times exterior elements such as low walls and gardens are visually extended through the glass and into the interior. The manner in which glass is rendered depends upon its size and location in a given building. The Lever House appears to be of transparent panes as part of what has been called the "cultivated elegance" of decorator architecture.[1] Other buildings have curtain walls to reflect sun rays and sky, and still others have sash which are playfully sized and located in the manner termed "brutal expression" ("the hard, dissident articulation of the individual parts of the building").[2]

But another element enters into the appearance of glass in a rendering. When heat-absorbing or glare-reducing glass is used, or when the sash are set deep in an exterior wall, the window openings will appear to be somewhat dark and of a bronze, gray, or green cast, according to the type of glass used. Occasionally a building will be designed so that its outer walls are of mirrored-type glass, which acts as a mirror when viewed from a brightly lighted side and is transparent to the viewer from the darker, opposite side. When clear glass is used in large openings, the delineator must, in an exterior view, show the furniture, furnishings, walls, floor and ceiling, interior planting, and any other objects in the design as if the glass wall were not there (Figure 5.4). Of course, the extent of

---

[1] Gerde Hatje, (general ed.), *Encyclopaedia of Modern Architecture,* Thames & Hudson, London, 1964, p.24.

[2] Ibid.

the interior that may be seen will depend upon the depth of interior spaces, the angle of the perspective, and the amount of sunlight that can reach the interior, as well as upon the interior illumination. In any event, such a view is always interesting since it shows a "living" building and draws the eye into important parts of the structure. Sometimes it is desirable to show reflections of trees, clouds, or buildings as well. An interior view, on the other hand, should whenever possible permit the observer to look outside.

What rules are available to the architect who wishes to make such a rendering? There are the sciences of perspective and of shades and shadows. Neither of these need be presented in detail here, since there are books which adequately handle these subjects—as sciences. Few books on shades and shadows, however, go into the subtleties of light and reflected light for the renderer. Since these are of the utmost importance in expressing the exterior-interior view and are certainly as important as the basic rules themselves, it seems worthwhile to examine them at some length.

Selection of Light Source

It is usual to assume a conventional light source for a rendering. This, as most renderers and architects will remember, is at an angle of 45 degrees from the left and 45 degrees from above. However, it must be realized that this is only a convention, and that while a design might look well with such 45-degree shadows cast upon it, as at noontime, the same design may not look well with shadows cast by an early-morning or late-afternoon sun at an angle of perhaps 20 degrees with the ground line. Therefore, it is well to study a design in several different light conditions before making a rendering.

If the conventional light source is at all suspect, perhaps it would be well to think out your problem even further before laying out your shadows. Some buildings, by the very nature of their use, might look better at one time of the day than at another. A church, for instance, may be used most during the early morning hours (Plate VII) when the sun's rays are still quite low. A dwelling is seen at all hours; therefore almost any light condition may be assumed. And yet, it may be located in a shady spot where it may rarely receive the direct rays of the sun, and where the most prevalent light might be reflected upon it. A client who bought a property because of its shade trees will not be impressed with a house shown in bright sunlight. A skyscraper may be so large that several different kinds of light will bear upon it at the same time (Plate V). Also, it may have cloud shadows on part of it. There is even a distinct possibility that a building may look best at night, or at dusk, as in Figure 8.7. And some renderers use no shades or shadows at all.

The selection of a light source, then, must always be thought out very carefully before a rendering is made. It is best to study all possibilities and make sure that the building will look well in any possible light condition, and then select the one most appropriate for the presentation.

Making a Value Study

Assuming that a daylight view has been chosen and that the 45-degree shades and shadows have been mechanically laid out, a value study may be made in charcoal or soft pencil on tracing paper placed over the perspective. The lightest values (other than the white of the paper) will be the *highlights* on pitched areas which receive the light rays most directly (see Figure 5.1, sketch 1). The *lights,*

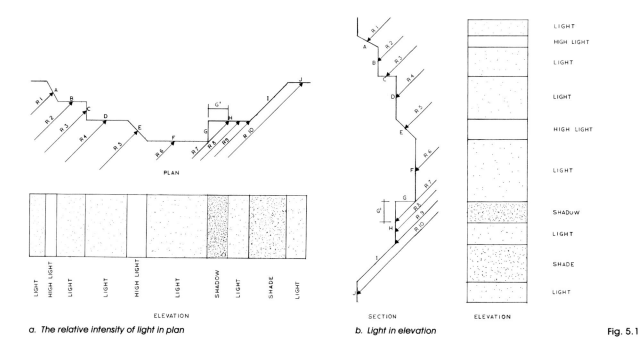

a. The relative intensity of light in plan

b. Light in elevation

Fig. 5.1

which are the next-lightest values, will be the glancing rays that fall on the vertical surfaces of the building, or on horizontal planes. Now turn sketch 1 so that plane A is at the top, and view it as a section (sketch 2). The undersides of planes with angles of 45 degrees or less to the horizontal will be in *shade* and will be dark in value. Dark areas cast by projections of the building or other objects interfering with the light rays are called *shadows* and are the darkest of all values. The darkest shadows are cast by edges of surfaces receiving the most direct light.

Whether the building is viewed as plan or section, it is assumed that all the light rays are parallel with each other, and that the rays shown in sketches *a* and *b* of Figure 5.1 are typical ones, selected for ease of illustration. Ray R5 strikes surface E perpendicularly; therefore surface E will be in highlight. Ray R1, which strikes surface A at a nearly perpendicular angle, therefore, would be in light and would be almost as light as the highlight. Rays R2, R3, R4, R6, R8, and R10 all strike their respective planes at an angle of 45 degrees; therefore, planes B, C, D, F, H, and J, are all in light. No direct rays strike surface G or I; therefore these planes are in shade. That portion of surface H marked G1 will be in shadow, cast by the edge formed by the intersection of F and G.

Figure 5.1, sketch *b*, also shows how light appears in elevation when its relative intensity is determined by the above principles.

Reflected Light

It must be remembered that light rays "bounce" from place to place, and in so doing modify shadows such as G1 in Figure 5.2. Let us examine the course of several such rays that ricochet from the ground in section. Ray RL1, bouncing upward at an angle of 45 degrees, strikes plane G near its outer edge, then rebounds at an angle of 90 degrees to the bottom of shadow G1. Ray RL3 acts in the same way, falling into shadow G1, near its top. The intensity of light diminishes according to the distance it travels. Ray RL3 + RL6, being shorter than ray

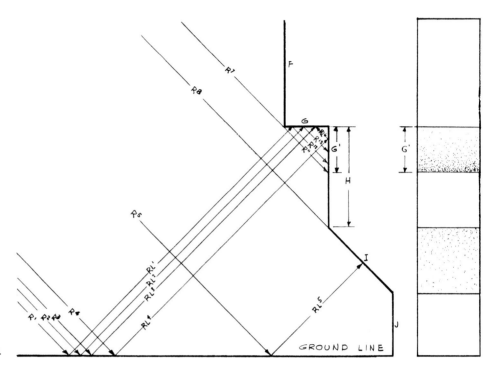

Fig. 5.2 The Workings of Reflected Light.

RL1 + RL2, will be the brighter of the two. Therefore, shadow G1 will be graded by reflected light, with its lower part darkest and its upper part lightest.

Shade, as on the underside of a sloping canopy, is also modified by reflected light (Figure 5.3). Ray RT1 bounds upon from the ground, rebounds from the building, as RC1, and strikes the underside of the canopy near its outer edge. Ray RC3 does the same thing as RC1, but travels a much longer distance from the face of the building. Therefore, the underside of the canopy, although in shade, will be graded from light at the face of the building to dark at the outer edge of the canopy.

When light rays strike a large pane of glass, they pass through it and ricochet inside the room (Figure 5.4). Since ray RT3 travels a longer distance than ray RT1, the ceiling will be darkest at the partition. These same rays, bounding farther than the ceiling, will strike the rear partition in such a manner that ray RT3 travels farther than RT1. Therefore the partition will be lightest near the floor and darkest near the ceiling.

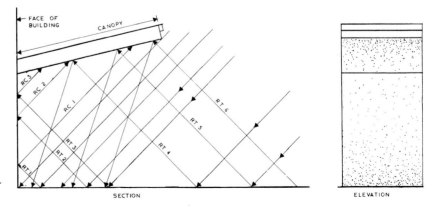

Fig. 5.3 Reflected Light on a Tilted Canopy.

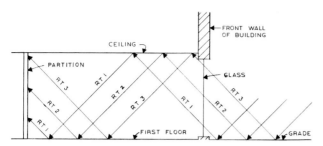

Fig. 5.4 Reflected Light Passing through Glass.

Double Gradation

Figure 5.5 illustrates double gradation in reflected light. A series of rays, typified by ray R1, casts a shadow X on wall Y. Reflected rays RL1, RL2, and RL3 bound off the ground and into the shade side of pier A, then rebound into shadow X. Since reflected ray RR3 is shorter than reflected ray RR1, the shadow will be graded from light at the pier to dark at its outer edge. The shadow, however, will also receive reflected rays, typified by RL4, RL5, and RL6, which bounce off the ground in a line perpendicular to the wall on which the shadow falls. Since reflected ray A is shorter than reflected ray C (in section), it is obvious that the shadow will be graded from light at the bottom to dark at the top.

Reflected Shadows

If an elevation is in sunlight, normal shadows will be cast by the direct rays of the sun at 45 degrees, and from the left, as in the left-hand portion of the plan (marked A) in Figure 5.6. If, however, the same elevation is entirely in shade, it may be assumed that reflected light, bounding from the ground in the reverse direction, will strike the facade from the right side, as in Figure 5.6. Thus, if there is a horizontal projection near the ground (see section), it will throw a reverse shadow on the face of the building (see elevation, portion B of Figure 5.6, which may be plotted in a manner similar to that used for ordinary shadows.) In

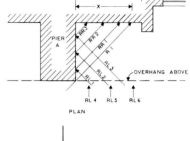

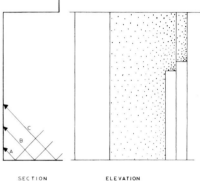

Fig. 5.5 Reflected Light in Elevation: Shadows.

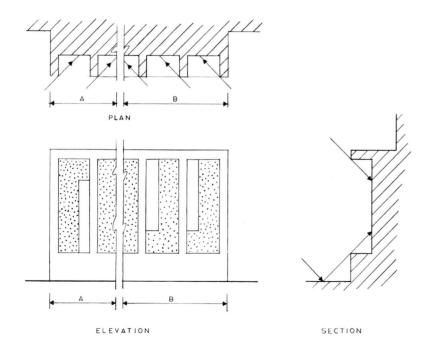

Fig. 5.6 Normal Shadows and Reflected Shadows.

the same way, back light throws shadows on the left and top sides of window muntins and mullions which are in shade, rather than to the right and bottom of these projections as when they are bathed in direct sunshine.

Light and Air

A problem which must be dealt with early in the process of making a rendering is the relative values of parallel planes. Considering that all walls of the hypothetical plan in Figure 5.1, sketch *b*, are of the same material — say limestone — which would be the lightest? To solve this problem, try to remember your last vacation in a mountainous area. If you will recall, the mountain that you stood upon always looked darker to you than a mountain in the distance. This was so because air — all air — has substance, and therefore has the ability to filter light and affect vision. The more air between the spectator and an object in the distance, the lighter that object will seem. If we adopt this rule as a convention in rendering, then it follows that in Figure 5.1, sketch *b*, wall F will be darkest, and walls B and J lightest, and walls H and D ranging between.

Light and Glass

The presence of glass in large areas of a perspective presents certain problems to the renderer. If there is a sheet of glass between the spectator and an object, the value of the object will be lightened somewhat. If there are two sheets of glass, the object will be lightened even more, and so on.

But glass presents other problems. For instance, the renderer must follow rules about glare. The presence of glare is easy to determine if the following rules are remembered: When spectators are directly opposite a glass area, at their own level, a small glass opening will appear dark, but a large glass area will be transparent. If they are either above or below the glass area, the glass will be in glare. For example, if they are standing at ground level and looking at a high building with a facade of glass, the glass will be darkest at the level of their eyes, and will become increasingly lighter as they look upward, with the greatest glare at the top of the building.

Similarly, if the spectators stand in front of a glass facade, the glass directly in front of them will appear to be darkest, while that at the ends of the building will be lightest, with the greatest glare at the ends of the building.

Theories and Observation

Keep the rules in this chapter constantly in mind. Observe the theories in action every day on actual structures as you walk along the street. Notice in particular that the vagaries of light and the presence of atmosphere cause constant changes in value and color in every wall surface, under every projection. Become aware of the differences in value and color of the many pieces of each building material, such as stone. Remember that no two things in nature are exactly alike. Notice that the texture and color of different pieces of the same material are affected in different ways by age and time of day. Also, as the sun becomes bright or dull, the same building will take on a hundred different degrees of brightness — sometimes within the space of a minute. When you have absorbed these phenomena and the general rules set down in this chapter, you will be in a position to develop your own conventions for rendering light and shade under any condition. From then on, you can apply these conventions and thereby avoid the deadly mechanical rendering which is the sign of the amateur.

chapter 6

Color—Fact and Theory

Until quite recently, color reproduction for books and magazines was of poor quality. It has always been expensive, and therefore less widely used than the black-and-white printing processes. People have come to accept black and white in pictures as reality instead of merely an abstraction of reality, which it really is. Yet the delineator usually finds that a rendering in color has a much greater appeal than one in black and white.

A rendering in color brings to mind real things and similar scenes that the spectator has experienced. Color enables the delineator to identify variations and textures in a rendering much more fully, and correspondingly helps the spectator to understand the message that the rendering is meant to convey. To prove the difference in the amount of appeal, it is only necessary to hang two skillfully drawn renderings of the same subject side by side—one in black and white, the other in color. Invariably the eye will go first to the one rendered in color, and only after this has been fully observed will it go to the black-and-white presentation.

Color and Light

Many theories have been advanced to explain color. Most agree that objects themselves do not have color, but that color is caused by their relative ability to absorb light rays. Because objects do not absorb the same quantity of light at each wavelength, different colors are produced. When light strikes the object itself, it penetrates the surface somewhat. The amount of penetration and absorption depends upon the texture of the object. If an object absorbs all colors except red, red rays are reflected to the eye and we call the object "red." White light is a mixture of all colors. These may be seen when sunlight, striking the curved surfaces of raindrops, is spread into a rainbow. The same effect may be obtained by causing a narrow beam of light to pass through a glass prism (Figure 6.1).

Fig. 6.1 Refraction of Light through a Glass Prism.

White surfaces reflect all colors, absorbing none. Black, on the other hand, represents a complete lack of light and color. Black surfaces do not reflect colors, but absorb them instead.

These basic facts are only a small part of the body of fascinating information about color and light amassed by scientists, especially those in the fields of optics and photography. But practical application of color by delineators and others who work with pigments must follow a slightly different path. For the purposes of this discussion, we shall consider color to be not merely reflection but rather an entity unto itself, with its own properties.

Properties of Color

Color may be described as having three outstanding properties: hue, value, and intensity. *Hue* means the name of the color, such as "blue," which differentiates it from another color, such as "green." *Value* designates the brightness of a color — that is, whether it is a light blue or a dark blue. *Intensity*, or chroma, denotes the extent to which the hue is free from any white constituent. The temperature of a color has no physical basis, but blue-greens and blue-violets, which seem to recede, are considered cool colors; and reds, red-oranges, and red-violets, which seem to advance, are considered warm colors.

Effects of Types of Light

Since color may be thought of as reflected light, it should be recognized that the kind of light that falls upon the object will affect its appearance. A color that appears to be bluish green when viewed in daylight will look yellowish green in incandescent light. Under daylight fluorescent lighting — which does not contain all the colors of the spectrum — the same color will appear to be completely blue. Because of this phenomenon the delineator should work by daylight whenever possible and should also arrange to show the rendering to all interested parties in the same light, so as to ensure color constancy.

If the light in which a rendering is to be shown is important, so are the surroundings, since any bright or garish wall colors near the presentation will vitally affect the appearance of the colors in the picture. The best surroundings are of a neutral tone.

Effect of Surroundings on Color

There are certain other phenomena which should be kept in mind in selecting colors for a rendering. An area of a picture rendered in a bright color will seem larger than it actually is, because a bright color is more stimulating to the nerves of the retina of the eye than a grayed hue. A white area enclosed by a darker area appears to swell in dimension. If the same color is used in several different parts of a picture, it may appear to be different in hue because of the different colors that surround it. An area painted yellow will seem larger than one painted orange, and an orange area will seem larger than one painted red. Invariably a blue area will seem larger than a black one.

That colors look different in different surroundings has led to many a disappointment when colors were selected for decoration with no thought of their eventual neighboring colors. Many a beautiful vase has been purchased because it looked magnificent in a carefully prepared display in a store, only to become just an extraneous item when it was placed in incompatible surroundings in the

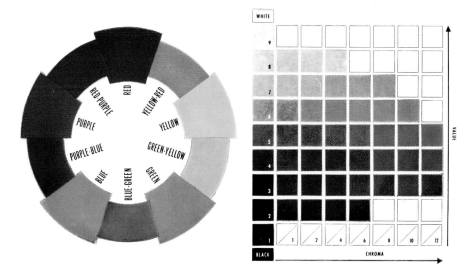

Hue circle (left) shows the principal hues, each of which is No. 5 of a family of ten adjoining hues. The chart at right shows all the variations in value and chroma for 5PB; the gray scale shows the steps between theoretical black and theoretical white. The color tree (below) illustrates the three-dimensional relationship of hue, value, and chroma. (Illustrations by Allcolor Company, Inc.; reproduced with permission from the Kodak Data Book *Color as Seen and Photographed*.)

Plate I

Munsell Color System

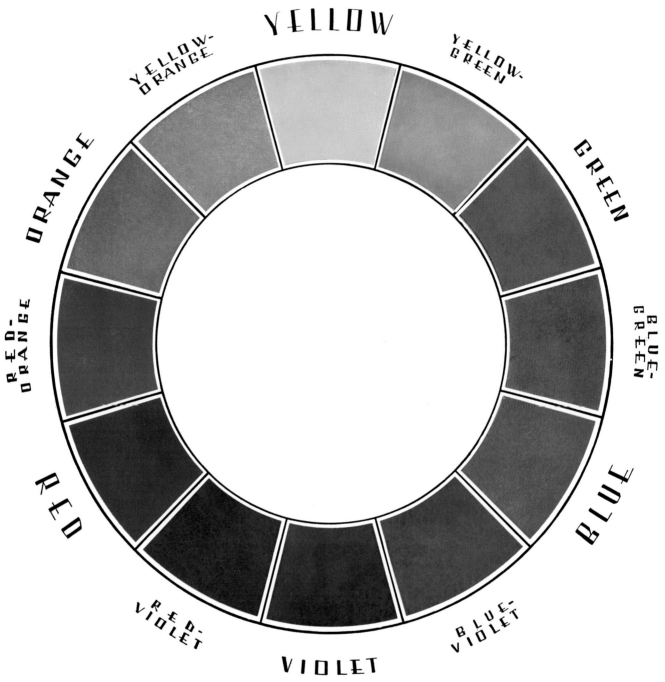

YELLOW

YELLOW-GREEN

YELLOW-ORANGE

GREEN

ORANGE

BLUE-GREEN

RED-ORANGE

BLUE

RED

BLUE-VIOLET

RED-VIOLET

VIOLET

Plate II

Twelve-Hue
Color Wheel

Plate III

Color Computer
(Courtesy of M. Grumbacher, Inc.)

Plate IV

Color Computer
(Courtesy of M. Grumbacher, Inc.)

home. This phenomenon is also responsible for the frequent disappointment that people feel when they actually wear clothes that looked very appealing displayed in a store under ideal conditions.

In rendering, colors of deep value will seem to be heavier than pale colors, and can cause an imbalance in a picture if too much of the deep color is used on one side. Finally, it should be remembered that light colors, or tints, always look brighter if they are viewed against a black background, while dark hues usually seem more dramatic against a white background.

If a room is painted with a cool color, the apparent size of the room will be increased. If a warm color is used, the room will seem smaller. Bright colors such as yellow-oranges, yellows, and yellow-greens have a luminous quality and should be used to lighten an otherwise dark room.

Psychological Effects of Color

It is probably well at this point to mention that colors affect people psychologically. Blue, for instance, reduces mental excitability and therefore helps one to concentrate. It is both cooling and sedative, but cannot be used indiscriminately, as too much of it will produce melancholia. These qualities were discovered during the Middle Ages, and are partly responsible for the use of so much blue in the stained-glass windows in the great cathedrals. Green is also cooling, and acts as an opiate. Yellow is cheery and stimulating and draws attention. Red is exciting and stimulates the brain; purple is sedative and soothing. Brown is restful and warming but should be combined with orange, yellow, or gold, because it can be depressing if used alone. Gray suggests color and like brown it is depressing unless combined with a livelier color. White, on the other hand, is cheering and reflects sunlight, particularly when used with red, yellow, or orange.

Color in Human History

People have always been interested in color, and have surrounded themselves with it. Cave dwellers of the Magdalenian period painted animals in color on the walls of their caves. During the earliest known ages in Egypt, color was used in religious rites and clothing, as well as in architecture. Temples were marked off in zones by colors in Mesopotamia and Asia, while in Greece, polychromy was developed to a high art, and red, blue, green, yellow, purple, white, brown, and black were used. During the Middle Ages color was used as a stimulus to emotion. However, during the Renaissance, color — at least in architecture — seems for a while to have been lost. This probably happened because, although Vitruvius amply discussed the influential architecture of ancient Rome, he made no mention of the use of color. In addition, some doctrines of the Reformation forbade adornment with color.

Chromatic Circles and Solids

As science developed, an increasing amount of attention was given to the secrets of color and their relation to mankind. Robert Boyle discovered in the seventeenth century that red, yellow, and blue came from white light by reflection and refraction. Sir Isaac Newton, while trying to solve the problems of the telescope in 1666, noticed the refraction and dispersion of light through a prism. He discovered that all color is contained in sunlight, and that when a beam of light

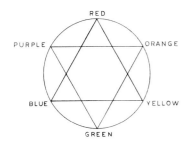

Fig. 6.2 Goethe's Color Wheel.

passes through a prism, the direction of the light waves is changed so that the violet waves, for example, are bent more sharply than red, and a rainbow results. See Figure 6.1. Having obtained this information, Newton then formed the first of all chromatic circles by bending these colors, pulling the red and violet ends around, and separating them with purple.

Johann Wolfgang von Goethe (1749 — 1832), the German poet, also dabbled in color, producing his own color wheel. See Figure 6.2.

The Munsell System of Color

In the United States today the best-known and most widely used system of color standardization is that invented by Albert H. Munsell. He became greatly interested in the practical application of color, and was disturbed by the fact that the popular names for colors do not describe them adequately for professional purposes. Colors are often named after flowers or plants (violet, indigo, old rose, primrose), fruits (peach, pomegranate, grape, avocado, plum) or places[1] (French blue, Naples yellow, Prussian blue). Others are named after actual persons, such as Davy's gray or Hooker's green.

Essentially, the Munsell system consists of an orderly arrangement of colors in the shape of a three-dimensional color solid roughly spherical in shape. See Plate I. It is based on a color circle of 10 major hues, made up of 5 principal hues (red, yellow, green, blue, and purple) and 5 intermediate hues (yellow-red, green-yellow, blue-green, purple-blue, and red-purple). Each of the 10 major hues, which appear to be about equidistant from the spectator, is No. 5 in a group of 10 numbers. Therefore, the whole hue circle is composed of 100 hues. A scale of reflectances, or "values" as they are known in the Munsell system, extends like a core through the center of the hue circle. A supposedly perfect white, having 100 percent reflectance, located at the apex of the value scale, is numbered 10. At the bottom, a supposedly perfect black (0 percent reflectance) is numbered 0. Nine graduated value steps connect these poles.

Radiating from this value scale, or central core, are the increments of saturation (called "chroma" in the Munsell system). These, too, seem to be about equidistant from the spectator. The numbers of these increments vary from 0 (a neutral gray) to as high as 16, according to the amount of saturation produced by a given hue at a given value level. Since colors vary in chroma or saturation, some colors extend farther from the neutral axis than others, and the solid is therefore not symmetrical. Pure red, with a chroma of 14, for instance, extends farther than blue-green, with a chroma of only 6.

Munsell Notation

In an intricate system of notation, each hue is described by a letter which locates it on the 100-step equator, a number from 1 to 9 which gives its value, and another number which locates it in relation to the neutral axis.

With this information it is possible to describe any given hue exactly and to locate its place in the color solid. Furthermore, as Munsell stated,[2] one can "select one familiar color, and study what others will combine with it to please the eye," by the use of three typical paths: one vertical, with rapid change of

[1] As Munsell has asked, "Can we imagine musical tones called lark, canary, crow, cat, dog, or mouse, because they bear some distant resemblance to the cries of those animals?"

[2] A. H. Munsell, *A Color Notation: A Measured Color System, Based on the Three Qualities, Hue, Value, and Chroma*, 2d ed., George Ellis Co., Boston, 1907, p. 87.

value; another lateral, with rapid change of hue; and a third inward, through the neutral center, to seek out the opposite color field. All other paths are combined by two or three of these typical directions in the color solid.

Possibly because this selective process is so complicated, the Munsell system is not generally used by artists or delineators. It is a splendid, methodical way of standardizing, categorizing, and identifying colors.

The Ostwald Color System

While on the one hand the various parts of the Munsell system are made up of hue, value, and chroma, the Ostwald system, also in use, concerns itself with hue, black, and white. The Ostwald solid (Figure 6.3a) is in the form of a double cone rather than a sphere. In this system there are 24 hues around the equator and 8 value steps from white at the top, or north pole, to black at the bottom, or south pole.

If the solid were to be cut in half vertically, the resulting section would be diamond-shaped, as in Figure 6.3b. Each side (left and right) of the diamond would form a triangle. All the colors in the left triangle, for instance, would be derived from hue 20 (green), and those in the right triangle from hue 8 (red). Hues 20 and 8 are complements, since they appear opposite each other on the hue circle. The entire solid is, of course, made up of 12 sections such as this.

Fig. 6.3a Ostwald Color Solid.

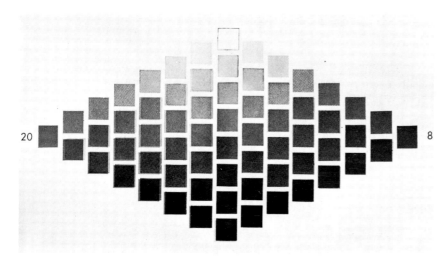

Fig. 6.3b Vertical Section through the Ostwald Color Solid.

Since each section is made up of 56 colors, the complete solid contains 672 chromatic colors, plus the 8 steps of the gray scale. In each color triangle, the vertical scales parallel to black and white (the isochromes) are equal in purity. The colors parallel to a line between pure color and white (the isotones), in the top portion of the cone, contain an equal amount of black. The scales parallel to a line between pure color and black (the isotints in the bottom) have equal white content. It may be seen from this description that the Ostwald system is based upon the assumption that all colors may be mixed from combinations of pure hue, white, and black.

Ostwald Notation

Combinations of various numbers and letters make up the Ostwald color notations (Figure 6.4a). The hues, all full colors (free of white and black) numbered from 1 to 24, are arranged in groups of three. These groups are called "yellow," "orange," "red," "purple," "blue," "turquoise," "sea green," and "leaf green." The gray scale is lettered from A for white at the top to P for black at the bottom (Figure 6.4b). Two of these letters are always required: The first indicates that the color contains the same amount of white as the gray of the gray scale (Figure 6.5), in which the series ends. The second letter indicates that the color contains the same amount of black as the gray of the gray scale in which the series ends.

In other words, any two letters will specify the amount of white and black of a color in terms of the gray scale. Any number from 1 to 24 specifies hue, and is written at the beginning of the notation like this: 22PA.

Like the Munsell system, the Ostwald color solid may be used for the selection of color harmonies. These are located according to geometric relationships within the various parts of the solid itself.[3] But this more or less mathematical system has not been accepted for general use by either artists or delineators, possibly because of its complexity but also because it is impossible with black and white paint pigments to obtain the colors in the Ostwald color solid.

---

[3] Egbert Jacobson, *Basic Color: An Interpretation of the Ostwald Color System*, Part II, Paul Theobald and Company, Chicago 1948, pp. 56–108.

Fig. 6.4a Hues around the Equator.

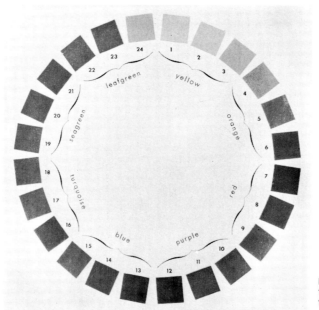

Fig. 6.4b One-Half the Vertical Section through the Ostwald Color Solid, Showing the Color Notation.

Black and white paints, instead of evenly lightening or darkening a given hue, change it. White, because it contains blue, "chalks" a hue, while black (which also contains blue) sullies it. If one attempts, for instance, to gray yellow by the addition of black, the result is green. So, while it is well for artists to know the Ostwald system, it cannot be used to advantage by those who work with paint pigments.

It is interesting to note that the colors of the Munsell system seem to lend themselves best to the development of standards in packaging and other manufactured products in general, while the colors of the Ostwald system have been used to a great extent by manufacturers of interior and exterior wall paints.

Differences between Light and Pigment

Unfortunately, the same laws do not apply to colors in light and colors in pigment. Physicists generally believe that red, green, and blue-violet are the true primaries. It is impossible, however, to obtain a full-intensity yellow with such a pigment mixture. Therefore, the color wheel that uses red, yellow, and blue as its primaries, while not agreeing with the theories of the physicists, is most satisfactory for the use of the artist. A large variety of colors can be obtained by mixing these three primaries: red, yellow, and blue. However, in order to produce as wide a range of colors as possible, the primaries would have to include a magenta-red and a blue-green instead of a blue. These are the primaries of printing rules. In other words, artists or delineators simply cannot make as perfect a chromatic circle with their pigments as can printers with their more nearly perfect inks. The qualities of the pigments themselves, and a knowledge of the ways that they mix and react with each other, are the important elements to artists — the elements which enable delineators to produce sufficiently well and with foreseeable perfection any architectural picture required.

Making a Color Wheel

From a practical standpoint, the delineator will find the simple color wheel (Plate II) of great assistance in determining color schemes and harmony. Neither the Munsell system nor the Ostwald color solid is easy or inexpensive to make, and since the color wheel provides a simple, yet adequate means of determining color schemes and color harmonies, it seems obvious that this is the tool to use. Although the color wheel shown in Plate II contains 12 colors, it can also be made with 18. In order to make such a color wheel, the procedure described below should be followed.

On a sheet of 140-pound cold-pressed stretched paper (stretched as in Chapter 10) or 140-pound cold-pressed illustration board, draw a circle 10 inches in diameter. Using the same center, draw an inner circle 6 inches in diameter. Then divide the ring between the two circles into 12 equal parts by making each segment 30 degrees. In order to keep the colors from running together, leave a space of about 1/16 inch between segments.

After the pencil drawing has been completed, the following materials should be assembled:

1. Watercolors (half tubes)
   a. Cadmium yellow pale
   b. Vermilion
   c. Alizarin crimson

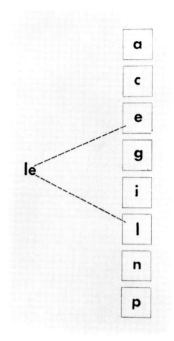

Fig. 6.5 The Gray Scale of the Ostwald Color Solid.

d. French ultramarine blue

e. Cobalt blue

f. Hooker's green

2. A small bucket or other container for water
3. A No. 4 watercolor brush
4. Six wash pans (white)
5. Several white blotters

Before applying washes of color, examine the 12-hue color wheel shown in Plate II and notice that the primary colors (yellow, red, and blue) are located at the third points of the color wheel. (The "primary colors" are so called because by mixing paints of these three hues, theoretically, at least, all other hues may be obtained. In actual practice, because of the limitations of pigments, as described above, this is not so.) Write these names lightly outside the segments in which they are to appear, and then identify the colors for the other segments in the same manner. The secondaries are located halfway between the primaries, and the tertiaries between the primaries and secondaries.

The colors for the 12 segments of the color circle may be purchased from any art materials shop. Grumbacher's colors are excellent for this purpose, but if you prefer to use the colors of the palette suggested later in this chapter, the procedure for mixing is discussed below.

Primary colors. Suggested pigments for the primary colors are

Yellow: Cadmium yellow pale

Red: Rose madder or alizarin crimson

Blue: Cobalt blue with a small amount of french ultramarine blue

Secondary colors. Each of the secondary colors — green, violet, and orange — is located halfway between two of the primary colors. Green is thus between yellow and blue, violet between red and blue, and orange halfway between red and yellow. Suggested pigments for mixing the secondary colors are

Green: Hooker's green with a small amount of cadmium yellow added

Violet: A combination of the proper amounts of the red and blue used for the primary colors

Orange: Vermilion with a small amount of cadmium yellow pale

Tertiaries. The tertiaries, the colors situated between the primaries and secondaries on the color wheel, are mixed as follows:

Yellow-green: Some of the yellow and some of the green previously mixed

Blue-green: Some of the blue and some of the green previously mixed

Blue-violet: Some of the blue and some of violet previously mixed

Red-violet: Some of the red and some of the violet previously mixed

Red-orange: Some of the red and some of the orange previously mixed

The pigments used for tertiaries cannot be mixed in equal amounts because of the differences in strength between the various pigments. Before applying each of your colors to the color wheel, it is well to place a sample on a piece of paper, let it dry, and then compare it with the color in Plate II, in order to ensure that your color is correct.

The 18-Hue Color Wheel

To make a chromatic circle with 18 hues instead of 12, proceed in the manner described above until you have developed the primary and secondary colors. To obtain the tertiaries, of which there will be two instead of one between each primary and secondary, proceed as follows:

The tertiary immediately to the right of the yellow primary will be yellow-green-yellow, followed by green-yellow-green. Between green and blue will be the tertiary green-blue-green, with blue-green-blue on its right.

The tertiaries between violet and blue will, of course, become violet-blue-violet, and blue-violet-blue. The tertiaries between violet and red will be violet-red-violet and red-violet-red. Those between orange and yellow will be orange-yellow-orange and yellow-orange-yellow.

Use of the Color Wheel

The color wheel is a means not alone for studying color, but also for locating harmonies. To begin with, it is a constant reminder of the relationship of colors one to another. This is a basic arrangement, each element of which can always be found in the same position. It provides simple color categories into which all pigment names must fall. It also provides a visual vocabulary of basic colors from which tints and shades may be made.

As in the study of color in light, the rules for obtaining color harmony with pigments are based on personal taste (that is, the personal taste of most people). The rules set down here will be found to relate closely to the rules that nature seems to use in colors. We seldom see colors used in full intensity in the world around us, and where intense hues occur, they are usually in small amounts. Greens in nature are not harsh, but are soft, grayed yellow-greens. The skies above us usually have very pale hues. Since the average people's minds are attuned to the world about them, they can accept such subtleties more readily than the harshness of loud, clashing colors.

Most art supply stores carry inexpensive color wheels which will help the beginning renderer to learn and experiment with mixing color, as shown in Plate III, Color Computer, and in Plate IV, Color Harmony Wheel. These are helpful reference tools which can be used when the renderer finds difficulty dealing with a color mix even while doing a rendering.

Color Schemes

It should be recognized at the outset that good color schemes are made of only a few colors, properly selected, mixed, and blended. The difference between good art, such as that found in the great museums of the world, and calendar art can be explained to a great extent by this phenomenon. The professional artist uses a few colors with many shades of these colors, while the amateur is inclined to use a great many more colors than needed for the situation—thus creating more problems than can be handled at one time.

One Color with White, Black, or Gray

The simplest of all schemes is that in which one color is used with white, black, or gray. The average book cover (without the dust jacket) is an example of this kind of color scheme.

The Monochromatic Scheme

The monochromatic color scheme, which can be very sophisticated, is one in which many shades of a single color are used. Of course, not all colors will lend themselves to a monochromatic scheme, simply because the lighter colors cannot achieve deep enough tones for emphasis. This automatically eliminates yellow, orange, and pale green.

The Analogous Scheme

The analogous color scheme permits the use of colors which adjoin each other on the color wheel (Plate II), such as yellow, yellow-green, and green, or red, red-orange, and orange. These colors are not necessarily used in their pure forms in different parts of the picture, but are mixed together in varying amounts so that numerous shades may be made from the few colors used. It is usual for one of the colors in such a scheme to predominate in a picture: that is, to be used in a larger area than the rest.

Analogous plus Complementary Accent

One of the most common color schemes consists of a series of analogous colors, plus a complementary accent, i.e., a color on the opposite side of the wheel to the center of the analogous run. For example, a scheme that uses yellow-orange, orange, and yellow-green could be combined with violet. By mixing these colors together in various amounts it will be found that the complementary accent (violet) will "gray" and soften the three analogous colors, deepen them for the darker tones, and at the same time complement them.

Complementary Scheme

For a simple complementary scheme, two colors opposite each other on the color wheel — such as blue-violet and yellow-orange — are used. Neither of these need be used in pure form, but literally hundreds of shades may be obtained by blending them together in varying amounts.

An interesting aspect of complements is the way they affect each other. In pure form they actually complement each other; each has the quality of making the other look better by its proximity. But as they are mixed together, they modify each other to a point where they finally form a neutral gray. It should be noted, however, that the neutral grays obtained by mixing different sets of complements will vary; sometimes a mousey gray occurs, and at other times a warm, brownish-gray. Grays can be formed by mixing two complements, such as red and green, yellow and violet, orange and blue, or red-orange and blue-green. A tie score is as unsatisfactory in rendering as in a ball game, and since completely neutral grays seem to have no color at all, they are to be avoided or used very sparingly. In other words, use more of one complement than the other so that the resultant mixture will appear to contain more of one color than the other.

Another interesting phenomenon is that colors that appear in neither pigment sometimes appear when the two complements are mixed. With certain proportions of yellow and violet, a rust color will appear. A little color experimentation will illustrate this point. Mix the various complementary colors together in pairs and watch what happens to each color as it is blended with its complement.

Near or Split Complements

A split complement takes the form of a Y on the color wheel, with one arm of the Y pointing, for instance, to yellow-orange, the other arm to yellow-green, and the stem of the Y pointing to violet. For example, the scheme could be composed of violet, plus two colors, one on each side of the direct complement, which in this case is not used. The split complement resembles the complementary scheme, but provides a slightly wider range of colors and shades.

Triads

Another excellent color scheme may be obtained by the mixture of triads: that is, three colors located equidistant from one another at three points of the color wheel. This combination provides a wide range of hues, shades, and tints.

Something to keep in mind regarding the last three color schemes discussed is that different kinds of colors and great variations may be obtained by varying the pigments that are used. In other words, the three different sets of orange and blue complements can be obtained by using three different kinds of blue in your palette, such as cobalt, French ultramarine, and cerulean. A red and green complementary color scheme permits the use of either Hooker's green or emerald green. A yellow-violet complementary color scheme can be carried out with either cadmium yellow pale or yellow ochre.

Browns are a mixture of orange with blue, green, or gray, while grays result from mixtures of three primary or two complementary colors. The type of gray — warm or cool — can be mixed to suit.

Colored Papers

No discussion of color would be complete without mention of colored charcoal and pastel papers. These are available at any art materials store in a number of shades, including gray, brown, yellow, green, orange, and red. (See the section on carbon pencil rendering in Chapter 9.) Orange and red may be quickly eliminated, since colors as bright as these are usually not suitable for renderings. Generally speaking, the more delicately tinted papers — such as cool brown, warm or cool gray, pale yellow, and pale green — are easier to work on, but there are times when the darker papers are required. A good rule to remember is that the delicately tinted papers lend themselves to transparent washes, either of watercolor or of body color of a thin or medium consistency, while the darker papers give sharper contrasts when these are desired, or when thick body color (tempera) is to be used.

Helpful Hints for Mixing Colors

As mentioned earlier, a sophisticated color scheme is usually the result not only of careful selection of the scheme and of the proper use of colors in proper areas, but also nearly always of mixing together for each part of the painting all the colors of your color scheme in varying amounts.

In general, two kinds of color schemes are used in rendering. In the first, the colors of nature are used, such as a blue sky and green grass. In the second, the colors of nature are modified. An example might be a blue monochromatic color scheme in which all the shades and tints are blue. In an analogous color scheme using yellow, yellow-green, and green, it is obvious that the sky cannot be blue, so it is likely to become a pale shade of green. An interesting fact about the use of such a stylized color scheme is that the eye will readily accept grass which is not green or a sky which is not blue. The result is often more dramatic than if the usual colors were used. In addition, skies in nature are rarely pure blue, but are likely at any time at all to contain green, yellow, orange, or gray. In similar fashion — this can be observed at almost any time of the year except perhaps in spring — lawns, trees, and bushes are not bright green at all, but are a mixture of subdued gray-green, yellow-green, orange-green, etc.

The renderer who recognizes these phenomena produces a much more realistic rendering than the amateur who uses pure hues. No two things in nature are exactly alike, and the numerous color schemes that delineators can include in their renderings have the benefit of introducing great variety and interest into the works.

Values and Color Choice

A successful rendering cannot be made without first determining the values of the various parts of the picture. Without contrast, even subtle colors do not show off to good advantage. Before proceeding with the application of any color, a value study must be made. Be sure that the colors you use are suitable. Bright red, for instance, would not give the desired effect in the rendering of a mausoleum, nor does it usually appear to be correct when used alone in a sky. The color chosen must be able to produce a deep value, if one is desired. The colors used in such incidental items as scale figures and automobiles must complement the colors in the building being rendered, and should not draw attention to themselves by their brightness or garishness.

The Color Study

It is well to make a color study before beginning work on the final rendering. This preplanning process is basic for even the experienced renderer. After selecting the several colors that you intend to use, which fall into one of the color schemes described above, put a little of each pigment on a piece of illustration board or paper similar to that upon which you are going to render. The possible range of your color combination can be ascertained in a few minutes by simply dabbling in these colors with a wet brush. For instance, if a scheme such as red, yellow, and blue is to be used, and you have decided upon cadmium yellow pale, cobalt blue, and alizarin crimson, you can quickly see by mixing them together in varying amounts that you can obtain anything from pure yellow, red, or blue, to grayish blues, reds, or yellows, warm browns, tans, and grayish tans. This is an enjoyable process which reveals all the potentialities and limitations of your colors. After this freehand color and value study, you are thoroughly prepared — at least in knowledge of color — to begin rendering.

Palettes

Before modern science discovered artificial ways of making them, paints were very rare, hard to obtain, and very expensive. Most artists made their own paints from earths such as the ochres, umbers and siennas; from minerals such as copper, lead, or iron; or from mixtures of burned wood and the blood of animals. Other items, such as burned teeth and shinbones of animals, were crushed and roasted. The soot of certain oils; burnt ivory; the ink bag of the cuttlefish; tiny snails; the roots, sap, and leaves of flowers and trees; berries; and the husks of nuts were also used. The processes of manufacture were secret and were passed from one generation to the next.

Ancient Greek literature speaks of the use of four colors: white, yellow, red, and black. The works of those times show a number of other shades that were obtained by mixing combinations of these four. During the Renaissance only a few colors were used; this limited palette consisted of red, yellow, blue, and black (and many shades thereof). The French Impressionists, who worked directly from nature in the 1870s and 1880s, used intense blues, greens, red, and purples. They renounced the use of black, reveled in strong and varied color, and were always conscious of the effect of light on colors.

More pigments, like ancient ones, are manufactured from a variety of substances, and their manufacture is accomplished by a variety of intricate processes. Earths such as the ochres, siennas, and umbers are used in the natural form or roasted. Animal materials, such as insects, provide certain colors. Stones, such as slate, are utilized, as well as the roots of plants, gum resins, and vegetables. Such metals as aluminum, cobalt, potassium, cadmium, copper, zinc, and iron play a part in the manufacture of pigments, as do charcoal, coal tar, and soot from certain oils. Many combinations are the result of a chemical reaction between a basic metal and another element such as oxygen, sulphur, chlorine, or arsenic. Since there are so many possible chemical combinations, there are literally hundreds of different pigments available.

Purchase of Paints

When shopping for paints, therefore, it is well to have a good idea of what you want to buy before you go to the art materials store. The author uses the following palette for watercolor, and recommends it because it permits the mixture of just about every hue, shade, or tint that the delineator needs.

Yellows
Cadmium yellow pale
Yellow ochre

Oranges
Cadmium orange
Vermilion

Reds
Alizarin crimson or rose madder

Blues
French ultramarine blue
Cobalt blue
Cerulean blue

Greens
Hooker's green dark
Emerald green

There are many possible palette variations, and each delineator or artist develops a personal palette, usually based on other artists' palettes and modified by experience. Examples of palettes, selected at random are shown below.

Palette 1

Yellows
Aureolin
Cadmium yellow deep
Indian yellow
Chrome yellow pale
Yellow ochre

Blues
French ultramarine blue
Cobalt blue
Cerulean blue
Antwerp blue

Oranges

Vermilion
Venetian red
Carmine

Green

Emerald green

Red

Indian red

Palette 2

Yellows

Cadmium yellow deep
Yellow ochre

Oranges

Cadmium orange
Vermilion

Reds

Alizarin crimson

Blues

French ultramarine blue
Cobalt blue
Cerulean blue

Brown

Vandyke brown

Earth color

Burnt sienna

Palette 3

Yellows

Cadmium yellow
Aureolin
Cadmium lemon

Oranges

Vermilion
Cadmium orange

Reds

Alizarin crimson

Blues

French ultramarine blue
Cobalt blue
Winsor blue

Greens

Hooker's green No. 2

Grays

Davy's gray (warm tone)
Payne's gray (cool tone)

Brownish gray

Sepia

Earth colors

Raw sienna
Burnt sienna
Raw umber
Burnt umber

Basic Pigments

From the palettes shown above, and from experience, the reader will discover that a number of pigments, such as those in the palette below, are basic and widely used.

Yellows

Cadmium yellow (pale or deep)
Yellow ochre
Aureolin

Oranges

Vermilion
Cadmium orange

Blues

French ultramarine blue
Cobalt blue
Cerulean blue

Greens

Emerald green

Reds

Alizarin crimson
Rose madder

Whatever colors you add to these will depend upon your personal taste and experience. Half the fun of being a delineator lies in the contemplation of a color you have not tried that lies temptingly in the showcase.

chapter 7

Work Area and General Approach to Rendering

One of the most enjoyable aspects of any new venture is the preparation for it, including assessing the many possibilities available for one's work environment, as well as the planning of that environment. The need for a proper work space, storage, lighting, and ventilation are important aspects of the planning program. The purpose of this chapter is to provide information on programming, planning, and equipping a studio. Specific equipment for special techniques will be listed separately in each chapter according to medium.

Studio Program

For the beginning renderer a studio is most likely programmed around limited available space, perhaps a spare bedroom, the attic, or a finished basement. While it is not always possible to have optimum conditions, the delineator should select a quiet spot where there is minimum or no general circulation, since the type of work will demand a great deal of concentration and privacy. Some basic rules should be considered in both the programming and planning stages for any studio.

A. Lighting requirements
   1. The most desired natural lighting is from the north and east.
   2. General area lighting should be incandescent or a 3-tube fluorescent fixture with warm white lamps.
   3. Task lighting at the specific work area should be used for detailed work.
   4. The most important point regarding the complex subject of lighting the work area is to avoid glare at all cost.
B. Heating, ventilation, and air conditioning
   1. Requirements vary depending upon the location of the studio and the medium being used.

2. Within a living space the normal heat and ventilation should be adequate. Basements and attics may require the addition of insulation, heating, and air conditioning. Ventilation is important if the medium being used produces disturbing or unsafe odors, fumes, or dust.
3. Design criteria for comfort will depend upon the amount of time spent by the renderer in the studio.

C. Electrical considerations
1. Normal convenience outlets for task lighting and equipment (eraser, pencil sharpener, etc.) should be adequate.
2. Supplemental electrical power will be necessary if additional equipment is required (copiers, drivers, etc.) To prevent possible fire hazard, an electrician should be consulted for such installation.
3. A telephone will be an important addition as the delineator develops a client base. And a telephone-answering machine is within the most limited budget.

D. Architectural considerations
1. A studio size of 10 × 12 feet (120 square feet) is ideal for the beginner.
2. A light, neutral color such as beige or off-white, with a high reflectance quality, is a good choice for walls.
3. The ceiling should be painted flat white.
4. Flooring, depending on the types of media to be used, may be a maintenance problem; therefore, vinyl asbestos tile (VAT), carpet tile, and linoleum should be considered.

E. Furnishings
1. A drafting table with or without adjustable top is the most important consideration. The table top should be covered with a protective cover, available from most art material suppliers. The minimum size for the drafting table is 36 × 60 inches. Another frequently used type of table is formed from a 36- × 84-inch (3 × 7 feet) flush door supported on a pair of 2-drawer file cabinets.
2. A reference table where drawings connected with a project may be kept, is a very important piece of equipment. The suggested place for this table, which should be as large as the drafting table, and which also may be a flush door supported by a drawing file, is immediately behind the renderer, although it will also be useful if it occupies a position at the side.
3. The drafting stool or chair, the height of which is determined by the type and height of the drafting table, is the most valuable consideration for long work periods. One rule of thumb in determining the height of the stool or chair is that it should provide a space of 5 inches between the seat and the underside of the drawing surface. The comfort and convenience of the individual renderer are the final determining factors.
4. A tackboard of cork, rigid insulation, or Homosote, upon which drawings may be fastened with thumbtacks, is a necessary item for the delineator. If possible, the tackboard should be located on a wall near the drawing board, so that value studies and other reference materials may be fastened to it for reference. While the tackboard can be as large as space permits, a good rule is to make it the same size as the drafting table.

The Commercial Studio Program

The studio requirements for the experienced delineator are much the same as for the beginning renderer. However, additional considerations arise because of increased overhead and operating expenses, as related to income.

A. Studio location
1. Urban, suburban, or rural.

2. Purchased or rented space.
3. Available mass transportation or automobile.
4. Need for parking.
5. Codes and zoning.
6. Access to art suppliers; delivery and receiving limitations.
7. Security of the studio.
B. Studio requirements
1. Large work area and layout area.
2. Photographic studio and darkroom, which require special lighting, plumbing, and ventilation.
3. Spray booth for airbrush with direct exhaust to the outdoors. There may be local zoning and code restrictions.
4. Copy requirements may include a photocopier, a diazo machine, a vacuum frame, and light tables.
5. Bulk storage for supplies, projects, and office equipment.
6. Conference area for meetings with clients.
C. Economic considerations
1. Purchased or leased space will require the aid of a lawyer to review all legal matters of a lease or mortgage.
2. Monthly costs for utilities, equipment rentals, insurance, and salaries will require accounting advice.
3. Construction for start-up will demand initial capital outlay which can be amortized over a number of years.
4. Miscellaneous costs:
   a. Stationery
   b. Logo design
   c. Building permits
   d. Mailing and shipping
   e. Telephone installation

General Approach to Rendering

At the outset, it should be recognized that there are many ways of producing a rendering, and the final result will depend upon such diverse factors as the renderer's training and experience, and the time available for producing the rendering. It should be made clear at this point, however, that there is a difference between a sketch — which is usually no more than a rough study for a rendering — and a finished presentation, which is the result of a preconceived and well-executed plan of procedure. One can see examples of both the quick sketch and the finished rendering in various architectural books and magazines.

The Sketch

The success of a spontaneous sketch depends upon skill and experience, as well as upon the renderer's emotional status at the time the rendering is done. The "arty" sketch, which looks as if it had been accomplished in a very short time, may possibly be the twelfth or thirteenth of a series. A noncreative period will show up in a rendering of this type, and since there is no way of predicting when such a period will occur, the architect must have a system that will produce a guaranteed result whenever needed. One must be able to know, when beginning a rendering, that it will be finished in good fashion at a definite time. Insofar as possible, it is the purpose of this book to provide, in the following chapters on techniques, procedures which will satisfy the architect's requirements and which, if followed, will produce the desired results.

Subjects for Practice

An architect's own designs are ideal for rendering practice, but these are not always available, numerous enough, or suited to the medium to be tried. Where, then, do renderers who have no designs of their own available seek a subject? Architectural magazines are filled with photographs of the latest designs, some by famous architects, and these can be enlarged to any desired size (14 × 21 inches is an ideal picture size) by means of the photostat or pantograph. After enlargement, the building can be traced on tracing paper (and the design modified if desired), and the photograph put aside, since the values and light source obtained by the photographer are usually not as good as the delineator can get in a value study. The photographer seeks an effect embodying stark contrasts which blot out much detail. The delineator seeks a different effect, in which all parts of the building design are expressed with the utmost clarity and honesty.

As for the building's surroundings, these can be changed or modified. Trees and bushes can be added or taken away, walks and roadways can be modified, or the building can be placed in an entirely different (and perhaps more inspiring) setting. A country house can become a seaside house, a building in a stark setting can be relocated in a verdant one, and so on. The amount of magic used in transporting the building is entirely up to the delineator. Renderers can do exactly as they wish while practicing, and no one can say nay.

One cannot begin a rendering without proper investigation of the project and proper preparation. The sight of a clean sheet of paper, whether it is for a letter or a rendering, is sometimes appalling simply because one is afraid to spoil it. However, clever writers know that they must write and then rewrite their letters, and thus they make drafts before attempting the final copies. So, too, the clever delineator realizes that there are many problems to be decided before attempting to work on the final sheet of paper, and makes preliminary studies.

The Value Study

A value study is the best way to begin your preliminary investigation, whether the rendering is to be in black and white or color. In a black-and-white rendering there will be no contrast if the values are not correct, and in a color rendering the colors will not look well if the values are not right. The value study is usually drawn on tracing paper which has been placed over the perspective line drawing on the illustration board below. It is usually drawn in charcoal or soft pencil. The author personally prefers a medium grade of charcoal, because changes may be made more easily in this medium than in pencil. Modifications or erasures may be made with the fingers, with a chamois, or with a kneaded eraser.

The value study should never require more than 10 or 15 minutes. It should be a spontaneous impression of the final picture, and not an attempt at a finished result (Figure 7.1). A short piece of charcoal, perhaps 1 or 1½ inches long, is ideal for this purpose. One should leave out all but the essential elements in the picture, and details should be only "indicated" or suggested. Such items as roof rafters, boards, shingles, and other details that would take a long time to draw should be mostly omitted, although a few may be quickly drawn in to tell all that is necessary about the detail. At this phase of the rendering, one is interested in finding solutions to the large problems, and not in the details.

Several value studies may be required before the renderer is satisfied that maximum success in planning the following aspects of the picture has been achieved.

Medium: Marker on Xerox enlargement.

1. Light source.
2. Proper relationship of values in building, sky, trees, bushes, and scale figures.
3. The focal point of the picture.
4. The location, character, and amount of entourage, such as buildings, background, walkways, roadways, trees, bushes, scale figures, automobiles, plots of grass, shadows, and bodies of water.
5. The size of the building in relation to the total picture. (See Chapter 4.)
6. The quality of the sky: clear or clouded, flat or domed.
7. Expression of building design through the use of contrast:
    (a) The building may be made light with dark surroundings.
    (b) The building may be relatively dark with light surroundings.
    (c) The walls may be light and the roof dark.
    (d) The walls may be dark and the roof light.
    (e) The sky may be either darker or lighter than the building.

When a value study shows a satisfactory arrangement and composition, as well as a pleasant relationship of values, fixative should be used and the drawing fastened to the tackboard. Then it can be assayed again from a distance before the next step is begun.

The Color Study

For renderings that are to be made in color — such as watercolor, tempera, or pastels — it is also necessary to make a color study. This may be done in a manner similar to the value study by using pastels on tracing paper, watercolor on tracing paper or watercolor paper, or perhaps tempera on tracing or watercolor paper. While it would seem that watercolor or tempera might seep through the tracing paper and damage the illustration board below, this will not happen if a good heavy grade of tracing paper is used.

The color study, like the value study, helps in deciding a number of things before the final rendering is begun. The palette must first be chosen, and upon this decision depends much of the final appearance of the rendering. The guesswork must be removed from the selection of colors for each portion of the building and each part of the surrounding area, including the sky. The color study shows how the various colors will combine and gives a quick idea of the final appearance of the rendering.

Realistic or Conventional Colors

The selection of the palette will depend to a great extent upon your client. Some people prefer the colors of nature as they see them — blue sky, green grass, green foliage. Others enjoy a slightly more sophisticated taste and would be appalled if you gave them natural colors. These more sophisticated clients are more likely to appreciate the off-tones and shades obtained by mixing together the several colors of a limited palette. They prefer to see anything but a blue sky and will be more satisfied with such tones as gray-green, blue-green, yellow, or orange. The grass in such a rendering may take such colors as gray-green, orange, yellow, brown, or even blue (in a monochromatic scheme).

Theory and Fact in the Selection of a Palette

Another problem that can be solved in the color study is the selection of the actual pigments of your palette in relation to the color scheme that you have selected. There may be limitation of palette if one must show the actual color of a material in the building, such as limestone, brick, or wood. The color of limestone, for instance, is mixed from the following pigments: cobalt blue, alizarin crimson, and yellow ochre. This means that these three colors must be included in the palette for a rendering of a limestone building. Actual material samples are helpful in choosing a palette.

An additional problem is the choice between clear and granulating pigments. If building colors and textures to be indicated require the pebbly appearance that can be obtained by the use of granulating pigments, this must be taken into consideration, as discussed in Chapter 12.

Using the palette suggested in Chapter 6 and looking at the color wheel, one of the following color schemes can be selected.

Monochromatic

1. French ultramarine blue
2. Cobalt blue
3. Hooker's green

Analogous

1. Cadmium orange
   Cadmium yellow pale
   Emerald green
2. Emerald green
   Hooker's green
   French ultramarine blue
3. Alizarin crimson
   Vermilion
   Cadmium orange

Analogous plus complementary accent

1. Cadmium orange
   Cadmium yellow pale
   Emerald green
   French ultramarine blue
2. Emerald green
   Hooker's green
   French ultramarine blue
3. Alizarin crimson
   Vermilion
   Cadmium orange
   Cobalt blue
4. French ultramarine blue
   Cadmium yellow pale
   Vermilion

Complementary

1. Alizarin crimson
   Hooker's green
2. Vermilion
   Cobalt blue
3. Vermilion
   French ultramarine blue

4. Cadmium orange
   French ultramarine blue
5. Yellow ochre
   French ultramarine blue

Split complementary

1. Alizarin crimson or rose madder
   Emerald green
   Hooker's green
2. Hooker's green
   Alizarin crimson or rose madder
   Vermilion
3. French ultramarine blue
   Vermilion
   Cadmium yellow pale

4. Cobalt blue
   Vermilion
   Yellow ochre
5. French ultramarine blue
   Hooker's green
   Vermilion

Triads

1. Yellow ochre
   Cobalt blue
   Alizarin crimson or rose madder
2. Cadmium yellow pale
   Cobalt blue
   Alizarin crimson or rose madder

3. Cadmium yellow pale
   French ultramarine blue
   Alizarin crimson or rose madder
4. Emerald green
   French ultramarine blue
   Vermilion

Color Experimentation

After the actual pigments have been selected for the project at hand, and even before the color study is made, the colors, shades, and tints that the chosen combination will produce should be investigated. In watercolor or tempera, this can be done by putting a small amount of each pigment on a piece of heavy white paper or illustration board, then pulling several colors together in varying amounts with a wet brush. If you are using alizarin crimson, for instance, with yellow ochre and cobalt blue, you will discover that not only can you get pure red, yellow, and blue, but by careful mixing you can achieve browns, purples, mauves, and gray-greens. If you are working in watercolor, lighter shades and tints can be obtained by the use of more or less water. If, on the other hand, you are working in tempera (see Chapter 13) with the colors described in Chapter 6, you will find that the colors may be lightened or darkened by the addition of white or black. If, after experimenting with the colors you have selected, you find that you cannot mix a color that you absolutely need, select a new palette and color scheme and go through the same process until you are sure that you can produce the color required.

The Finished Rendering

Having completed the value and color studies, you are well prepared to begin the final rendering. You will meet problems that you did not anticipate and that you have not settled, but these will be few and minor. It should be remembered that the end result will be a combination of the correct values of the value study and the colors of the color study, and that the final rendering will be an interpretation and improvement on these preliminary studies. If the preliminary studies look well, the final rendering will be successful. If there are basic errors in the preliminary studies, they will show themselves clearly in the final rendering.

The actual technique for making a rendering is described in the following chapters on techniques, but the method for appraising renderings is common to all and can be discussed here. Often the delineator is too close to the project to see its basic mistakes. Sometimes renderers become so absorbed in each detail that they do not realize that there is something basically wrong with the project as a whole. The author cannot stress too strongly the importance of systematically checking your own work by looking at the drawing at various stages from a distance. If the drawing board is too heavy to lift, stand on top of a fixed (not revolving) stool and look down upon it. If the drawing board is light enough to move, stand it against the wall and look at it from a distance of 10 or even 15 feet. If you have a diminishing glass, you may leave the drawing in its original position and see the whole picture through the glass. During these viewings — which are also valuable as moments of relaxation — compare the values with those in your preliminary studies. Any basic differences will quickly manifest themselves and should be noted so they can be corrected immediately. Even when the rendering is finished and the values and colors seem correct, look at it again with a critical eye to see if there are any changes or additions to be made, then make these while you are standing away from the board in a direct, fresh, manner. This procedure will sometimes suggest the perfect note to bring your rendering to life.

Matting

While great care should be taken during the making of the rendering to keep the edges reasonably square and clean, the addition of a mat helps to "clean up" the edges. It also acts as a foil for values and colors in the rendering itself. Generally speaking, the width of the mat should vary according to the size of the rendering. A general rule for 14- × 21-inch pictures, for instance, is to make the sides and top of the mat 2½ inches wide, and the bottom 3½ inches wide.

There are many mat-board colors to choose from; some are listed below.

Antiques

Charcoal	Fabric white	Dove gray	Off-white
Slate	Brilliant white	Pearl gray	Autumn brown
Light gray	Crimson	TV gray	Cream
Dark blue	Ivory	Warm gray	Sea foam
Canary	Dark green	Pastel gray	Ivy
Maroon			

The above are available in 32 × 40 inches. In addition, brilliant white, ivory, and off-white are also available in 30 × 40 inches.

Tones

Black	Horizon blue	Turquoise	Bayberry
Chestnut	Autumn gold	Deep coral	Pumpkin
Rose	Forest green	Terra verte	Terra cotta
Fern	Pussy willow	Meadow green	Paloma
Tan	Caribbean blue	French blue	Gobelin blue
Aquamarine	Stone gray	Ecru	Pink

The above are available in 32 × 40 inches, while black is also available in 30 × 40 inches.[1]

Gold-colored mat board is available in a smooth finish, size 32 × 40 inches. Single and double thicknesses of pebble board are available in sizes 16 × 20 inches, 20 × 30 inches, 30 × 40 inches, and 32 × 40 inches, in the following colors:

Pebble finish

Off-white and white
Cream and white
TV gray and white
Light gray and white

Special deluxe qualities are available when required, as well as extra-large sizes up to 30 × 60 inches. Boards in the 32- × 40-inch size with special coverings are available as follows:

Burlap

White	Eggshell	Natural	Chocolate

Linen

White	Highland green	Nutmeg
Natural	Brandywine	Heraldry
Gray	Eggshell	Ginger twill
Firethorn	Loom state	

Silk

Alice blue	Pearl	Nile
Raspberry	Tiffany	Eggshell
Chamois	White	Black
Ecru	Sand	

Grass cloth

Natural	Rik-rak	Rush
Sandalwood	Driftwood	Honshu
Eggshell	Rattan	

Suede

Death Valley	Rye	Sonoma
True Brit	Targa	Jacana

In addition, a special museum mounting board, pure rag, is available in various sizes and plies in solid ivory and solid white. Acidfree conservation board is also available in numerous colors and dimensions similar to those found in the standard board.

Care should be taken in the selection of the mat since the wrong texture or color will detract from the color balance of the picture or overwhelm the values of a black-and-white rendering. Remember that the eye is drawn to bright colors, and they may take attention away from the rendering itself. A good rule is to use white, cream, buff, or eggshell, either matte, pebble, or linen finish and to beware of the brighter colors, at least until you have had much experience.

An inexpensive mat can be made for your own use from kid-finish bristol board which comes in one, two, or three plies, 23 × 39 inches. However, in

---

[1] Courtesy Charles T. Bainbridge's Sons, Brooklyn, New York.

order to show the rendering at its best to anyone else, it is advisable to use mat board.

Cutting the Mat

First draw the picture size on the mat, and then cut the opening with a beveled edge, which gives the mat an appearance of greater depth and provides an interesting surrounding shadow line for the rendering.

Protecting the Finished Rendering

Information is given in various chapters on techniques for "fixing" renderings which require it. If a presentation is to be framed and glazed after it is matted, it will not need further protection. If, on the other hand, it is not to be framed and will be handled by a number of people, its face should be covered with a sheet of transparent plastic material, which may be obtained in varying sizes from any art materials store. This should be of sufficient thickness so that it will not buckle from dampness or handling. It can be attached to the back of the rendering or mat with drafting tape.

Photographing the Rendering

The period following the completion of a rendering is usually quite hectic, and there is often a strong temptation to deliver the original drawing without first having had it photographed. Once a drawing leaves your hands, however, getting it back is hard, and so, at all costs, it should be photographed before delivery. Photographing artwork is a specialty, and you should have your renderings photographed by a competent specialist in this exacting field. In a well-equipped photography studio, all the conditions can be controlled. The lighting will be correct, and straight lines can be kept true. In addition, the professional photographer may use a large view camera that can take an 8- × 10-inch negative. With a negative of this size, almost any size print can be made with maximum clarity.

The photographer is armed with four different kinds of black-and-white and color films for photographing these four types of architectural subjects:

1. Line drawings
2. Black-and-white drawings with halftones, such as pencil renderings
3. Colored renderings that are to be photographed in black and white
4. Colored renderings that are to be photographed in color

Black-and-white line drawings (item 1 above) photograph most clearly if no washes are used on the drawing, since a special film, sensitive only to jet black and pure white, is used for line drawings. If shadings are required, it is preferable to do them either with Zip-A-Tone (with dots) or by hatching with a fine pen.

Photographs can be made any size or shape, but for economy's sake, choice should be limited to the standard sizes (in inches) listed below:

8 × 10	20 × 24
11 × 14	30 × 40
14 × 17	40 × 60
16 × 20	

These sizes are the same for black and white or color.

If the photographs are to be reproduced, glossy prints should be ordered, since the smooth surface preserves even the finest details of a picture. As a matter of fact, matte and pebbled finishes are often used to subdue detail (as in portrait photography). For presentation-type enlargements, however, prints should be matte (pebble grain).

Color Photographs

As mentioned above, color photographs are available in the same sizes as black and white. They are, of course, more expensive than black and white. To keep costs down and still retain a color record, some delineators prefer 35-mm transparencies. If the job warrants the purchase of color prints, a negative should be made.

It frequently happens that the time available for photography is minimal and the rendering can be in the hands of the photographer for only a short time. The most expeditious way of handling the photography of a rendering is to deal with a photographer who specializes in this work. If an appointment is made in advance, the photograph can be taken in 10 or 15 minutes.

When pressed for time, photographers may use a color standard which consists of the primary colors of the Kodak Type C process. The colors of the Type C color standard, also called the "color-control patch" are printed on a strip of cardboard. These colors, selected as representative of the colors commonly used in photographic reproduction, are black, three-color (brown), white, cyan, violet, magenta, primary red, yellow, and green. When the rendering is photographed, the color-control patch is attached to the background near the rendering. Then the rendering and the color standard are photographed in the same light. Color prints can thus be made with perfect color match, without the presence of the original renderings. (For black-and-white reproduction, the gray scale is used in the same manner as the color standard.)

The Color Transparency

If a rendering is to be reproduced in color in a magazine or a book, a color transparency is required. Such a transparency should be taken directly from the original rendering.

Mounting Photographs

If the photograph is for reproduction, mounting is not required. However, if it is to be part of a presentation, mounting will keep it from curling and will improve its appearance. All good architectural photographers have a dry mounting press, heated by electricity. In this pressure-under-heat process, a sheet of transparent dry mounting tissue is placed between the print and the mounting material, and the three pieces are placed in the hot press. Then the finished print is removed from the press and allowed to cool.[2]

---

[2] Information on photography courtesy of Gil Amiaga, architectural photographer.

chapter 8

Rendering the Entourage

The building itself is the major element in the completion of a rendering, yet it cannot stand alone. Surrounding it, according to its location, may be trees, bushes, grass, roadways and walkways, adjoining buildings, scale figures, water, automobiles, trucks, trains, airplanes, and above all, a sky. Since each is an important part of the total abstract composition of a rendering, and since even the lay person can detect poorly drawn or poorly located surrounding elements, each item should be rendered with the greatest of skill. If this is done, the entourage can complement the building and lead the spectator's eye to a desired focal point. If, on the other hand, the entourage is drawn unskillfully and located without plan, a spectator will be unimpressed with the rendering. Therefore, a detailed examination of the elements that go to make up the entourage of the average rendering is worthwhile.

Trees and Bushes

The lives of humankind have long been enriched by the trees of the earth. Few of us realize how much we depend upon the tree. We use it for shade, and for protection against the elements. Wood is used for the building of houses and ships, in the manufacture of furniture, for the tanning of leather, for fuel, for medicine, and for the making of hundreds of other objects closely related to our daily lives. But our affection for trees goes further than the utilitarian. Trees are things of beauty and symbols of abundance, and most peoples have learned to use them to enhance their surroundings and thereby establish a close connection with nature. Trees are an inseparable part of human life.

Importance of Trees

Trees help to identify the setting of a building in a general way, since particular species are associated with definite parts of the country. Some grow only near water, others in flat areas, while still others grow only in mountainous areas. To render a tree that cannot possibly grow on the site might invite embarrassing questions. It is wise to use the correct trees and draw them at least moderately well, particularly as regards shape and proportion. The client will be impressed with them and with the entire rendering.

The exact methods for drawing trees are discussed in the chapters on the various techniques, but before any method for rendering can be evolved or used, the structure of the tree itself must be thoroughly understood. The novice who does not understand the structure invariably produces a lollipop stick with a series of cotton balls stuck to it, and calls it a tree. The more experienced delineator constructs the entire framework of the tree first and then applies foliage to it, remembering that each foliage mass must be supported by a part of the tree structure. Also, the root system of a tree is as much a part of it as the portion above ground, and the trunk rises not only from the ground itself, but from a series of roots, some of which show aboveground, particularly in soil that has been eroded. To show these roots gradually disappearing into the ground is to indicate a well-supported tree.

The diameter and height of the trunk itself will vary according to the age and species of the tree. So will the type of structure. Some trees, such as the white willow, start to divide into large branches close to the ground; others, like the elm, begin to divide higher; while still others, like the Virginia pine, have one trunk for the entire height of the tree. The general shape of the tree also varies with the species. The poplar, for instance, fits into a high, narrow oval. Most oaks fit into a circle, while the apple tree fits into a low, flat oval. The general shape, outline, texture, branch arrangement, and bark are sufficient to identify the species. The rest we leave with the botanist.

Obviously, a great deal of information about trees, particularly those in a given location, can be memorized. Those not often used are difficult to remember, however, and so it is well to accumulate a complete file of tree photographs and sketches for use in delineating buildings in areas outside your normal theater of operations.

Where possible, a set of photographs of trees on the site under consideration should be made. An owner who is fond of the trees and plans to keep them will expect to see them faithfully duplicated.

Basic Methods for Trees

Three basic methods are used for rendering trees, as follows:

1. Draw the structure of the tree alone, or with a few small bits of foliage.
2. Draw the tree structure, then apply foliage masses upon it, with parts of the tree structure showing in the spaces between the foliage masses.
3. Lightly draw the shape of the tree; paint the foliage in simple, relatively flat masses; then paint the trunks and a few branches to support the foliage. This method is applicable to ink and watercolor rendering only.

Most renderers agree that trees should be suggested by simple means. If a tree is believable in shape and structure, little else needs to be done to make it three-dimensional. Therefore, the best ways to practice basic forms of trees are by drawing or painting them in silhouette (Figure 8.1) and by drawing their skeletons alone (Figure 8.2).

Some trees that the renderer should practice drawing and painting are listed below.

White oak Alpine fir Red cedar White birch Black walnut

Norway pine Hickory Willow Elm

Sugar maple White oak Yellow poplar Weeping willow

Live oak Honey locust Long-leaf pine Fig. 8.1 Trees in Silhouette.

Elm, American white — maximum height 180 feet

White oak — maximum height 150 feet

Black oak — maximum height 150 feet

Scarlet oak — maximum height 150 feet

Live oak — maximum height 60 feet

Beech — maximum height 120 feet

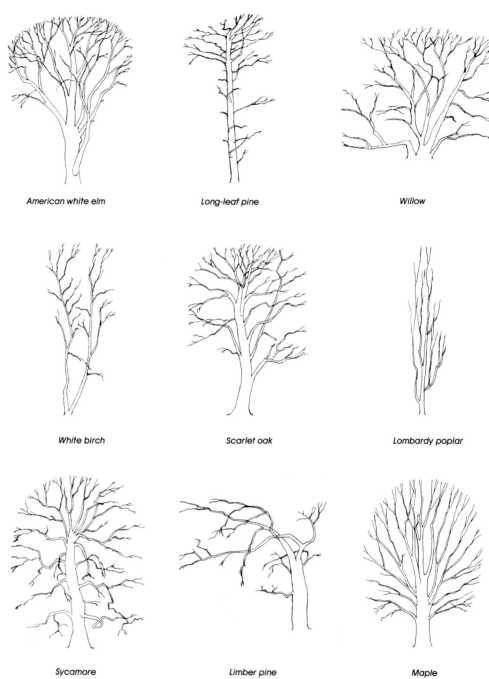

American white elm   Long-leaf pine   Willow

White birch   Scarlet oak   Lombardy poplar

Fig. 8.2 Trees in Skeleton Form.   Sycamore   Limber pine   Maple

Shagbark hickory — maximum height 140 feet

Black walnut

White pine — maximum height 250 feet

Limber pine

Willow

Poplar

Sycamore — maximum height 150 feet

White ash

Maple

White birch — maximum height 180 feet

Dogwood

Black locust

Red spruce

White spruce — maximum height 150 feet

Balsam fir — height 60 feet

White fir — height 275 feet

Eastern red cedar — maximum height 50 feet

Western red cedar — maximum height 200 feet

Palm

The rendering will benefit if these trees are painted in silhouette, using a small brush and a jar of dark showcard color or ink. The tree skeletons should be drawn with a sharp pencil. In drawing the skeleton remember that it needs to be correct not only in proportion but also structurally; that is, each branch must spring in a believable way from the trunk, each smaller branch must spring in turn from the larger branches, and a sufficient number of twigs must be shown to make the structure seem complete. A good general rule for determining the diameter of each branch is this: The sum total of the sectional area of all the branches at any point should be slightly less than the cross-sectional area of the trunk or branch from which they spring.

General Values of Trees

Dark trees should be used behind light building masses, light trees behind dark masses. Trees located in front of a dark building or tree masses are usually left light, while those located in front of a light surface are usually made dark.

Trees, Atmosphere, and Perspective

Remember that trees in a perspective will diminish in size according to their distance from the eye of the spectator. Those in the foreground will be large and the leaves may be quite detailed. Those in the mid-distance may be generalized and lighter, while those in the distance may consist of nothing more than flat planes with a few trunks and branches. The distant trees will be the lightest ones in the perspective.

Trees and Composition

Rarely is one tree used alone, because one tree, like one scale figure, has a lonesome appearance. It is best to use a number of trees relatively close together (Figure 8.3). After the charcoal study is made, it should be examined to make sure that the trees do not hide the design. This is a good time also to decide just how complete and textural the trees should be in order to complement and not compete with the architecture. They should be believable in size, shape, and location. Finally, all the trees and bushes except those most important in the composition should be eliminated. Also, make sure that one tree or tree mass is higher than all the rest, to establish a dominant note.

The textures of trunks and branches will vary with the kind of tree being shown, but if it is kept in mind that each portion of the tree structure is round in section, rendering it intelligently will be easy. The light source should be kept in

Fig. 8.3 Tree Groupings. Design for Office Building. (Architect: The Eggers Group, P.C., Architects and Planners.)

Fig. 8.4 Details of Trees and Flowers.

mind. In sunlight, even though the value of the tree itself may be dark, parts of the structure may be rendered as light as the paper itself. In shade and in shadow, the values may be very dark. It is permissible to take liberties in selecting the values of the structure throughout the tree, showing light branches against dark foliage masses, or dark branches and twigs against light foliage masses. Accents such as shadows, cast by branches or foliage upon branches and trunks below, should be drawn around the members upon which they fall, as shown in Figure 8.4.

Rendering Foliage

The actual method for rendering foliage in each medium is discussed in the appropriate chapter. Generally speaking, however, the foliage should not be applied until a correct structure has been drawn. Obviously, foliage may be placed only where it can be supported by branches or twigs.

Tree Shadows on the Ground

The shadow of a tree on the ground will, of course, depend upon the shape of the tree and the source of light. The length of the shadow can be determined if the tree height is known. Simply draw (in section) a ray of light from the top edge of the tree to the ground. The average tree is made up of spherical or partially spherical forms, and the shadow in turn is made up of intersecting ellipses and partial ellipses (Figure 8.5, sketch a). When these are constructed, it will be found that small light areas, irregular in shape, are left between the shadows of the small ellipses. When the intersecting elliptical shadows are joined, and the

Fig. 8.5 Construction of Tree Shadows on the Ground.

a   b

Fig. 8.6 Tree Shadows used to Indicate Change in Level. Design of Snowcreek at Mammoth Lake. (Architect: Berkus-Group Architects. Renderer: Richard Yaco.)

shadow of the tree skeleton is made a part of the shadow, a believable shadow results (Figure 8.5, sketch *b*).

The casting of a tree shadow should be done with care; it must be quite foreshortened or it will appear not to "lie down" upon the ground. The value of the shadow upon the ground will vary with the material upon which it falls. A shadow will be darker on grass, for instance, than on a light path. Tree shadows are an important means of showing rises and falls in terrain, flights of steps, and other changes in level. See Figure 8.6. If shadows fall upon the building itself, they should not be deep in value, since deep shadows camouflage rather than express the form of the structure.

Grass Areas

Any grass area shows a wide deviation in value, color, or both, throughout its plot. Variations in tone are caused by several factors, including difference of light, showing through of the soil beneath, variation in the natural color of the grass itself, and shadows on the grass. While the actual execution of the grass will depend upon the technique in which it is rendered, there are several different methods of approach.

The first is to apply a graded wash, starting with light in the background and changing to dark in the foreground, using horizontal strokes. The second method is to use the same kind of wash, but to introduce light and dark variations as the wash is run. The white (or color) of the paper should be allowed to show through the wash in a number of spots in order to obtain a light, effervescent appearance. Generally speaking, grass areas should have a sunny appearance so that shadows falling upon them need not be too dark.

If the grass areas look uninteresting and unfinished after they have been done by the above method, they may be stippled or stroked with short, vertical strokes, relatively close together. These are usually slightly darker than the base tone. If the rendering is in color, a graded wash, as described above, may first be applied; then another wash, slightly darker, may be run over the first, care being taken to let a good deal of the first wash show through the second. Additional interest may sometimes be obtained in grass areas by sandpapering sections which lack interest, particularly if rough-textured paper is used.

Roadways and Walkways

Roads and walks are usually kept light in value, but should be varied in tone. After the base tone is put on the paper, additional interest can be given them by

Fig. 8.7 Building Reflected in Wet Roadway and Sky. Meadowlands Arena. (Architect: Grad/DCOP. Renderer: Licht/Levine.)

the use of lighter and darker streaks which simulate tire marks, shadows, etc. Expansion joints should be lightly shown in order to help provide scale. If the building is relatively placid in appearance and seems to need a "lift," it is sometimes desirable to assume that the walkways and roadways are wet, and to show reflections of the building in them (Figure 8.7).

Surrounding Buildings

The problem of how to render surrounding buildings is easily solved if they are kept indistinct and uninteresting. They should do no more than frame the building and locate it in time and space — in other words, identify the neighborhood. They should be definitely lighter or darker than the building being rendered, according to the values required to make the new building stand out. It is also usual to draw or paint them rather loosely, in a less precise manner than the subject. If the rendering is in color, the same palette used for the building itself should be used for mixing the colors for the surrounding buildings.

Skies

Like the other accoutrements, the sky exists only to complement the building. Too often the novice gets so interested in the sky that it becomes an end in itself. The result is that the viewer is more interested in the sky than in the building. Sometimes it is unnecessary to draw or paint a sky at all, but if one is required, or desired, it should usually be kept relatively simple.

A cloudless sky can be domed by grading it from light at the horizon to dark at the top of the picture, or vice versa. The texture of a sky, or the clouds in it, may be arranged to perform a function. If the perspective of the building is so sudden that it seems to run off the sheet, clouds or the texture of the sky itself may be arranged to counter this motion (Figure 8.7).

As a general rule, the type of sky required will depend upon the building itself. If the building is complicated and has a dynamic quality, a quiet sky is best. On the other hand, if the building is placid and unexciting, or lacks movement, a sky with plenty of clouds and variations in tone or color may be used (Figure 8.8).

There are, of course, many different kinds of clouds, and the various types may be seen in books specifically related to the subject. An analysis of actual clouds will reveal that generally they are less round than one might think. Many have edges which are rectilinear or almost straight. No two cloud areas will be alike.

Fig. 8.8 Clouds Used to Add Interest.

In drawing them, care must be taken that they do not acquire the appearance of faces, animals, or geometric forms. They should not be made overly conspicuous.

The delineator will sometimes be tempted to render either a sunrise or a sunset, but these should be strictly avoided; the results obtained are greatly outweighed by the problems involved and created.

Water and Reflections

In rendering water, the delineator must first decide whether it is to be made placid, slightly rippled, or rough. If it is to be placid, the reflection will look very much like the building itself, in an inverted position (Figure 8.9). On the other hand, if the water is rippled or rough, the depth of the reflection will vary according to the roughness of the water; the height of the building will be greater in the water than in actuality because of the reflection of the building in waves far in front of the building itself (Figure 8.10a and b).

The principles of reflection may best be understood by examining buildings located near water. In Figure 8.11, sketch a, the building is resting at the same level as the water and its reflection is exactly the height of the building itself. The height of each corner of the tower is reproduced beneath the level of the water, and the ends of these lines are then joined.

When a building does not rise from the water, but is located a short distance back from the water's edge, the reflection is determined by dropping true heights from the base of the building, as above, imagining that the water extends to the foundations of the structure itself. See Figure 8.11, sketch b.

If the building is raised above the water, as in Figure 8.11, sketch c, its reflection will begin as far below the surface of the water as the bottom of the building is located above the surface of the water. In a domed building, the depth of the reflection below the horizontal axis of the dome will be the same as the height of the building above the axis (sketch d). The reflection of any odd-shaped object lying in the water or at the water's edge will generally follow the same rule.

The same principles used for determining reflections in placid water, with the building located on the water itself, are used in plotting the reflection of a room

Fig. 8.9 Reflections in Placid Water.

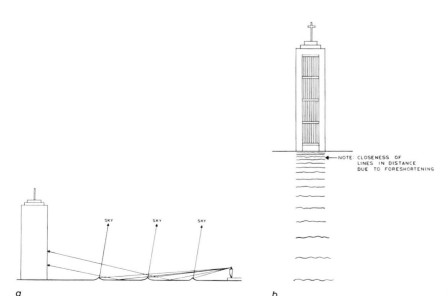

a b Fig. 8.10 Reflections in Rippled Water.

NOTE: CLOSENESS OF LINES IN DISTANCE DUE TO FORESHORTENING

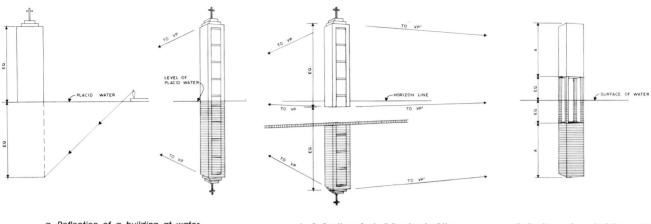

a. Reflection of a building at water level when water is placid

b. Reflection of a building back of the water's edge

c. Reflection of a building raised above water level

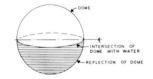

d. Reflection of a domed building

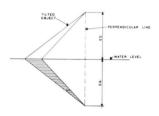

e. Reflection of a tilted object

Fig. 8.11

in a mirror. Any point in the reflection should appear to be located as far behind the surface of the mirror as it is actually located forward of the mirror in the room. Constructed in perspective, the room will look the same in reflection as in reality. It will, of course, be reversed.

To draw the reflection of a tilted object in water, first drop a perpendicular from its top extremity. The distance from its top to the waterline will be the same as the distance from the waterline to the end of the object in reflection on a perpendicular line. See Figure 8.11, sketch e.

For most purposes it is wise to make the reflection appear not mathematically conceived but rather casual. Usually the water can be assumed to be slightly rippled — enough, that is, to deform the line of the building in the reflection at least slightly. The height of the building will be elongated. The various lights and darks reflected in such a body of water will appear wavy (Figure 8.10), broken by streaks of light or dark. It is usual to permit the white of the paper to appear in such a reflection in generous amounts, usually in a horizontal motion, to simulate the slight roughness of the water. Reflections of buildings, tree trunks, etc., can be shown vertically, or at an angle if they are actually tilted (Figure 8.11). The very indistinctness of the outline of a building reflected in slightly rippled water adds a great deal of charm, and the eye is more likely to accept such a reflection than one that is too distinct. This is particularly true of the reflection of tree masses in water. Often the tops of trees in a reflection are permitted to be hazier and less distinct in outline than the trees themselves.

One final word: Water should be either lighter or darker than surrounding elements. As to value and color, it should be remembered that the color of the water is made up of the color of the sky that is being reflected in it; the color of the water itself; the color of the bottom on which it rests; and the color of buildings, trees, and other objects around the water. If the rendering is in color, the colors of the building reflected in the water area will be modified by all the colors that affect the color of the water, with perhaps an occasional small spot of true building or sky color in the reflection. While there will be times when rough water needs to be shown, the waves and reflections in it generally tend to attract too much attention to themselves.

As to the general gradation of water — where it should be dark and where light — the following rules should be remembered: Water will be light wherever it can reflect the bright value or color of the sky. If the sky is dark, the water will be dark. A large body of water is usually light in the distance, since the light sky at the horizon is reflected there, and dark in the foreground, where the darker value or color of the sky above is reflected. In addition, water is usually shown dark when smooth and light when rough, because of the refraction of light by the many small waves.

Reflections of buildings in wet streets, as mentioned previously, are sometimes helpful in adding interest to an otherwise overly quiet rendering. If a wet street is used, the same principles hold true as for a building on a placid body of water, with the addition, of course, of the reflection of scale figures and perhaps automobiles. In night renderings, the reflections of lighted glass areas are graded so that they are brightest near the base of the building and gradually diminish in intensity toward the bottom of the picture.

Scale Figures

Most renderings include scale figures. If the structure is to be used by great numbers of people, groups may be shown. No matter how many figures are indicated, they should be located so as to draw the spectator's eye to a focal point — usually the entrance to the building. This may be done by drawing a few figures in the foreground at large scale, a few more to the left or right in mid-distance, and several more near the entrance itself (Figure 8.12). If figures are distributed indiscriminately, the eye will travel back and forth between them a number of times before it locates the focal point of the picture.

Because styles in clothing change rather rapidly, extreme styles should be avoided. Very short or extremely long dresses for female figures, or wide shoulders in male figures, quickly date a rendering. Facetious figures may be fun in school, but have no place on the professional rendering. The figures on many renderings in this book are seriously drawn, but not too detailed.

Automobiles, Trucks, Trains, and Airplanes

Trucks and trains may be drawn if their presence helps to explain the uses to which the building is to be put, and to give it scale. Neither changes too rapidly in style. Automobiles and airplanes, however, do change in style so rapidly that

Fig. 8.12 Use of Scale Figures. Descanso Gardens in La Canada, California. (Architect: Berkus-Group Architects. Renderer: Richard Yaco.)

their presence dates a building—often before a year has passed. It must be remembered that a rendering is part of a general presentation. Sometimes approval for construction is quickly obtained, but on other occasions, as with government buildings, approval may not be forthcoming for a number of years. If a rendering with automobiles or airplanes on it is shown to a committee for final consideration several years after it has been drawn, the committee is likely to conclude that the building design, like the automobiles or airplanes, is already out of style. It is well either to omit such embellishments or to draw them in such a general way that their style is not very obvious.

Renderings of industrial establishments frequently require the indication of trains. Locomotives rarely need to be shown. Freight cars may be indicated on sidings, but if too many are shown, they will tend to distract the viewer's attention from the building. If a locomotive must be shown, do not indicate smoke or steam issuing from it, as this would attract attention away from the building.

Boats

Nautical scenes invariably require the indication of various kinds of boats. Since these are not so quickly outdated as automobiles, they may be shown in greater detail. As a matter of fact, groups of boats often create a very pleasing pattern.

chapter 9

Pencil Rendering

The Graphite Pencil — Where Did It Come From?

The graphite pencil as we know it is not a very old instrument. Its predecessor the lead pencil, however, is mentioned in Egyptian history and supposedly was used for making preliminary lines which were then drawn over with brush and ink. Use of lead continued into Elizabethan times, although it was far from satisfactory as a marking or writing tool. After the famous Borrowdale Graphite Mine was discovered in Cumberland, England, in the sixteenth century, pencils were made of pulverized graphite cemented into solid blocks, but even these were not practical.

The difficulty of using blocks and sticks for writing and drawing was overcome in 1795 when N. J. Conté first made pencils by grinding graphite with certain clays, pressing the compound into sticks, and firing it in a kiln. The demand for graphite was so great that its use was restricted at the time of James I in order to preserve the supply, and the mines were used for only a few weeks of the year. For the rest of the year they were flooded.

Types of Lead

Our common "lead" pencils are really made of graphite and China clay. The current supply of graphite comes from Ceylon or Mexico, while the clay which is mixed with the graphite comes from central Bavaria. Generally speaking, there are four different types of "lead":

1. Ceramic lead, used for drawing and writing pencils
2. Colored lead, made of a paste of metal, cellulose wax, and pigments, and not baked because the heat would destroy the color
3. Soluble or indelible lead, which contains aniline dyes
4. Wax crayons

For the ceramic lead, the graphite in its crude form is first purified and broken down into minute particles. Similarly, the clay is pulverized, washed, and purified. When it is combined with the graphite, the resultant mixture is a fine powder. The preparations of clay and graphite vary, depending upon the degree of softness or hardness required. The more graphite, the softer and blacker the "lead" will be. The more China clay, the harder and lighter (in value) the pencil will be.

After the powder of graphite and China clay has been made, water and certain chemicals are added to it and it is mixed under pressure. Sometimes wax is added for smoothness. The resultant mass is then compressed under tremendous pressure and forced through a die to emerge as a soft, solid "lead," of pencil length. These leads are soft and unusable—almost the consistency of spaghetti —until they are put into grooves in boards and tempered by baking at 2000°F or higher. The tempered lead is then encased between two pieces of aromatic cedar wood, grooved to make a depression for it. The halves are fastened together by vinyl resin, clamped, and heated at a low temperature. The individual pencils are then cut to size, sandpapered, and lacquered with six to ten coats. The ends are sliced clean, and the name and grade stamped on the side with a hot dye. Although the Bureau of Standards in Washington has tried to standardize the grades of pencil, the grades still differ according to manufacturer.

Equipment Required

Pencils are graded from hard to soft, as follows:

H indicates hard.

F indicates firm.

B indicates soft.

The grades available are 9H (hardest), 8H, 7H, 6H, 5H, 4H, 3H, 2H, and H, F, HB, 2B, 3B, 4B, 5B, and 6B. Of these, the soft pencils are best suited for freehand sketching and rendering, although some papers require harder pencils than others. There are two schools of thought on this: some delineators prefer to use only one or two of the softer pencils, such as 2B and 4B, while others prefer the effect obtained by varying the pencils according to the paper used.

Graphite sticks are graded from hard to soft as follows:

2B indicates hard.

4B indicates medium.

6B indicates soft.

Soft graphite sticks are used for both layouts and sketching. They are excellent for the broad stroke, where large areas of graded graphite are required. Sizes available are square (¼ × ¼ × 3 inches) and rectangular (½ × ¼ × 3 inches).

Coarse papers, such as Canson and Mongolfier, demand relatively hard pencils such as HB, F, and 2H, while layouts are made with an even harder pencil. The reason for using harder or softer pencils according to the quality of the paper is that paper is made of a weblike mass of interlaced fibers. When a pencil is passed over these fibers, it is worn down by the file action of the paper, which holds its particles in slight concavities. The rougher the paper, the more readily this file action occurs. The smoother the paper, the less the file action and the softer the pencil required.

Extremely rough paper, such as Canson and Mongolfier, is usually satisfactory for a large drawing and unsatisfactory for a small one, since drawing fine detail upon it is difficult. Medium-rough-surfaced paper, such as kid-finish bristol board, Strathmore paper, or rag-bond tracing paper, is best for general work, while pencil sketch-pad paper is fine for small studies.

Choice of Subject

Almost any subject can be rendered with the graphite pencil. It must be remembered, however, that the pencil is a relatively pointed medium, and therefore is best suited for buildings with small detail and least suited for those with large, plain areas.

Preparing the Pencil

There are several basic methods of preparing the pencil for rendering, but before the point can be made ready for any of these methods, about ⅜ inch of the graphite must be bared with a knife, at the end opposite the grade mark. After

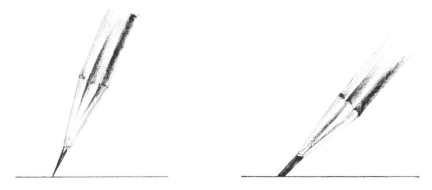

Conical Point
Bare ⅜ inch of graphite and form conical point on sandpaper block.

Broad Stroke
Make point conical; then form flat surface by stroking it across a piece of scrap paper.

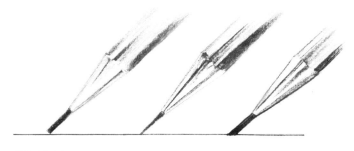

Chisel Point
Step 1: Bare ⅜ inch of graphite.
Step 2: Flatten both sides of point on sandpaper block.
Step 3: Flatten bottom of chisel to desired angle.

Very Broad Stroke
Bare ⅜ inch of graphite and flatten lower side on sandpaper block.

Fig. 9.1 Ways of Preparing the Graphite Pencil.

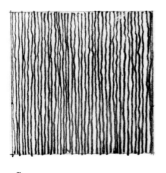
a

b

c

d

e

Fig. 9.2 Practice Strokes.

this has been done, it must be decided how the pencil is to be used: as a penlike point, as a broad stroke (at an angle of about 45 degrees), as a very broad stroke (by holding it at an angle of as little as 20 degrees with the horizontal) as a chisel, or as a pencil "wash" (obtained by holding the side of the pencil practically flat with the paper). See Figure 9.1. Mechanical pencils are readily available for both fine-line detail drawings and broad-stroke sketching.

No matter what point is desired, it can be worn to the desired shape by the use of a sandpaper block, fine files, or mechanical sharpener. After this, it should be smoothed down on a piece of scratch paper and wiped with a cloth to remove any loose graphite. For quick identification, some delineators prefer to mark the various grades they are using with notches or cut-in rings, or with grade painted on all sides of the pencil. No matter how they are marked, time and effort can be saved by keeping the pencils in order, either on the drawing board or in the hand. For practice, sharpen four grade B pencils in the ways shown in Figure 9.1 and make the five different sets of practice strokes indicated in Figure 9.2 and described in the list below, using kid-finish bristol board.

    a. Penlike strokes made with a conical point
    b. Pencil wash made by holding a conical point flat and moving it lightly back and forth across the paper
    c. Broad strokes
    d. Very broad strokes, made with pencil held at 20-degree angle (or less) with paper
    e. Chisel-point strokes

Note: A pencil can be used in many ways. Try them all and see which you like best.

Make these practice strokes carefully, deliberately, and as beautifully as possible. Each stroke should abut the next, with perhaps a small amount of white between them. Try building up values not only by strokes of even pressure, but by varying hand pressure (Figure 9.3), as follows:

Fig. 9.3 Strokes Made by Varying Hand Pressure.

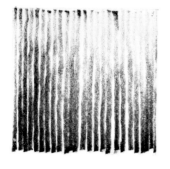
a

b

c

d

a. Begin with light pressure and end with heavy.

b. Begin with heavy pressure and end with light.

c. Curve strokes by bearing down on one side of the pencil point more than the other.

d. Grade by use of graduated pressure or by building graded values with the side of the pencil.

Further exercises utilizing various grades of pencils will now be helpful. Remember that each stroke on a final rendering should be clean and concise, without fuzzy edges or a fuzzy texture. The pencil chosen will vary according to the value desired. An HB or F pencil will give a sharp, clean stroke on the light side of the building, while a 2B or 3B pencil will give a similar clean, but darker, stroke on the shade side.

Practicing Materials and Textures

Before beginning a final rendering it is a good idea to practice various parts of it on the same paper that is to be used for the final rendering, and at the same scale. Since each person's individual style will differ, only general suggestions for technique can be given here, but no matter what the technique, one major premise must be kept in mind: The renderer should not attempt to capture the realism of a photograph, or the drawing will be monotonous and lack interest and life. There will be occasions when more or less contrast than a normal photograph will be required. What is more important, the light and dark masses of the sketch must be manipulated so that they form a pleasing composition. If the normal pattern of light and dark is followed, the picture may become complicated and trite. Generally speaking, the major effect of such a picture pattern will be determined by the dark mass, and all other parts of the pattern must be related to it. Compare Figure 9.4, Relation of Dark Mass to Pattern, with a similar final rendering, Figure 9.19. Care must be taken in the indication of subordinate parts of the picture to fit them into the predetermined general pattern; otherwise camouflage, instead of clarity, will result. Similarly, if completely accurate rendering of local color and detail results in spottiness, these elements should be subordinated. Remember that the form of the building or object must be easily understood when the rendering is finished.

Fig. 9.4 Relation of Dark Mass to Pattern.

Methods of Indicating Textures

Roof shingles. Cover the roof area with some strokes parallel to the ridge and with others parallel to the pitch of the roof (Figure 9.5, sketches a1 and a2). These can be drawn in relatively short strokes, leaving plenty of light between them and between groups of strokes. When this has been done, shingle butts and joints between shingles can be drawn over the base wash in wavy, varying lines, using a pointed pencil. Purposely avoid drawing too many of these, particularly joints between shingles. The base washes will vary in intensity according to the local color of the shingles to be used. For a white roof, for instance, no general value need be laid down first.

Tile roof. Follow the same procedure for flat shingles, except that the edges of the tile, like the single butts for flat shingles, should be drawn with the sharp point of the pencil (Figure 9.5, sketches a1 and b2).

Wall shingles. To render shingles in sunlight, give the wall a pencil wash similar to that described for roof shingles. To render them in shade, render each shingle separately, using vertical strokes, leaving the vertical joints white. Then draw

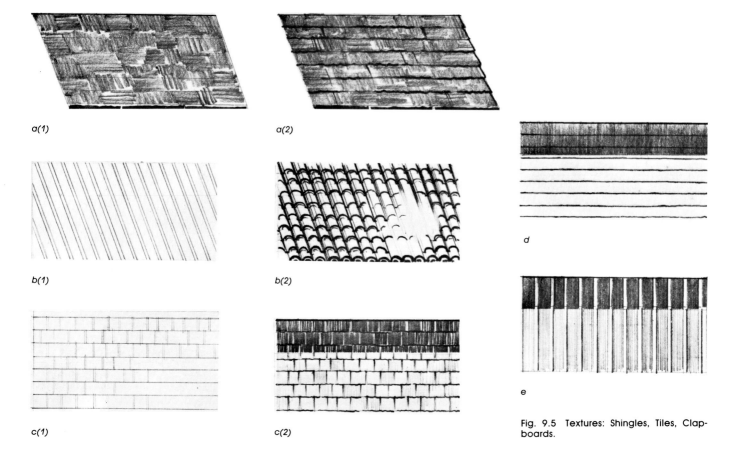

a(1)

a(2)

b(1)

b(2)

d

c(1)

c(2)

e

Fig. 9.5 Textures: Shingles, Tiles, Clapboards.

in dark, wavy lines under some of the shingle butts (Figure 9.5, sketches c1 and c2).

Siding or clapboards. Draw the joint lines lightly. Then add a light wash with perhaps an H or F pencil over the entire area, varying it so that it is lighter here and darker there. Draw slightly wavy, freehand shadows under the butts and at the joints. Vary these in intensity and leave some of them out in order to avoid monotony (Figure 9.5, sketch d).

Flush boards. These can be rendered similarly to siding or clapboards. The joints between the boards should be kept thin, and can be drawn in with a T square and a sharp-edged pencil, using a wiping motion to avoid monotony (Figure 9.5, sketch e).

Stucco or Cement

The value of stucco or cement will depend upon its actual local color, as well as how it will fit in with the total pictorial composition. It should be remembered that even white stucco will have a light-gray quality in shade. If any value is given to the stucco in sunlight, it should be done with an H or 2H pencil. Sometimes it is best not to put a wash on the light side at all, but to indicate texture by the use of dots made with a fairly hard pencil (Figure 9.6, sketch a).

Stone

Cut stone. Cut stones, such as limestone or granite, are rendered in a manner similar to stucco, except, of course, that joints must be indicated. If the entire

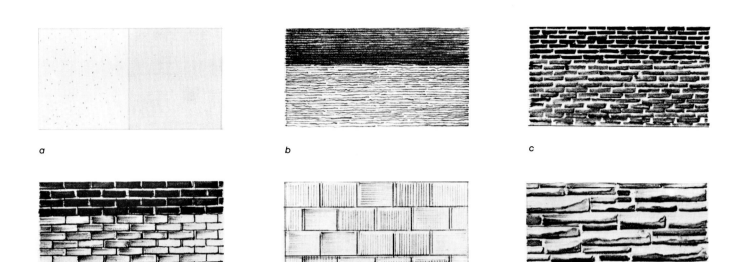

a   b   c

d   e   f

Fig. 9.6   Textures: Stucco, Stone, Brick.

wall is covered with joints, they will be monotonous; therefore eliminate many of them, making them appear "washed out" by bright light in certain areas (Figure 9.6, sketch e).

Fieldstone. Draw the pattern of fieldstone with a sharply pointed B pencil. Remember that its local color will vary from very light to medium dark, and therefore each stone must be rendered separately. Try using vertical lines to express the verticality of the wall. Generally speaking, it is advisable not to render all stones, but only enough to express the texture of the wall. In most cases this means showing the stones at the edges, top, and bottom of the walls. A pleasing pattern can be formed by leaving streaks of white running in the direction of the sun's rays, with perhaps an occasional stone or joint breaking into this area (Figure 9.6, sketch f).

Brick.   There are two ways of rendering brick in pencil, according to the scale of the drawing. In both cases the brick joints should first be drawn in lightly. For a small scale—say ⅛ inch = 1 foot—a general wash, varying in intensity, should first be put upon the wall surface. Remember to leave plenty of light areas. The brick joints can then be put in with slightly wavy lines, varying in intensity throughout the drawing. Here and there the faces of a few of the bricks can be rendered (Figure 9.6, sketch b).

Bricks at larger scale — say ¼ inch = 1 foot — can best be rendered by a broad stroke, the width of a single brick course, leaving the joints white. Monotony can be avoided by the occasional omission of bricks and the inclusion of diagonal strokes made in the direction of light rays (Figure 9.6, sketch c).

Bricks in shade are merely rendered darker by the use of a softer pencil. In shadow, bricks are rendered individually with clean, sharp strokes, leaving the joints white and giving an occasional shadow next to or on top of some of the bricks (Figure 9.6, sketch d).

Rendering Windows

As mentioned in Chapter 5, one of the most important things to remember in rendering windows is that sash and glass usually occupy a position slightly back

a

b

Fig. 9.7 Rendering of Windows. Housing Project. (Renderer: Schell Lewis.)

from the face of the wall. In addition to the outside reveal thus formed, an inner reveal, which may or may not be covered by curtains, also exists. In small window openings (particularly if venetian blinds, shades, or curtains are used) the amount of the inside of the building that can be seen is so limited that dark shading of varying intensity can be used to indicate the interior.

A small window such as the one shown in Figure 9.7a is best rendered as follows:

1. Draw the window complete with shade, blinds, curtains, etc.
2. Darken that portion of the window not obscured by the items as shown.
3. Put in shade at head and jamb.

4. Put in shadows cast by muntins and meeting rail on curtains and blinds.

5. Put in shadows cast on glass by muntins and meeting rail.

In order to avoid monotony, use a varying line pressure when doing the above five steps.

If the glass opening is large, and the glass is not in glare, the glass itself can be treated as nonexistent. Furniture and furnishings inside the building must be meticulously drawn and shaded in values that will not conflict with those on the exterior of the building. Plants and patterned materials inside the glass opening should be rendered in a subdued manner so that they will not attract undue attention in relation to the whole picture.

Rendering Entourage

Foliage. Foliage should be practiced before it is drawn on the final rendering. Its location and size can be determined in the value study. Remember that while there may be large trees and certain bushes on the site that cannot be moved, those that you add can be placed wherever you wish. When you practice drawing foliage, keep the following rules in mind.

1. Limit the amount of foliage to the necessary minimum. Too much will draw attention away from the building itself.

2. Remember that foliage should complement the architecture and not detract from it; therefore, do not make it more conspicuous than the building itself.

3. Show only live-looking specimens. This is no time to indicate trees that have been struck by lightning or otherwise partially destroyed.

4. Rarely, if ever, should only one tree or bush be indicated in any location; a grouping is always much more pleasant to look at.

Realism in the indication of trees comes with the realization that a tree is never an isolated thing. The greatest realism in shrubbery is obtained by drawing generalized, light-valued trees in the distance, slightly detailed; larger, darker trees in the mid-distance; and still larger, darker, and more detailed trees in the foreground (Figure 9.8). The latter are near the spectator's eye, and therefore the bark, tree structure, and leaves must be exceedingly well drawn. A

Fig. 9.8 The Perspective of Trees.

general description of tree structure is given in Chapter 8, so we will confine our discussion here to the various ways of rendering trees in pencil.

To draw trees in pencil, first block out the rough shape of the tree with a 2B pencil, then draw the trunk, branches, and twigs lightly but as completely as possible. Remember that the branches and twigs radiate from the trunk in all directions, not only to the left and right. Remember also that the total cross-sectional area of any particular group of branches, twigs, etc., must be slightly less than the part of the tree from which this group springs. Draw all parts of the tree from the ground up, using "growth-motion strokes" as shown in Figure 9.9. Most of all, remember that even though it will take some time to do it, the *entire* structure of the tree, including a number of twigs, should be drawn or it will not look real. A rule of thumb is to always draw the tree structure from the ground up, as the tree grows, and in short, straight strokes, each deviating in direction from the previous one below.

Strokes. In drawing the structure of the tree, some of the shading strokes may follow the length of the members that they fall on, and some strokes, particularly shadows, can be drawn around the members. As in all pencil work, leave some areas of the tree structure white.

Foliage in the mid-distance. As foliage is made up of a series of masses, it is first necessary to block these in lightly. Leave holes in the foliage masses and draw branches in these spaces. Using the side of the pencil (and remembering that there should be no hard edges to the foliage masses), practice making light strokes. Use an F pencil for the foliage in sunlight, and a B or 2B for foliage in shade and shadow (Figure 9.10, sketch *a*). Touch the paper with the flat of a broad-stroke pencil and go back and forth in as many different directions as you can without taking the pencil off the paper, turning the pencil as you go. This method can also be used for bushes (Figure 9.11).

Fig. 9.9 Drawing the Tree Structure with Growth-Motion Strokes.

Note: Always draw tree structure from the ground up, as the tree grows, and in short, straight strokes, each deviating in direction from the one below.

a. Branches of a foreground tree
b. Radial broadstrokes used for foliage of a mid-
   distance tree
c. Locating shade areas
d. Leaving the pencil on the paper and radiating
   strokes in all directions

a

b

c   d

Fig. 9.10 Drawing Foliage Masses.

Trees and bushes in the foreground. For detailed trees or bushes in the foreground, groups of individual leaves must be shown (Figure 9.10a–d and Figure 9.11a and c). The shape of the leaves will vary with the species shown.

Trunk textures. The trunk texture, of course, depends upon the kind of tree. It need not be detailed, but can be shown in a generalized way. Texture on tree trunks in

a

b

c

d

e   f

g   h

a.–d. Four methods of rendering shrubbery
e.–h. Tree trunk textures:
e. Paper birch, f. Sycamore, g. Shagbark history,
h. Black locust

Fig. 9.11 Bushes and Tree Trunks.

the foreground should be detailed as carefully as possible. Some suggestions are shown in Figure 9.11e–h. Generally, if one remembers that a tree is made up of a series of cylindrical (not flat) members, more realistic tree drawings will result.

Rendering Grass

Grass can be rendered in several ways:

1. By parallel vertical strokes for the entire grass area
2. By some vertical strokes for only those areas of grass which are in shadow, leaving the remainder of the lawn white
3. By horizontal strokes

No matter what technique is used, the grass will become lighter as it recedes into the distance.

Tree shadows on grass. Shadows on grass areas should first be constructed on tracing paper so that they look realistic. First draw the shadow of the tree trunk and its branches upon the ground, remembering to foreshorten the total shadow sufficiently so that it appears to lie flat on the ground. Each portion of the foliage mass, which is approximately spherical in shape, will cast its own small elliptical shadow upon the grass. These will overlap to form a shadow which will have a number of light areas in it (see Figure 8.5). Grass in the shadow areas will, of course, be darker than grass in the sun. Effort should be made to minimize detail in the shadow; otherwise it will detract from the building.

Walkways and roadways are generally kept light. It is usual to show roadways without texture, but some delineators prefer to indicate the motion of traffic by an overlapping series of tire marks. Walkways, on the other hand, may be built of any of several materials of distinctive texture, such as brick, flagstone, or cobblestone, and for these the foreground at least may be detailed by shading the individual components of the walk, joining the values together here and there by the use of an H or 2H pencil. Whatever joints are indicated, either in roadways or walkways, must be drawn with a fine light stroke, since they are invariably seen in quite a foreshortened manner.

Outdoor steps. Vertical strokes are usually used to express the verticality of outdoor risers and to draw attention to them.

Remember that the value of a shadow, wherever it falls, is determined by the material it falls upon. On grass, it is quite dark. On a roadway or walkway made of light material, it is correspondingly light. As with shadows on lawns, tree shadows on roadways and walkways should be constructed so that their appearance is believable.

For additional interest, streets and walks may be assumed to be wet, as from rain, and reflections of the building, passers-by, automobiles, etc., may be shown in them. This is particularly successful if the scene is taken at dusk or at night (see Plate IX).

Skies

Some delineators prefer to leave all skies in pencil renderings white. A number of others, however, prefer to shade skies or to render clouds in them. If a sky is rendered, it should complement the building; that is, it should be dark if the building is light, and light if the building is dark. A good rule of thumb is this: If the building has a static quality and is so quiet that the picture appears to require more life, then a cloudy, busy sky will help. If, on the other hand, the building is dynamic, with many exciting elements, the sky should be quiet, without clouds and with a minimum of textures.

If the perspective of a building is so sharp that the drawing seems to slip out at the side, the motion can be stopped by using a sky made of strokes which counter

Fig. 9.12 Office Building. (Renderer: William Spence Black. Student project.)

MATERIALS: Kid-finish bristol board; HB, B, 2B, 4B, and 2H; Pink Pearl, Ruby; clear pastel

the movement (Figure 9.12). This can be a plain sky or a cloudy one, depending upon the type of building.

Since the pencil strokes themselves are so definite that they do not lend themselves to clouds, the clouds are sometimes rubbed down and softened in the surrounding areas by the use of a cardboard stump. Some delineators find that the side-of-the-pencil technique is better for skies than the broad-stroke technique, because it minimizes texture.

Scale Figures

See the discussion of these embellishments in Chapter 8.

Making a Pencil Rendering

To create the rendering shown in Figure 9.12, a line perspective was drawn on white bond tracing paper. Another piece of tracing paper was placed over the perspective and the lines of the building and the surrounding areas were traced upon it. This paper was then turned face down, and each line was drawn on the back. Then this drawing was placed right side up on top of a piece of kid-finish bristol board, with the perspective in the proper position, and each line was traced with an HB pencil. Care was taken not to groove the bristol board, since grooves show up as white lines in a finished rendering.

Charcoal Study

Next, a new piece of tracing paper was placed over the tracing-paper perspective and a charcoal study was made as described in Chapter 7. In this charcoal study, it quickly became apparent that the perspective of the building at the left side of the sheet would have to be stopped in some way, so several trees and a tree branch in the sky were introduced. The horizontal sky accomplishes a similar task. A light source from the front and upper right was chosen because it gave the opportunity to express the forms of the building most clearly. It was decided at this time that the roof fascias of the building should be left light and that a dark sky and trees behind it should be used to make the building stand out.

Shading

1. The first values to be rendered were those on the sides and soffits of the grid. All these, except those on the second floor, were put in with an HB pencil with a broad-stroke point, and were drawn in perspective in order to help express the shape of these members. The shading on the first floor was purposely made vertical to relieve the monotony.

2. The light values on the glass of the upper floor were next washed in with an H pencil, and the shadows upon the glass were rendered with long, clean strokes, using a 2B pencil.

3. On the shade side of the building, the smooth-cut stone was shaded with an F pencil, the strokes being made in perspective. The cut stone was shaded by rendering each stone separately, some light, some dark, for interest and local color. The joints were permitted to remain white, and the monotony of the stonework was eventually relieved by creating white streaks with a Ruby eraser.

4. The shadow on the adjoining portion of the building was rendered with HB and B pencils, and reflections on the lighter part of the building were introduced with a Ruby eraser.

5. The lower portion of the building was rendered with an F pencil for the

Fig. 9.13a Preliminary Study for a Church. (Architect: O'Connor and Kilham, Architects. Renderer: Schell Lewis.)

light areas and a B pencil for the dark areas. The street and the building in the distance to the left were put in with an HB pencil, as was the sky.

6. The stone of the plant pocket at street level was rendered with H and HB pencils, while the shrubbery and the palm trees were indicated with F, B, and 2B pencils.

7. The perspective was fixed with clear pastel fixative.

Pencil Drawings on Tracing Paper

Schell Lewis makes his pencil renderings on tracing paper, using a rag bond with a good "tooth" — not slick or smooth. After a perspective line drawing and a preliminary study (Figure 9.13a) are made, another sheet of tracing paper is placed over the line drawing, and the finished rendering is made, beginning at

Fig. 9.13b Partially Completed Rendering of Preliminary Study. (Renderer: Schell Lewis.)

the left and finishing at the right, as shown in Figure 9.13b, being guided by the line perspective which can be seen through the top sheet of tracing paper.

An analysis of Schell Lewis's technique of indicating building materials reveals some interesting things. Brick is made in single strokes, with a pencil point the exact width of one course. Its pattern is purposely made imperfect so it will not appear stiff. Some stones are treated with great tonal variation. Sometimes stones are plainly shown; elsewhere they are so light that they are left the color of the paper. Occasionally stones are omitted altogether, and angular smudges as well as white spaces are used to relieve the monotony. Where stones are in shadow, they are rendered dark, and the joints are left white. But aside from the variation of the stones themselves, notice that there is a definite gradation from dark at the bottom of the building to light at the top. In Figure 9.14a

Fig. 9.14a Study for a Church. (Architect: O'Connor and Kilham, Architects. Renderer: Schell Lewis.)

Fig. 9.14b Completed Rendering of a Church. (Architect: O'Connor and Kilham, Architects. Renderer: Schell Lewis.)

and *b*, however, the brick is graded from dark at the top to light at the bottom. Each is interesting in its own way.

Foliage is rendered with rather wide strokes about ¾ inch long, most of which are diagonal. Shadows cast on trunks and branches by foliage masses are soft in quality and have wavy, indistinct edges. Finally, some trunks and branches are outlined for emphasis.

The skies in Schell Lewis's renderings were made with broad strokes of the pencil, the washes then being muted by rubbing with a paper stump.

Scale figures and automobiles complete the renderings.

Shortcuts in Pencil Rendering

Many renderers save time in pencil work by using a good grade of rag tracing paper for the final rendering. Instead of laboriously transferring the perspective from one sheet to another, they merely place a clean sheet of tracing paper over the line perspective, and, after making a value study, render.

Tracing paper requires the use of slightly harder pencils than kid-finish bristol board, but provides an excellent surface. When the rendering has been finished it may be fixed with pastel fixative, and either the original may be shown to the client or any number of copies may be made from the tracing. If the tracing paper is to be mounted, it can be fastened to an illustration board with Scotch tape, or it can be "floated" on the illustration board by the following method:

1. Mix a batch of Sanford library paste to a creamy consistency (free of lumps) in a cup or other container.

2. Turn the tracing drawing side down on a smooth surface and thoroughly saturate it with the paste, using a sponge. Remove the excess.

3. Sponge an illustration board larger than the drawing with the same paste.

4. Hold the illustration board on one edge next to the tracing, then let it fall onto it (Figure 9.15). When you turn the illustration board upside down, the tracing will be fastened to it, but will be wrinkled. To remove wrinkles and any excess paste, cover the drawing with a clean piece of tracing paper, and, using the edge of a large triangle, gently stroke outward in all directions, radiating away from the center.

An illustration board that is wet by such a mounting process will usually curl. To counteract this, another sheet of tracing paper should be paste-mounted, as described above, on the back of the illustration board; or, if the board is quite thick, merely wetting the back will do. Finally, the mounted drawing should be

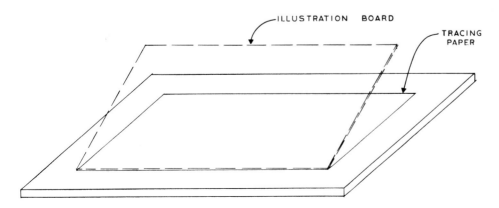

Fig. 9.15 Dropping the Illustration Board onto Tracing Paper.

placed on a flat, even surface, covered with clean paper, and weighted with heavy books until it is thoroughly dry.

It is possible to avoid curling and the need to counteract-mount if all mounting is done on foam-core board, which is faced on both sides with white paper and is available as follows:

1/16 inch thick in sizes 30 × 40 inches, 40 × 60 inches, and 48 × 96 inches

1/8 inch thick in sizes 32 × 40 inches and 48 × 96 inches

1/2 inch thick in sizes 48 × 48 inches and 48 × 96 inches

Mounting with rubber cement is another method, more commonly used than paste mounting. By mixing 50 percent rubber cement with 50 percent rubber cement thinner, it is possible to obtain a better, longer-lasting and more workable mounting medium. Once mixed, it is best to spread a thin, even coat of rubber cement on the mounting board and the back of the illustration to be mounted. When both areas are completely dry, it is then possible to float the mount as explained above. In working with rubber cement, it is necessary to avoid wrinkles because this method of mounting will not permit any movement of the float once it is in contact with the illustration board.

The Carbon Pencil

The carbon pencil is a much more versatile instrument than the graphite pencil. Basically, a combination of carbon and a sort of gum paste is pressed into a stick, and then encased in a wooden container in much the same way as a graphite pencil. Beyond this basic similarity of general appearance, the two have little in common. Whereas the graphite pencil glides across the paper, the carbon pencil grips it. When it is drawn across the paper it produces a clean, dry line, jet-black in tone, velvety in quality.

The carbon pencil, of which the Wolff pencil (made in England) is most widely known, is made in six degrees:

HH very hard
H moderately hard
HB middle degree
B black
BB very black
BBB extra black (this is also made in extra heavy)

It can be used in various ways, such as:

1. Strokes
2. Hatched strokes
3. Hatched strokes smudged with chamois
4. Strokes combined with chalk
5. Strokes combined with white pencil
6. Strokes combined with tempera

The carbon pencil is one of the fastest and easiest media to use, and is capable of producing a wide range of effects. It erases fairly easily with a kneaded eraser, and produces dramatic effects when used on the proper paper or board. It has a fabulous quality when used for indicating detail with a minimum of effort. It may be used on a variety of papers or boards, but is most effective when used on a soft-textured paper such as kid-finish bristol board, tracing paper, vellum, charcoal paper, pastel paper, or any of the colored illustration and poster boards. Its sole disadvantage is that the point breaks easily; for this reason, it is advisable to hand-sharpen the pencil very carefully with a sharp knife, exposing only about ¼ inch of the carbon. Care must be taken not to nick the carbon during the removal of the wood. As with the graphite pencil, the final shaping of the point is done on a sandpaper block or a fine file.

The carbon pencil is effective on colored as well as white paper, particularly when it is combined with white pencil, chalk, or tempera. American-made charcoal paper, which is available in a standard size of 19 × 25 inches, comes in about thirteen colors. Colors which are relatively "grayed" are most suitable for use in architectural rendering, and these have been marked with an asterisk in the following list.[1]

*Fog blue	Golden brown	Black
Powder pink	Minton yellow	*Bright white
*Pottery green	*Velvet gray	Maize yellow
*Peach glow	*Storm gray	Autumn brown
*Cadet blue	*White	Harvest gold

Poster boards are available in more colors than colored papers. One company makes forty-one colors, including colors representative of the entire spectrum. As with colored papers, only the relatively grayed colors are suggested for architectural renderings, because bright colors detract from the rendering itself. Some of the colors that are useful for rendering are:

Brown	Ecru
Dark green	French blue
Silver gray	Dull white
Charcoal	

Some colored poster boards are coated on one side, others on both sides. The standard size for these 14-ply boards is 28 × 44 inches, and they can be cut to the size desired.[2]

Herga (English-made) pastel papers are also excellent for use with carbon pencil, and these are available in many colors. The author recommends the colors marked with an asterisk for architectural renderings.

*Light gray	*Light brown	*Light green
*Dark gray	Brown	Blue
*Green	*Buff	Black

These papers are sold in size 22 × 30 inches.[3]

Equipment Required

The equipment required will be determined by the color of the paper used. The supplies in the list below will enable complete experimentation in the various techniques described in the following pages.

---

[1] Strathmore Paper Co., courtesy Robert Rosenthal, Inc.

[2] Charles T. Bainbridge's Sons, courtesy Robert Rosenthal, Inc.

[3] Winsor & Newton, Inc., courtesy Robert Rosenthal, Inc.

1. A sheet of soft paper
2. Black carbon paper
3. White carbon paper
4. B, BB, and BBB pencils
5. Kneaded eraser
6. Chamois
7. Jar or tube of Chinese white or poster color
8. Jar of black poster paints or tempera
9. Several sticks of white chalk
10. White pencil
11. Jars of warm gray tempera in grades 0, 1, 2, and 3
12. Pastel fixative

Example: Pencil Rendering of a Meeting House

The entire perspective for the rendering in Figure 9.16 was constructed on tracing paper and then reproduced on charcoal paper by placing a large sheet of white carbon paper between the tracing paper and the charcoal paper (carbon side down). Each line of the perspective was traced with a 3H pencil, lightly but firmly, to reproduce it on the rendering paper below. It is necessary to use carbon paper because the carbon pencil will not "take" on lines which have been drawn by a graphite pencil, but will slide off.

Charcoal study. While the value study was being made in charcoal on tracing paper, the following decisions were made:

Fig. 9.16 First Unitarian Meeting House, Madison, Wisconsin. (Architect: Frank Lloyd Wright. Renderer: Jaroslav Sichynsky. Student project.)

1. The light should come from above and to the left in order to express the architectural forms most strongly.

2. The trees should occupy the position shown in the final rendering in order to stop the violent perspective motion of the roof line.

3. The grass, trees, and flowers in the foreground should be made dark in order to "push the building back" into the mid-distance, while the trees in the background at the right side of the drawing were placed there to keep the building from "falling out of the back of the sheet."

4. No clouds were necessary, and the color of the paper alone provides a sufficiently luminous sky.

a

Shading. The strokes used for textures and shading were differentiated according to location, the texture to be indicated, the direction of the plane, etc., as follows:

1. The shade side of the building at the left, as well as the eaves, was rendered individually in strokes with a pointed B pencil (Figure 9.17, sketch *a*).

2. The windows in this area were darkened by hatching with the flat side of a BB pencil. Edges were kept straight with a triangle which was held in place as the pencil was moved back and forth (Figure 9.17, sketch *b*).

3. The shaded area under the roof was rendered in the same way. The outer edge of this wash was made darker than the inner edge because of reflected light.

4. The shadow on the glass area was put in by hatching with a BBB pencil and was finally darkened by the use of strokes with the dulled point of the BBB pencil.

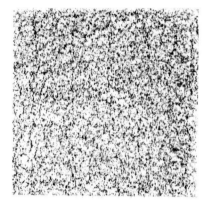

b

5. Shadows on the mullions were put in with a B pencil in short strokes, care being taken to permit the color of the paper to shine through for the effect of reflected light.

6. Stonework: The stonework of the side wall in sunlight was indicated by a series of rather isolated stones set in a gray tone (Figure 9.17, sketch *c*), since an attempt to show more than this in the charcoal study took away the sunny effect it was felt that this wall should have. The stones in the shade area cast by the roof at the left were indicated completely before they were hatched vertically with a BB pencil.

7. The shadows under the mullions were put in freehand in continuous strokes.

8. The complicated texture of the roof was simplified by using large freehand strokes to simulate the shadows under the shingle butts. If these had been put in solidly, the roof would have been monotonous in appearance; therefore they were made in a series of short, slightly wavy strokes with a B pencil. The small roof at the right and the low roof at the left were made by a series of strokes parallel to the roof in both directions, with some of the paper allowed to shine through.

c

9. The shingles of the roof in the lower portion of the building at the right were indicated in the same way with a B pencil.

10. The dark windows were indicated by hatching with the point of a BBB pencil, leaving the mullions the color of the paper.

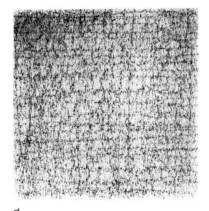

a. Pointed pencil
b. Side of pencil (cross-hatched)
c. Hatched, rubbed with chamois
d. Hatched, rubbed, and textured

Fig. 9.17 Shading Made with a B Carbon Pencil.

d

11. The shadow on the ground was indicated by short vertical strokes with a sharp BB pencil.

12. The stonework in this area was indicated by drawing an occasional stone and then placing a smooth wash of white pencil over the stone area.

13. White pencil was also used at various places such as the edges of the roof at the right, parts of the shingle roof at the left, and the stones of the wall in sunlight in the foreground.

14. The grass in the foreground was indicated by the use of a B pencil held as flat as possible. Strokes about 1½ inch long were made, care being taken to vary the intensity here and there and to allow the color of the paper to shine through in order to prevent monotony. The grass in the immediate foreground toward the bottom edge of the picture was darkened considerably with the same horizontal strokes in order to help provide a dark frame for the picture.

15. The flowers and grass in the immediate foreground were put in with pointed pencils varying from B to BBB. The strokes were made from the ground up with a wiping motion in order to achieve a natural-looking growth pattern. The details were made individually with a pointed BB pencil, beginning with

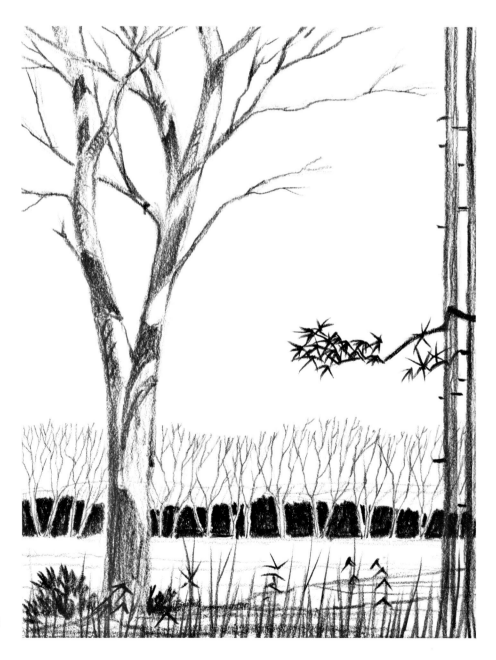

Fig. 9.18 Details of Trees, Flowers, and Grass in Carbon Pencil.

strong pressure and ending with no pressure (Figure 9.18). Some of the flowers were whitened with the white pencil.

16. The trees were put in last, the bark being indicated with B and BB pencils by a combination of strokes around the trunks, as well as vertical strokes. The branches were shaded on the underside with a BBB pencil, and the pine needles were put on last with the same wiping motion as described above and shown in Figure 9.18.

17. Pastel fixative was used to fix the finished drawing.

Example: Pencil Rendering of an Office Building

Preparation for Figure 9.19 was similar to that for Figure 9.16, but a black carbon paper was used to transfer the perspective drawing.

E.D.WHITE

Fig. 9.19 An Office Building, New York City. (Renderer: Edward Devine White, Jr., Student project.)

MATERIALS: Sheet of black carbon paper; American-made charcoal paper, 19 × 25 inches; B, BB, and BBB pencils; kneaded eraser; chamois

The value study in charcoal disclosed that the most dramatic effect could be obtained by the selection of a light source from above and to the left, giving definite light and dark sides to the building and providing a dark form of low adjoining buildings as a base. It was decided to make the tower darkest at the top and at the edges next to the sky.

Detail in this project was almost eliminated because of the smallness of scale. A general impression was sought, rather than a detailed rendering. The dark shadow in the foreground (from a building assumed to be behind and to the left of the spectator) and the two scale figures were included in the position in order to push the building into the mid-distance.

Shading. This rendering was made by the smudge process; that is, strokes were applied and then smudged with a chamois as follows:

1. A general gray value was given to the shade side of the office building by hatching with the side of a BB pencil in several directions. Then each portion of this side was in turn masked with 8½- × 11-inch pad paper and rubbed with a clean chamois (see Figure 9.17, sketch *d*). The spandrels were then given the same treatment in order to make them darker than the glass areas. They were shaded with a BB pencil.

2. The general light-colored, grayed tone on the light side of the building was applied by hatching, care being taken to darken the left upper edge.

3. The spandrel areas were then lightened by masking each spandrel with 8½- × 11-inch pad paper and erasing with a piece of kneaded eraser. The strokes in the erasing process were made from the left- and right-hand edges of the spandrels.

4. The small dark openings in the center of the light side of the building were applied with a BB pencil, and each opening was made separately in order to obtain gradation.

5. The upper left-hand section of the light side of the building tower was then darkened by hatching softly with the side of a B pencil.

6. Shadows cast by spandrels were introduced by the use of a T square and a loosely held B pencil. Reverse shadows on the shade side were cast by the same method.

7. The dark areas at the top of the tower were next indicated by hatching, using clean, short strokes with a B pencil. Shadows were added in the same manner.

8. After the entire office building had been rendered, rough edges (places where hatching had gotten into the sky area) were cleaned with a kneaded eraser by masking the building with pad paper and then erasing in a wiping motion away from the building.

9. The low surrounding buildings were next rendered by hatching in several directions with the side of a BB pencil, masking with pad paper, and then rubbing with a chamois. After the general tones had been put in, cornices, window, canopy, and other details were drawn by hatching with the point of a BB pencil. The low building at the right of the picture was indicated in the same way.

10. The values on the street were put in unevenly to avoid monotony, and a dark shadow cast by a building to the left of and behind the spectator was added in the immediate foreground.

11. Scale figures were distributed throughout the picture to draw the eye to the entrance of the building. Like all values, these are dark in the foreground and lighter in the background, and were drawn with B, BB, and BBB pencils.

12. Reflections in the street were made with a wiping motion by the use of a kneaded eraser held against a T square tilted at an angle.

Example: Product Design of an Engine

Figure 9.20 was made by using carbon-pencil strokes and chalk in a manner similar to that described for Figures 9.16 and 9.19. White pencil may be used instead of chalk in this type of rendering, the difference being that the white pencil has a waxy quality which does not permit any overlaying of carbon-pencil lines.

Fig. 9.20 Product Design of an Engine. (Renderer: William C. Wilkinson. Student project.)

Example: Porch Detail

After the perspective for Figure 9.21 was transferred to the pastel paper by using white carbon paper, a value study was made over the tracing-paper perspective. It is impossible to make a value study over a dark sheet, as the values become confused.

The light source was assumed to be directly behind the spectator, since this would create shades and shadows which would best express the architectural forms.

Shading. This rendering was executed with carbon pencil combined with chalk on Herga green pastel paper.

1. The shade under the canopy was made by hatching in the direction of the perspective with B and BB pencils. Care was taken to leave the inner edge of this shade area lighter — almost the color of the paper itself — to create the illusion of reflected light. The shade under the other members of the canopy was put in by the use of a T square and a BB pencil.

2. The interior was drawn and shaded with B and BB pencils, care being taken to show the chair and to indicate some other pieces of furniture inside the glass.

Fig. 9.21 Porch Detail. (Renderer: Emil Kempa. Student project.)

Variations in value with the dark portions next to mullions and wall area were introduced into this area as well as into the partly drawn curtains.

3. The beams above the glass were drawn with a T square and a sharp B pencil.

4. The shadows on beams, glass, mullions, and stone were rendered by strokes made with the side of a BB pencil. The outer edges of the mullions were then darkened in order to make them stand out.

5. The top of the shadow on the building cast by the canopy was kept lighter than the bottom edge in order to give the feeling of reflected light.

6. The front fascia of the canopy, the front edge of the mullions in sunlight, other portions of the front face of the building, and the sky were permitted to remain the color of the paper itself, as were portions of the porch floor.

7. The shadows in the vertical joints of the boarding at the front of the building were introduced by using a loosely held, sharp B pencil and a T square. Care was taken to draw them with varying intensity in order to avoid monotony.

8. Stonework in sunlight was drawn with joints the color of the paper, with only an occasional joint darkened with a B pencil. Because of the angle, and in order to obtain a definite break, the narrow edge of the masonry mass was rendered darker than the longer side of the masonry mass, and the stone was hatched with a B pencil here and there, the joints remaining the color of the paper.

9. In combinations of white chalk or other kinds of white with carbon pencil, care must be taken to limit the amount of white, because too large an area will reduce the importance of the carbon pencil itself. A careful analysis in the value study indicated the use of white in the places shown on the finished rendering.

The chalk was first sharpened so that it made a conical point similar to that of a pencil used for writing. The graining on the board at the left of the rendering was put in freehand. The highlights on the sides of the vertical boards at the front are indicated with a wavering line of chalk, put in with a T square. Some highlights on the curtains to the left and right were put in freehand with a curved motion to simulate the folds of the curtains. The highlights on the lower portions of the window mullions were added by masking around those areas with pieces of pad paper as previously described, and then hatching them over and over with the chalk. The light portions of the roof overhang were done in a similar manner, except that some strokes were introduced at the left.

10. The flagging in the porch floor was whitened with strokes and counterstrokes in perspective. The floor was graded from solid at the left to paper color at the right. The grass in the joints was then drawn with a B pencil held flat. The steps were rendered in strokes. The ground was rendered by holding a B pencil at an angle of 20 degrees with the paper and making strokes in perspective. The hill in the back was rendered in the same way, except that the strokes were pitched in order to indicate the slope. The trees were first constructed with a loosely held, sharp BB pencil. Portions of the tree trunks were permitted to remain the color of the paper, and shading was made with short strokes around the trunks themselves (Figure 9.18).

11. The tree mass at the right was indicated by first softly delineating the mass with a BB pencil held flat, and then shading the foliage with a series of short converging strokes. The flowers in the foreground were drawn freehand with a sharp BB pencil and chalk.

As this rendering was being made, errors in carbon pencil were corrected by masking around the area to be changed with pad paper and erasing the unwanted portions of the wash with a small piece of kneaded eraser, wiping it away from the edge of the pad paper.

Fig. 9.22 Visualization Based on the Architects' Plans, United Nations Headquarters, New York. (Architect: United Nations Headquarters. Planning Staff: Wallace K. Harrison, Director. Renderer: Hugh Ferriss.)

12. At the very end of the job, small tree shadows were introduced with short vertical strokes made with a B pencil, held lightly.

13. A small amount of charcoal fixative was applied from a distance of about 5 feet. Note: Too much fixative will diminish the white value of chalk areas and make them disappear.

The Lithographic Crayon Pencil

While the carbon pencil has a slightly gritty feel when used on paper, the lithographic crayon pencil is smooth and somewhat waxy. It is used in the same manner and on the same kinds of paper as the carbon pencil (when it is used alone) and is capable of producing the same jet blacks, atmospheric effects, and tonal variations. The best known is Korns Lithographic Crayon Pencils, which are made in the following grades:

No. 1, soft   No. 4, extra hard
No. 2, medium   No. 5, extremely hard
No. 3, hard

Like the carbon pencil, the lithographic pencil is excellent for indicating large expansive projects without actual detail, as shown in Figure 9.22, drawn by Hugh Ferriss. In this powerful rendering, the eye is drawn to the center of interest because the tones in that area were left light, and because the focal points were surrounded with rather deep (sometimes almost black) values.

Direction is given to the various planes in each rendering by the simple expedient of building tones with final strokes in perspective. By placing wash upon wash, and by leaving small spaces between strokes, lightness and transparency are obtained. The appearance of natural or artificial light is skillfully reproduced in this rendering by the use of sharp value comparisons: light areas are permitted to remain very light, and are always adjoined by dark building surfaces. Gradually diminishing the intensity of light on the wall and street surfaces also contributes to the extraordinary illusion of reality: the farther an area is from the light surface, the dimmer its light becomes.

chapter 10

Ink Rendering

The Pen

The pen existed as a writing instrument long before it was used by artists and architects. Pens were first made of bamboo roots or other hollow woody plant forms, with the ends prepared by fraying. It was the Greeks and Romans who cut reeds to a point and slit them like modern pens. Eventually, pens were made of such metals as copper and bronze; these imitated in form the earlier pointed reeds. Use of goose quills, which were easily prepared, came later.

The modern pen dates from the latter part of the nineteenth century, when it was mechanically (and therefore cheaply) produced in England by Joseph Gillott. The form and style of pens have been improved, and they have been standardized according to number and produced in many sizes. The smallest of the modern pen points is called the "crow-quill point," and the earliest of these was actually copied from the quill form. The better drawing pens are produced by Gillott in England and the Hunt Manufacturing Company in the United States. For the purpose of simplification, the numbers of pen nibs specified in this chapter will be those of the Hunt Manufacturing Company, but the accompanying table gives the corresponding sizes of Hunt and Gillott pen nibs.

Although there are more than 35 different styles and sizes of pen nibs available, only about ten of these are generally used for drawing. The finest of this group is the crow-quill point, Hunt No. 102, which is very flexible and can produce a moderately wide line if pressure is exerted upon it. Another small nib is the flexible quill, Hunt No. 108, which is a bronze-finish quill pen for cross-hatching. The hawk quill, Hunt No. 107, has a superfine point but is stiffer than the crow-quill nib and very durable. It is also used for cross-hatching.

For larger drawings, Hunt's No. 99 round-pointed drawing nib is popular, and this, used in conjunction with Hunt's No. 22-B extra fine (medium-stiff) nib and Hunt's No. 56 school drawing pen, provides an assortment adequate for nearly all work. There will be occasions, described later in this chapter, when broader lines are desired, and these can be made by using Hunt's No. 512 bowl-pointed nib, Globe 513-EF, and the Speedball pens, such as B-6 and C-6.

Gillott and Hunt Pen Sizes*

Gillott	Hunt
1	101
13EF	514
14EF	513
41	67
51	67 (nearest)
61	59
81	67
91	69
102	35 (nearest)
105	X98
170	99
290	100
291	103
292	35 (nearest)
295	35
303	22B
351	22B
390	67
404	56
425	69
427	67
601	59
603	5
604	35
659	102
837	107
849	38 or 65
850	108
878	97B
908	98
909	5 (nearest)
1000	104
1008	38 or 65
1009	38 or 65
1010	38 or 65
1043	38 or 65
1044	59 (nearest)
1045	69
1046	59 or 69
1047	67
1060	97B
1065	35
1066	35
1067	67
1068	59 or 69
1071	38 or 65
1083	65
1087	6
1089	69
1095	98
1096	59 or 69
1100	38
1102	38 or 65

Gillott and Hunt Pen Sizes (Continued)

Gillott	Hunt
5005-1	400-1
5005-1½	400-1-1½
5005-2	400-2
5005-2½	400-2½
5005-3	400-3
5005-3½	400-3½
5005-4	400-4
5005-4½	400-4½
5005-5	400-5
5005-5½	400-5½
5005-6	400-6

* Courtesy of Hunt Manufacturing Co., Philadelphia, Pennsylvania, and Heidl Slocum Co., Inc., New York, U.S. sales representative for Joseph Gillott & Sons, Ltd., England.

Penholders. Since penholders are inexpensive, it is usual for the delineator to keep about a half dozen on hand. The crow-quill nib requires a special holder, available with or without a cork cushion. All other nibs fit the average writing holder, which must, however, be small enough to fit into the neck of an ink bottle. A renderer who does a great deal of pen-and-ink work may wish to buy penholders of different colors, or to identify them by notching, so that the desired nib can be chosen quickly and easily.

Pen Wiper. A soft, pliable chamois will be found ideal for cleaning pen nibs, as it absorbs ink and will not injure delicate points.

Inks

The earliest inks, like the early pens, were employed for writing rather than drawing. They were made of vegetable stains; berry juices; and mixtures of soot, charcoal, resin, and sometimes schist, a crystalline rock. Ink was used in China as early as 2500 B.C., and at approximately the same time in ancient Egypt by the ruler Ptahhotep, who used both red and black ink.

Chinese ink and stick inks in general are made ready for use by grinding sticks of ink in water, straining the solution, and carefully storing the ink in an airtight container. Tube ink, also, is mixed in water and strained. Today's high-quality liquid inks, which are available in various colors, make it possible for the renderer to begin working immediately — thus saving time and avoiding the mess of mixing, straining, and storing which is associated with Chinese ink.

Modern inks used by delineators are, for the most part, black. If ink is to be used in conjunction with watercolor or other washes, waterproof ink is chosen. For delineators who wish to use them, the following colored inks are available:

Yellow	Violet	White
Orange	Blue	Brick red
Red orange (vermilion)	Turquoise	Russet
Red (scarlet)	Green	Brown
Carmine red	Leaf green	Indigo
Red-violet (purple)	Neutral tint (gray)	

Some manufacturers of American inks are Higgins Ink Co., Inc., Artone Color Company, and F. Weber. A superior drawing ink is Pelikan, manufactured by Gunther-Wagner, Germany.

Ink-bottle holders. Use a simple and inexpensive bottle holder to reduce the possibility of tipping. These holders are commercially available.

Fountain-Type Pens

Some renderers prefer a fountain-type mechanical pen such as Koh-I-Noor Rapidograph or Pelikan Graphos.

The Rapidograph pen uses special ink and is available in fifteen point sizes,[1] which are interchangeable, as indicated in the accompanying table.

Point size*	Approximate line width, inch	Pen no.
6X0	0.004	086471
5X0	0.006	032597
4X0	0.008	025627
3X0	0.010	104159
00	0.012	113078
0	0.014	113069
1	0.019	113022
2	0.023	113031
2½	0.0275	113087
3	0.0355	113041
4	0.052	113096
6	0.067	025636
7	0.080	025645
8	0.098	025654
9	0.118	025663

* Courtesy Rosenthal's, New York.

The Pelikan Graphos pen is a precision drawing-ink fountain pen with interchangeable points for ruling, lettering, and drawing. It has an ink-cartridge fill system with an ink regulator to maintain a uniform flow of ink for all point sizes. A typical renderer's set contains a pen, bellows, cleaner, compensation clip, six blank ink cartridges, four B points (0.1, 0.2, 0.3, and 0.4), and eight D points for lettering and drawing (0.3, 0.4, 0.5, 0.6, 0.7, 0.8, 1.0, and 1.2).

Paper

As discussed in Chapter 1, early papers were made from the bark of trees and from papyrus. In addition, vellum and parchment were produced from the skins of calves and sheep. Parchment, although it was very expensive, replaced papyrus because changes could be made upon it, because it had two usable sides, and also because it was thick. The combination of parchment and the pen resulted in greater facility, and hand-lettered illuminated books came into existence as early as the fourth century, developing to their highest point during the next two or three centuries.

There are a number of types of modern paper which lend themselves to pen-and-ink work. Such papers should be fairly smooth and firm, and should accept erasures without any obvious change in the surface. Among those that fit this description are the following:

1. Ledger bond paper.
2. Tracing cloth or Mylar.
3. The better grades of firm tracing paper.
4. Hot-pressed paper, which can also be purchased mounted.
5. Cold-pressed paper, which, though rough, will accept pen-and-ink work as well as watercolor washes. The watercolor washes can be made over waterproof ink.
6. Plate-finish bristol board, which has the most desirable surface for pen-and-ink work since it has a smooth surface across which the pen may glide. It will accept gently rubbed erasures without damage and is made in two- and three-ply thicknesses, either of which is thick enough to form a good cushion.
7. Kid-finish bristol board, which is preferred by some delineators to the smoother plate-finish bristol board, even though the surface is fairly rough.
8. Colored illustration boards.
9. Prepared acetate.

Advantages and Limitations

It should be recognized at the outset that pen and ink should be reserved for small-scale drawings. The very fineness of the pen point is at once an advantage and a disadvantage. Small details may be easily rendered, but the illusion of reality in larger areas is obtained by building values of appropriate combinations of lines or dots of various kinds. Thus, careful selection of line groupings allows easy and magnificent indications of wood grain, stone, trees, foliage, etc.

Something else as exciting as these realistic effects, however, can also be achieved in pen and ink: the logical expression of architectural form by the use of abstract conventions. In this approach all but the most important elements in a picture are eliminated, and those that are included are rendered in lines and combinations of lines and dots arranged in a striking manner. The success of such a presentation will depend upon the "readability" of each portion of the picture, as well as the manner in which the various parts fit into a meaningful whole.

Getting to Know Your Pen

Before attempting the more complicated means of producing tones, textures, and values, it is well to familiarize yourself with your pens. Using a piece of the same paper or board on which you intend to draw your final rendering, take a medium-nib pen, dip it into the ink, shake off the excess, and hold it in a manner similar to that used for writing. Then practice the following series of strokes (see Figure 10.1):

a. Sets of straight strokes from left to right, about ⅟₃₂ inch, ⅟₁₆ inch, and ⅛ inch apart, with even pressure. As you draw the pen across the paper, notice that holding it lightly causes the pen nib to work in a natural way, and the average line for that pen nib will result. Certainly every pen nib can be caused to make a wider line than its average, and in some cases this is desirable, but such treatment will quickly wear out the pen nib.
b. Similar sets of vertical straight strokes.
c. A set of horizontal wavy strokes.
d. A set of vertical wavy strokes.

When you have filled a space about 10 × 12 inches with such experimental strokes, you are ready to practice the various kinds of strokes and combinations

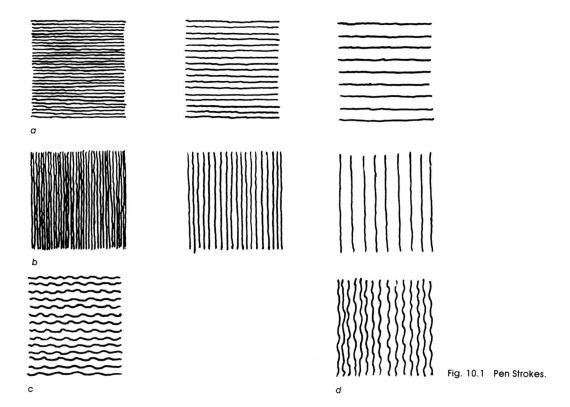

<table>
</table>

a

b

c   d   Fig. 10.1 Pen Strokes.

thereof normally used in the rendering of a building. Among these are the following (Figure 10.2):

a. Short parallel vertical lines
b. Short parallel horizontal lines
c. A combination (hatching) of items a and b
d. Straight lines at an angle of 45 degrees from right to left
e. Straight lines at an angle of 45 degrees from left to right
f. A combination of items d and e
g. Wavy lines at 45 degrees
h. Wavy lines with steady pressure, in two directions at 45 degrees
i. Vertical strokes beginning light and ending dark
j. Vertical strokes beginning dark and ending light
k. Horizontal straight strokes with 45-degree hatching
l. Crosshatched parallel curved lines
m. Flat C's
n. E's
o. Water-wave strokes
p. Dots
q. Circles
r. Plus marks
s. Graining
t. V's

It is useful to keep in mind the conventions described below, when rendering pen-and-ink trees.

1. Generally speaking, trees in the background are shown by a simple combination of vertical straight or wavy strokes (Figure 10.3, sketches b and c). Trunks may or may not be shown in these areas as white spaces (sketch a).

Fig. 10.2 Devices for Forming Tones.

a. *Short parallel vertical lines*
b. *Short parallel horizontal lines*
c. *A combination (hatching) of items a and b*
d. *Straight lines at an angle of 45 degrees from right to left*
e. *Straight lines at an angle of 45 degrees from left to right*
f. *A combination of items d and e*
g. *Wavy lines at 45 degrees*
h. *Wavy lines with steady pressure, in two directions at 45 degrees*
i. *Vertical strokes beginning light and ending dark*
j. *Vertical strokes beginning dark and ending light*
k. *Horizontal straight strokes with 45-degree hatching*
l. *Crosshatched parallel curved lines*
m. *Flat C's*
n. *E's*
o. *Water-wave strokes*
p. *Dots*
q. *Circles*
r. *Plus marks*
s. *Graining*
t. *V's*

2. Trees in the mid-distance are usually shown in quite a developed manner, with the complete tree structure indicated, but with small circles or ovals, or perhaps dots, for leaves (Figure 10.4, sketch *d*). Sometimes foliage masses are shaded with lines forming continuous convolutions over the foliage areas (Figure 10.3, sketch *f*).

For best results, block the trees lightly in pencil, and then use a lightly held crow-quill pen. Thin lines will produce the illusion of reality and distance.

3. Trees in the foreground are usually quite detailed, in both trunk texture and

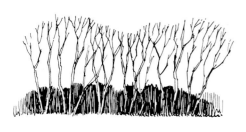

a

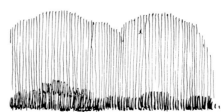

b

c

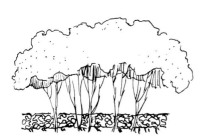

d

e

f

Fig. 10.3 Background Trees.

Fig. 10.4 Simple Tree Indications.

a

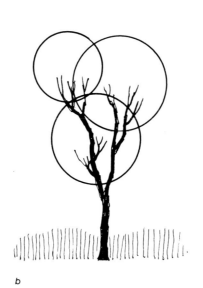

b

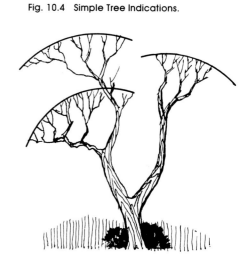

c

d

e

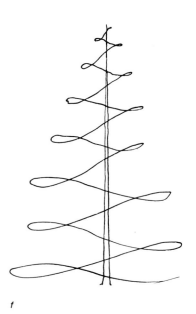

f

leaves. Leaves should be characteristic of the type of tree indicated. Pine trees may be shown by combinations of needle groupings. Sometimes these groups are hatched with vertical lines. Individual leaves in the foreground may be abstracted; that is, only a few may be shown, and these may be shaped with simple vertical parallel lines. As in all types of rendering, only a relatively few leaves should be included to express the idea, and these should complement the architecture rather than draw attention away from it. If realistic leaves are desired, each leaf must be carefully drawn around previously constructed tree or bush structures.

The shading and texture of trees is accomplished in several ways, but usually by a combination of lines that parallel the shape of the tree structure with short, curved strokes around the tree structure. Figure 10.4 shows a number of simple tree indications.

Grass

Grass can be shown in many ways: by a combination of short, vertical strokes; by individual clumps of grass made with fine strokes of varying heights covered by light crosshatching; by convolutions; or by a combination of short, parallel, horizontal, wavy lines. As in pencil drawing, only a small portion of the actual grass area should be indicated, and only in areas receiving shadow.

Water

Water may be represented by a series of short arcs facing upward, or by wave forms. It may also be indicated by combinations of thin, relatively horizontal lines, with a wavy reflection here and there, or by a series of "moving" wave forms. See Figure 10.5.

Procedure for Rendering

As in pencil rendering, the perspective drawing should be transferred to the rendering paper with a graphite pencil (see Chapter 3). Extreme care should be

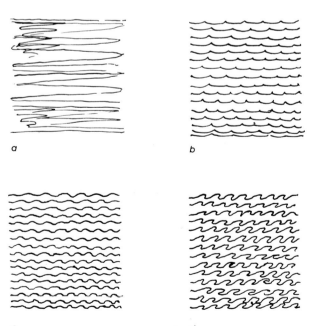

Fig. 10.5 Ways of Drawing Water.

taken not to dent or gouge the paper, since the pen is easily caught by such irregularities.

Value Study

A charcoal study is particularly important in making a pen-and-ink rendering, since it determines not only the light source, locations of trees and bushes, size of the picture, shades and shadows, etc., but also the exact proportion of white, gray, and black. While this is important in any black-and-white medium, it is doubly important in pen and ink, as the white, gray, and black areas must be delicately balanced in order to produce a successful picture. A picture with no black in it has no punch, but if there is too much black, the gray areas — important as they may be — are lost. If a sufficient amount of white is not left in a rendering, neither the gray nor the black areas have any meaning at all. In addition, the black areas must be strategically located so that they do not form an unpleasant pattern which camouflages rather than expresses the form of the architecture. The same can be said of local color, which, while it may be important in the finished building, sometimes must be modified in order to fit into the total picture.

Before the final rendering is begun, a preliminary pen sketch should be made on a sheet of tracing paper placed over the perspective drawing. This, of course, should not be a complete rendering, but rather an experimental drawing in which various parts of the building and textures can be studied. In particular, this study should determine what kinds of lines will be used and where they are

Fig. 10.6 Sol Friedman House, Pleasantville, New York. (Architect: Frank Lloyd Wright. Renderer: Homer King. Student project.)

MEDIA: Hunt pens (crow-quill and No. 99, No. 22B, and No. 56); Higgins' waterproof black ink; plate-finish bristol board, three-ply; chamois; and Ruby, glass, and artgum erasers.

to be located. The exact pens to be employed can be selected at this time, and generally it will be found that the broadest pens will be used for lines in the foreground, pens of medium width for lines in the mid-distance, and fine pens, such as the crow-quill pen, for lines in the distance. This is an important secondary means of expressing perspective in pen and ink.

In making the value study shown in Figure 10.6, it was decided that because of the building's rather plain exterior quality, additional interest could be given the rendering by a carefully studied tree disposition in the foreground. The simplification of the architecture was enriched by the delicacy of the network of trees in this splendid setting. Liberty was taken in the relocation of actual trees on the site in order to accomplish this. In addition, a feeling of sunlight on the ground was introduced by the use of long shadows and a pattern of fallen leaves. It should be noted that the foreground is smaller than the building in both area and total intensity, and that it therefore complements rather than competes with the building.

The building itself was rendered in hatching and dots, and a wash made by adding water to a small amount of ink was applied with a No. 4 brush to the sunlit portions.

Ink Washes

When you have mastered the basic skills in pencil, graphite, and pen-and-ink rendering you will be ready to try the most basic of all liquid media. Dry media are applied directly to the paper without mixture with any vehicle, and ink is usually applied with a specially designed instrument, the pen. However, such liquid media as ink, watercolor, and tempera are applied with brushes after they have been mixed with water. The use of water, of course, creates an entirely new set of problems. Liquid media are applied in washes, by dropping and scrubbing into wet surfaces, by the stipple method, by spatter, and by spraying with an airbrush.

Preparation of Ink

Media of the watercolor type, including diluted ink, are prepared by suspending particles of the pigments themselves in water. Sometimes watercolors that do not suspend evenly in water are used deliberately, as described in Chapter 12. But to make a rendering of clear, unadulterated, transparent washes, ink is the best choice. Applied correctly, this medium makes possible amazingly real illusions of light, space, and air. It is a good choice for renderers who wish to present their designs clearly, concisely, and beautifully.

As previously mentioned, Chinese ink, stick ink, and tube ink are mixed with water, strained, and carefully stored in airtight containers. Chinese ink in stick form (the way it was originally prepared in China and Japan), is made of finely ground lampblack baked with a glutinous binder. The better sticks are delicately perfumed, and the older a stick is, the better it is considered to be. Some sticks 300 to 400 years old are still in use.

Materials

Paper

Handmade watercolor paper is available in three different finishes; cold-pressed (medium texture), hot-pressed (smooth finish), and rough (used for watercolor paintings).

For ink washes medium texture is best, since it accepts washes more easily than the other two. There are a number of good brands of paper, with different countries of origin, such as the French D'Arches, the Italian Fabriano, the English J. B. Green, the English Royal Watercolor Society, and the American Strathmore. Each sheet of RWS paper is inspected separately, individually marked, and embossed with the seal of the Royal Watercolor Society. Using an appropriate weight of paper (based on the weight of a ream of standard size) is as important as choosing a good brand. Watercolor papers are available in 44-, 72-, 140-, and 300-pound weights. Too light a paper will not stand up to the rigors of stretching, nor does it have the body to withstand sponging. Therefore, it is best to use a paper no lighter than 140-pound, based on the imperial size, 22×30 inches.

An increasing number of delineators are using illustration board, which consists of several thicknesses of cardboard faced with watercolor paper.

It is wise to look at a sheet of paper carefully before purchasing it. Since it is handmade, it may have imperfections. If you hold it up to the light and see any thin spots, or if you discover any mounds on the surface, return it and ask for another sheet. Do not be concerned if the paper appears to be old and creamy rather than white, since the older the paper, the more seasoned it is likely to be.

Brushes

Good brushes require a major expenditure, but they may be used for watercolor as well as ink rendering and will last virtually a lifetime. The best available are red sable, made by Winsor & Newton, Inc., and are known as series 7, Albata. The seventeen brush sizes in this series are numbered from the smallest, No. 000 (1/32 inch), to the largest, No. 14 (1 17/32 inch). If money is no object, buy a No. 4 and a No. 12. If the budget must be considered, a No. 4 red sable in the less costly series 133 or series 33 (which offers fourteen sizes) and a large camel's-hair brush, which is much less expensive, will do.

As a brush is a major investment, each individual brush should be selected with care. There are several ways of testing brushes. To begin with, do not buy the first brush that you look at; ask the dealer to show you several brushes in the size and brand you plan to buy. Take them in hand and look at them carefully. If you discover a loose ferrule, put that brush aside immediately. But even more important, ask your dealer for a small container of water and dip each brush in it. Move the brush around in the water to get all the air out of it, then take it out of the water and hold it vertically. If the brush is conical, comes to a sharp point, and does not have any loose hairs sticking out at the sides, it is a pretty fair brush. Now look more closely. Dip it in the water again. Shake the water out by holding the handle firmly and slatting the brush toward the floor. If it comes to one point and is smooth and symmetrical, you are ready to try it further. Wet it again and, holding it like a pencil, draw it across a sheet of paper, pressing down upon it as you do so. If the brush springs back into a conical shape after you have done this, it is a good brush, but if it stays in a bent position, it is not good.

In addition to the red-sable and camel's-hair brushes, a Chinese bamboo bristle brush is also frequently helpful. These are inexpensive and may be discarded when they become too frayed, but when they are new they hold a good point and are extremely helpful in many ways.

Care of the brush. Moth larvae enjoy chewing on red-sable brushes; therefore, when these brushes are not in use they should be kept in a box with a few mothballs. Make sure that the brushes are dry before putting them away. After use, rinse them thoroughly. Above all, never leave them standing in water; they may acquire a bend that can never be corrected.

Miscellaneous Supplies

Some other supplies that will be needed for Chinese ink rendering are the following:

1. A bottle of Higgins' waterproof ink
2. A silk or "baby" sponge
3. A small box of alum
4. A small box of cheesecloth
5. Six or more white wash pans (enameled metal or plastic)
6. A water bucket or other container that will hold at least a quart of water.
7. A squeeze bottle of Elmer's Glue-All or Sobo glue
8. A half dozen white blotters
9. A drawing board about 3 inches larger all around than the rendering you intend to make

Preparation of Paper

White cold-pressed, hot-pressed, and rough watercolor paper may be purchased mounted in the form of an illustration board, but a tougher, tighter surface may be made by stretching the paper on a drawing board. But why is a stretch necessary? The answer is that any liquid medium has a tendency to buckle the surface of the paper upon which it is used. Just place a few drops of water on any sheet of paper and you will see. While a sheet of paper which is made taught and drumlike by a stretching process may temporarily buckle, it will immediately become flat again as the washes dry. Since there will be occasions when the entire sheet is wet by brushing or sponging, the importance of a stretch can easily be seen.

Before proceeding further, look carefully at the drawing board that you intend to use. It should be clean and free from lumps of glue or dirt which would be magnified by the stretch. If you discover such imperfections, try gently scraping them off in a way that does not further mar the surface of the board. If there are any large, open cracks in the board, it is well to discard it and get another.

Cutting

For practice rendering throughout this book, 14 × 21 inches is suggested as a picture size; therefore, the sheet of paper that you intend to use should be cut to a minimum of 20 × 26 inches. But before you cut the paper you will want to know which side you will work upon. Hold the full sheet that you have purchased up to the light and you will see a watermark (usually the name of the manufacturer) in one corner. The side from which you can read this watermark is the side upon which you will render. The other side is the one to be glued. To avoid confusion, mark a small X with a graphite pencil in the center of the usable side of the paper.

Now mark the size that you want your paper to be and cut it to this size with scissors, sharp knife, or razor, being careful not to cut it on the drawing board that you intend to use — or on your best table.

After you have cleared away the scraps of paper, cover the drawing board entirely with several thicknesses of newsprint paper to protect it from moisture. You are now ready to soak the rendering paper, in order to relax the fibers, then to stretch it. When the paper dries, the fibers will again draw close together.

Soaking

The paper can best be soaked in a large, flat, clean, tray-type sink, but if the paper is larger than any sink available, a clean bathtub will do. Fill the sink or tub with 3 or 4 inches of cold water and place the paper in it. It will float at first, so force it under the water. Let it soak for no more than 2 minutes; oversoaking (or soaking in warm water) will eventually totally disintegrate the fibers of the paper. At the end of 2 minutes, and if possible with an assistant's help, lift the sheet out, let most of the water drain off, and place it drawing side down upon the newsprint paper on your drawing board.

Blotting

Using clean white blotters, blot about 1 inch of the entire edge of the paper on all four sides. Make sure that these edges are entirely dry. Open the squeeze bottle of glue and take a generous amount of the glue upon your forefinger. Spread this generously, but not wastefully, upon the dried area on all four sides of the paper. Make sure that you do not miss any spots. Then wash your hands, and close the bottle of glue.

Lift the watercolor paper again, holding it by two corners. Have your assistant first remove the wet newsprint from the drawing board and then hold the other two corners of the watercolor paper. Reverse the sheet so that the rendering side is up and the glue side down, and place it in the center of the drawing board and as parallel with its edges as possible. Now you are ready to stretch the paper.

Stretching

Pulling too hard may break the paper, so always pull gently. Starting at the top corner, pull gently in one direction while your assistant pulls gently in the opposite direction. When this section has been stretched, move down about 2 inches and repeat the process. When the paper has been stretched in one direction (Figure 10.7), change directions and stretch it the opposite way.

Now, using your fingers or the bottom of the glue bottle, press the glued edges of the paper tightly upon the board. Start at one corner and, moving your hand or the bottle, press down and pull the edge of the paper toward your body for a

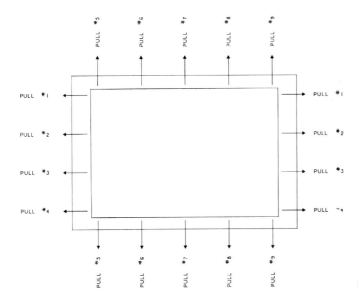

Fig. 10.7 Stretching the Paper.

distance of about ¾ inch. Repeat this process all around the edge of the paper until you can see no place where the paper has not been adequately fastened to the board. Using paper towel, facial tissues, or clean rags, remove the excess glue that has been squeezed from under the paper. Wash your hands again. Using clean water and the silk sponge, dampen the picture side of the paper — though not the edges under which the glue is located — being careful to remove any puddles of water which may form.

When you have completed the stretch, lay it aside (being careful not to put it near a heat source such as a radiator) while it dries. After about 10 or 15 minutes, look at it again and see if any of the edges of the paper have risen from the board. If so, take a small amount of glue on the end of a pen knife and insert it under the paper at these areas, then carefully press the paper into position again. Stubborn spots such as these may be held in place with a thumbtack until they have dried, after which the tack should be removed.

If this procedure is carefully followed, a good stretch should result. If the paper does not remain tautly glued when it dries, do not try to rescue it, but remove it from the board and start over with a fresh piece of paper, being careful to follow the steps described above. The remnants (the glued edges of the paper) may be removed by scraping with a knife after they have been soaked by placing wet newspaper upon them for about half an hour. Do not attempt to lay a second stretch while remnants of the first stretch are in place, or while the board is still wet. If the opposite side of the board is in good condition and dry, it may be used.

Preparation of the Mother Wash

The mother wash, from which all the lighter washes in the rendering are made, can be made by mixing water and ink to the consistency desired.

Practice Washes

As perfect as it is, pure mother wash cannot be applied undiluted to the paper. Instead, it is mixed with water in a clean pan and used in a series of light washes. Washes such as these provide an opportunity for greater uniformity, since it is easier to build a tone of a number of light "layers" than it is to make it of one heavy wash. In addition, such heavy, carbonaceous washes have a dead look. To begin with, practice laying the various kinds of washes used in rendering. The simplest wash is, of course, a flat wash of uniform intensity throughout. It is made as described below (Figure 10.8, sketch a).

Tilt the board about 10 or 20 degrees by placing books or a wood block under the edge farthest from you. Using a small brush, place several drops of the mother wash in ¼ inch of clean water in a wash pan. Stir until the ink is thoroughly mixed. For practice, a cold-pressed illustration board rather than a stretch may be used. Draw six graphite pencil rectangles on the board, each about 4 inches wide and 6 inches high. Dilute a few drops of Higgins' waterproof ink in some water and outline each of these rectangles with a pen. After the diluted ink is dry, remove the graphite lines.

Making a Flat Wash

Before making any ink washes it is well to dampen the surface of the paper with clean water, using a No. 12 brush. When the paper has dried to the point where it no longer feels cool to the back of a finger, it is ready to use.

Take your large brush (not the one which was used for mixing the ink), dip it into the wash that you have prepared, and move it around until all the air has

Fig. 10.8 Ink Washes.

been removed from the brush. Gently shake off the excess wash, and holding your other hand under it as you cross your illustration board, begin by wetting the entire top of the first rectangle. Draw this down about an inch, using a rotary motion with the brush, being sure to touch only the liquid and not the surface of the paper.

Take another brushful of wash and drop it into the first wash above the puddle created by the tilt of the board. Mix this with the same rotary motion and draw it down another inch. Repeat the process, being careful not to touch the paper, until the wash has reached the bottom of the rectangle. It is important to keep the wash within the inked lines of the rectangle.

The puddle at the bottom can be removed by shaking or squeezing the wash from your large brush and touching it to the puddle, squeezing the brush out, and repeating the process until the puddle is all gone. It will dry evenly if the board remains tilted.

Superimposing Washes

Since just about every section of a rendering will be made up of more than one wash, it is worthwhile to experiment with superimposed, uniform flat washes (see Figure 10.8, sketch b). Each wash is done as shown in Figure 10.8, sketch a. Care must be taken that the first wash is dry before the second one is applied.

Graded Washes

Graded washes can be run most easily from light to dark (Figure 10.8, sketch c). In laying a graded wash, the simplest method is as follows:

Use two wash dishes, one containing about ⅛ inch of clear water, the other

Ink Rendering / *129*

containing mother wash. Place a pencil dot at 1-inch increments along the height of the rectangle to be washed. Use two brushes as before — the smaller one for handling and mixing the wash, and the larger one for running the wash itself. Begin by introducing two small drops of mother wash into clear water and mixing thoroughly with the small brush. Dip the large brush into this mixture and introduce it to the top of the rectangle as in Figure 10.8, sketch a, being careful to keep within your inked lines. Carry it down to the first increment, then introduce two more drops of mother wash into the mixture with the small brush. Mix this thoroughly and again take up a brushful of the new mixture with the large brush. Drop the new wash into the one previously made, as before, and mix it in with a rotating motion, carrying it down to the next increment. Repeat this process, introducing the same amount of additional mother wash each time, until the bottom has been reached. Remove the excess wash as before, keeping the board tilted until the wash dries.

Graded washes are built up in the same way as flat washes, but the first wash must be discarded and the entire process repeated, beginning with water and mother wash.

Gradations from dark to light are made as follows: Make a mixture of medium-intensity wash by mixing water and mother wash; about ⅛ inch in the bottom of a pan will do. Divide your rectangle into increments as before, and after introducing the medium wash at the top of the rectangle, carry it down with a rotating motion for about an inch. Introduce a small brushful of clean water into the medium wash and mix it thoroughly with the small brush. Use this new mixture, and (dropping it in above the puddle, using a rotating motion, and being careful not to touch the paper) carry it down to the next increment. Repeat the process until the bottom of the paper has been reached. Remove the excess, as above.

Double-graded washes. In making an actual rendering, it is often necessary to reverse the gradation of washes during a single wash (Figure 10.8, sketch e). This can be accomplished as follows: Begin by grading from dark to light, but prepare two wash pans full of the same medium-intensity wash. When the halfway mark has been reached, begin adding a couple of drops of the medium-intensity wash into the mixture in order to darken it. Keep adding the same amount for every increment so that the wash will be dark at the bottom.

It is often necessary — as when a sky is being rendered — to run two washes simultaneously, keeping them at an even gradation (Figure 10.8, sketch d). This process can be practiced if a rectangle piercing the sky is drawn about two-thirds of the way down from the top. The height of the rectangle should be divided into increments as before, and the wash, which we assume will run from light at the top to dark at the bottom, is run as in sketch e, except that the wash of equal intensity should always be introduced concurrently at the left and right sides and carried down. Care must be taken that the washes are moved along quickly enough to prevent formation of horizontal lines by settling wash.

French Method of Gradation

This is a surefire method of grading washes. Divide the rectangle into increments as before, but this time actually draw a horizontal line with dilute ink at every increment. Assuming that you wish to make a gradation from dark at the top to light at the bottom, you would proceed as follows (Figure 10.8, sketch f):

Use a light mixture of wash, perhaps placing three drops in ¼ inch of water, and place a wash over the top segment. When this is dry, place a wash over the top two segments, then over the third, fourth, etc. The last segment, of course, will be covered by only one wash, and an excellent gradation will result. To make the gradation from light at the top to dark at the bottom, you would begin by rendering the bottom segment first, then moving toward the top, following the same procedure as described above.

Wash Failures

Now that you have completed a practice sheet of washes, you might benefit by a constructive analysis. As in any other newly learned process, imperfections of various types can creep in. They may fall into any of the following categories:

1. If horizontal brush strokes show, the wash was probably run too dry, or one pigment was not thoroughly mixed, or you may have used the wrong brush for making the wash.

2. If the edges of the wash dried with dark crusts, you probably used too large a puddle of water.

3. If the wash dried dark at the bottom, the puddle was not adequately removed.

4. If the wash dried with a light, uneven ending, too much of the puddle was removed, or the brush touched the paper when you were removing it.

5. If a jagged, fan-shaped imperfection formed at the bottom, the wash was permitted to dry with a puddle at the bottom, and this puddle was drawn up into the dried area above it.

6. If white, uneven spots showed up during the wash, there is a good chance that perspiration from your hands was absorbed by the paper, and those areas, being oily, resisted the wash.

7. In graded washes, if the gradation is uneven, you may not have made the mixture at a steady rate; that is, you may have added more water or wash at one place than at another.

Hints

Before attempting a rendering, read the following helpful hints:

1. Keep all parts of every wash equally wet, and complete the wash to its conclusion, no matter how light it may seem to be.

2. Do not try to "feather off" the edge of a light wash.

3. Keep to the limiting lines of the wash, whether they are straight or curved, neither overrunning nor falling short of such lines. If, however, the washes somehow manage to run over the edges that they are meant to meet, they should be repaired immediately by blotting the overruns. If the overruns may still be seen after drying, they should be scraped with a small brush and clean, cold water, and blotted. This process should be repeated until they have disappeared. This removal process should be used only when a single overrun is discovered, since if several overruns occur in the same area, it is almost impossible to remove the defect.

4. Once a wash has been started, do not let it stand for any time, since a horizontal line will always appear where applications overlap.

5. Do not touch the paper with the brush; touch only the surface of the wash.

6. Mix the wash thoroughly as you are drawing it along, with a rotary motion.

7. Limit the size of puddle that you render with, since too large a puddle may

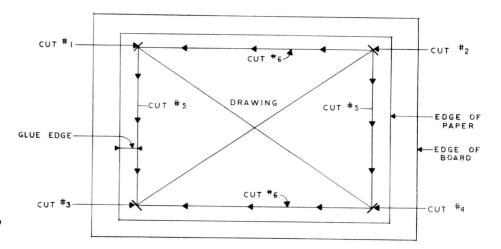

Fig. 10.9 Cutting the Stretch from the Board.

suddenly run to the bottom of the board, or may cause the wash to dry with a hard edge.

8. In running a graded wash by the French method, crusts may appear at the edge of each subsequent wash. These will disappear when additional washes are run over them, if the washes are run as described above. If an attempt is made to run such graded washes by giving each small area its proper number of washes separately, hard crusts will form between them.

9. In overlaying a previous wash with another, be sure that the first wash is thoroughly dry before proceeding.

10. If a drop of wash falls upon a drawing, blot it immediately, first with the corner of a blotter, being careful not to spread the blot. Wet the drop with clean water and blot it again. Repeat this process until the spot has been removed.

11. If the blot cannot be removed by the foregoing method, carefully erase it so that it is lighter than the adjoining areas, then shade it to match the surrounding tones by stippling or hatching with a fine brush. Be careful not to let the stippling or hatching run into the surrounding areas.

Example: A Carillon Tower

While making the charcoal study for the carillon tower shown in Figure 10.10, the renderer decided to make the tower dark at the base and light at the top, so that the dark bells would stand out.

In making the actual rendering, No. 4 and No. 10 brushes were used, the smaller for mixing and the larger for rendering. Before the rendering was started, the paper was given a wash of alum mixed in water in order to recalender the paper and neutralize any possible greasy perspiration spots. This alum wash was made of a tablespoon of alum in a quart of water.

The outlines of the building were reproduced on the sheet with graphite pencil. Then each line was in turn drawn with a pale, thin, diluted waterproof-ink line, using a ruling pen with T square and triangle. The shadows were cast and outlined in the same manner.

It was decided to make the gradation in the sky light at the bottom and dark at the top. The framework of trees in the mid-distance beside the platform frames the tower and locates it, at the same time permitting and encouraging the eye to look around the tower into the distance. When the charcoal study was completed, another study to determine the number of washes for each area was made

Fig. 10.10 A Carillon Tower. (Renderer: James Stevenson Whitney. Student project.)

on tracing paper over the line drawing which had previously been inked, as in the practice washes.

It was decided that the left side, which was to receive the direct sunlight, would be given one wash. The bright side of the left fin and the edge of the fin facing the spectator would receive five washes, the shadows would be made of ten washes, the sky of four washes, the grass area in the foreground of four washes, the trees in the distance and the risers of the steps of three washes.

The trees were first textured with convolutions, using a freehand pen and dilute waterproof black ink, and were then modeled with washes and stippled to create the illusion of form. The grass areas were also stippled.

The first washes were put on the sky, the board being turned upside down for this purpose. Two pans were used, one with water, the other with a medium wash. The washes were begun at the ground line and were run over the trees. Because of the height of this wash, it was graded at 2-inch increments. The sky was completed before the tower was begun.

After the second and fourth washes, crusts around the tower were removed by sponging. Sponging is an important part of ink rendering, because it permits the delineator to correct errors, get rid of crusts that have formed, and remove surface ink. When an ink rendering has been completed, the ink should look as if it is a part of the paper and should not stand on the surface. Sponging, as well as the transparency of the washes, contributes greatly to the atmospheric quality of this medium.

The tower was rendered in a manner similar to that for the sky, the light areas being rendered first. No two adjoining areas were rendered at the same time or in sequence, because to do so would have been to cause one wash to run into the other.

The shadows in the foreground and the trees were built up simultaneously until they had achieved the darkness indicated by the charcoal study. The bells were rendered individually; those at the top were made darker than those at the bottom in order to gain maximum contrast with adjoining areas. The bells were rounded by introducing a medium-gray wash at the sides and front, then joining them into surrounding areas with a damp brush. The trees were then given additional form by stippling, and the scale figures were painted in.

When the rendering was completed, it was removed from the rest of the stretch by cutting along the borderlines with a sharp knife. A short 45-degree cut was first made at each corner (see Figure 10.9). The top and bottom were cut first; then the sides were cut. A word of caution: If possible, the rendering should be cut by two people, one person cutting one side while the other cuts the opposite side. If the cut is synchronized so that the two knives are exactly opposite one another, the pressure of the stretch will be gradually released. Large stretches, especially, sometimes crack if they are carelessly cut from the board.

Example: Guggenheim Museum

The rendering in Figure 10.11 illustrates two important points of technique. The drum of the building was rendered by the French method. Since the drum diminishes in diameter at the bottom, the diminishing of the various steps was achieved as indicated in Figure 10.12. After the highlight and darkest dark had been located in Figure 10.13, the rendering became a mere matter of applying washes from light at the highlight to dark at the right side, and from light at the highlight to dark at the left point of tangency of the drum, and from the darkest dark to a light gray at the extreme left (Figure 10.11).

The small circular elements to the left of the drum were, on the other hand, graded by the experimental method described above, in the section on double-graded washes (see Figure 10.8, sketch e). The small square areas behind the drum on the upper part of the flat facade were rendered by applying mother wash to the top and right side of each opening, then cleaning the brush and placing clean water in the rest of the opening so that the mother wash blended with it. The darks were later reinforced.

Fig. 10.11 Guggenheim Museum. (Architect: Frank Lloyd Wright. Renderer: Philip Gordon McIntosh. Student project.)

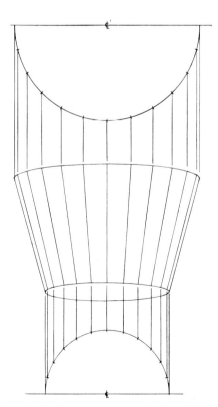

Fig. 10.12 Laying Out the Facets of the Drum for the French Method.

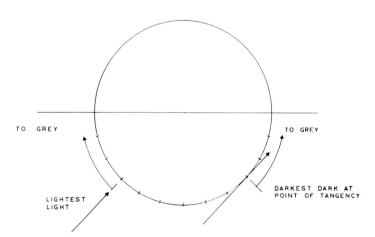

TO GREY

TO GREY

DARKEST DARK AT
POINT OF TANGENCY

LIGHTEST
LIGHT

Fig. 10.13 Determining Lights and Darks of the Drum.

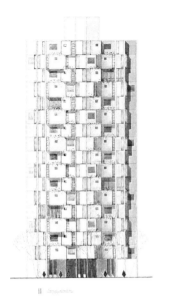

Fig. 10.14 Student Design Project. (Renderer: Arnold Syrop.)

Wet-into-Wet Method for Trees

Several methods for rendering trees in wash have been mentioned: for instance, that in which the trees are first drawn and then textured in dilute waterproof ink, and also that method in which the tree foliage masses are formed by flat washes or stippling. Another method, looser in appearance, is described below.

The tree masses are blocked out in pencil. A pale wash of dilute ink is then put on each foliage area to approximate the shape of the mass. After this has dried, each tree is rendered by first wetting a spot about ¼ inch larger than the foliage mass with clear water. While this is still damp, the foliage mass is formed by dropping a brush of fairly dark wash on the part (usually near the center of the foliage mass) which is to be darkest. This spreads with a feathery edge which is controlled by the use of a blotter. When its movement has stopped, it is brushed rigorously with a 45-degree motion, pressing the brush on the surface of the paper, thus intensifying or decreasing value as desired. As each foliage mass dries, the process is repeated until the desired values are obtained. The tree trunks and branches are added after the foliage masses are dry, and these are varied in intensity according to their location, the darkest being in the foreground, the lightest in the distance.

Rendering Trees in Plan

To render trees in plan, first draw them in dilute waterproof ink, then dampen each tree with clean water. When this has almost entirely dried, place dark dilute ink wash on the shade sides of the trees, and grade to light at the opposite side by adding water to the wash as you proceed to the light side. Of course, even shown in plan, a tree, like any other element, is certain to cast a shadow on the ground. The renderer should take advantage of this opportunity to show ground material in shadow, and should also use reflected light to highlight the tree foliage on the shade side of the tree.

Pen and Ink with Ink Wash

Illustrated in Figure 10.14 is an elevation which combines the pen-and-ink technique with that of the ink wash. There are many advantages to this method, but the most significant is that details may first be developed by using pens of various sizes and larger areas may later be graded with diluted ink washes.

The delineator must depend upon an accurate value study to determine which areas of the drawing will be detailed and the areas to be graded with ink washes. Once the details have been drawn on the final rendering, the addition of the washes is a very quick process. Should an error occur, it is easy to correct, when dry, with a pen and ink.

It should also be noted that this technique requires less masking — thus saving time, which is most necessary when a rendering is near completion.

Charcoal and Pastel Rendering

Subject and Medium

The subject to be rendered often determines the medium to be used. Pencil and pen are pointed and therefore are ideal for rendering buildings heavily textured and fine in detail. Smudge charcoal, on the other hand, is well suited to rendering structures or interiors which have large plain areas and are fairly large in detail (Figures 11.1 and 11.2) It is a fact that more renderers can obtain a fine finished result with smudge charcoal the first time they try it than with almost any other medium. It is easy to apply and is by nature such a loose, soft medium that it is almost impossible to produce a tight, uninteresting rendering with it. What, specifically, is the smudge-charcoal technique? It is a rendering process in which powdered charcoal is applied to a rather rough paper by means of absorbent cotton, stumps, or the hands. The smudge-pastel technique is similar, except that colored pastel chalk sticks are used instead of charcoal. Smudge charcoal is used on renderings that are to be reproduced in black and white, smudge pastel on those to be reproduced in color.

Charcoal

Materials

A quality grade of white linen-finish charcoal paper, such as Fabriano Ingres (Italian), should be used in this type of rendering. Avoid the cheaper brands of paper because no matter how hard you work with these, the results will be poor. Not only does the texture quickly wear or become "tired" when it is worked upon, but the color of the paper is usually off-white and therefore does not permit sharp contrasts.

Powdered charcoal can be purchased, but one can also use a medium grade of stick charcoal, such as Weber vine charcoal, which will be powdered and ap-

Fig. 11.1 The Interior of a Chapel. (Renderer: Joan Willet de Ris. Student project.)

plied with absorbent cotton. For masking, it is best to use 8½- × 11-inch thin but firm pad paper without ring binder or other holes and with straight, clean edges. In addition, you will need several stumps, which are made of thin paper strips wound to a point and can be purchased at any art materials store. A kneaded eraser, a sandpaper block, a Ruby eraser, and charcoal fixative complete the equipment required.

Procedure

Since the process that you are about to try involves the use of pressure on the drawing board, it is wise to make sure before you begin that your drawing board is clean, and as free of imperfections as you can make it. It should then be covered with one or more sheets of detail paper to form a cushion. If detail paper is not available, several sheets of charcoal paper may be used. These should be firmly fastened to the board with thumbtacks, with the sheet of charcoal paper that is to be used on top. When handmade charcoal paper is held up to the light, the side from which the watermark or name can be read is the right side to use. If no watermark can be found, either side can be used.

Fig. 11.2 Detail of a House. (Renderer: Paul Hilary Pinter. Student project.)

Assuming that you have already drawn your finished perspective at a size of about 14 × 21 inches on a sheet of tracing paper, and have it backed up as described for pencil rendering in Chapter 9, you are ready to reproduce it on the charcoal paper. This must be done with extreme care, as an erasure on the charcoal paper at any stage of the rendering, before the finishing touches, will show up in the finished rendering as a black smudge that cannot be removed. Similarly, any grooves made by the heavy pressure of the pencil will show in the finished rendering as white lines; therefore, the drawing must be pressed through to the charcoal paper with a light but firm stroke.

Freehand Charcoal Study

Before proceeding with the actual rendering of your perspective drawing, you should make a freehand stick or block charcoal study, as described under ''The Value Study'' in Chapter 7. This will permit quick experiments with various light sources, value comparisons, and sheet composition. Fix this study and hang it on your tackboard or on the wall in front of you, so that you may use it as a guide during the progress of your rendering.

You are now ready to prepare the charcoal. Fasten a large sheet of pad paper on a table or board next to your drawing board with drafting tape — on the right side if you are right-handed, and on the left side if you are left-handed. Correct placement is important so that you can avoid crossing your entire drawing with the powdered charcoal while you are using it. Now make a pile of powdered charcoal, about 1½ inches in diameter and ¼ inch deep, by rubbing the stick charcoal across the sandpaper block. Do this slowly, so that the charcoal is finely and evenly powdered, with no lumps. If the charcoal scatters, it may be drawn together with penknife or palette knife.

The powdered charcoal, at least for most large areas, is applied by dipping a piece of absorbent cotton into the pile of powdered charcoal, tapping it on a piece of waste paper to remove the excess, and rubbing it on a previously masked area. It can be applied in long, overlapping strokes (Figure 11.3, sketch b), or in long strokes in several directions (Figure 11.3, sketch c). Variations in tone and gradations are obtained by taking more or less charcoal on the cotton, by varying hand pressure, and by applying more or fewer coats of charcoal. See Figure 11.3, sketch d (light to dark), sketch e (dark to light), and sketch f (light at the upper left to dark at the lower right).

It is well to wash your hands often when working in this medium, since oil marks from the fingers will stain the renderings.

Because of the fugitive nature of powdered charcoal, the rendering is best accomplished in three steps:

1. A general attempt is made to obtain the correct relative values in the several parts of the drawing.

2. The values obtained in step 1 are refined and corrected.

3. Further refinements and corrections are made, the darkest tones are deepened, textures are inserted, and erasures are made for highlights.

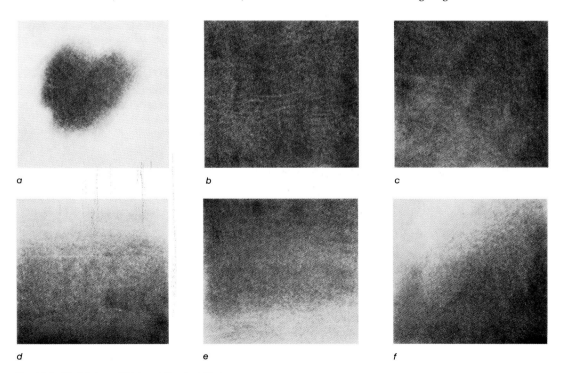

Fig. 11.3 Trial Rub and Flat and Graded Washes.

Order of Drawing

Masking paper is used to surround the edges of the area to be rendered, and as many sheets as the area has sides will be required at one time. Since it is difficult to hold four sheets with one hand while applying charcoal with the other, you may find it helpful to make two right-angle templates, which can be used together to lay down a rectangle or square of any size easily and in a short time (Figure 11.4). If your rendering has large curved areas, these may be masked by forming the curves with a number of sheets of overlapping pad paper, as in Figure 11.5, or by cutting a piece of pad paper to the exact curve.

Step 1. An appropriate place to start a rendering of an interior such as that in Figure 11.1 would be the ceiling. Place a sheet of masking paper on each edge of this area and hold them firmly in place with your fingers. Dip a piece of cotton about the size of a walnut into the charcoal and tap it lightly on a spare piece of paper to remove any excess charcoal. Also take a trial rub on the spare piece of paper to make sure that there are no lumps and it will make a smooth wash (see Figure 11.3, sketch a). Then apply the charcoal to the masked area of the rendering. Gently brush the cotton into the area in long, clean, overlapping strokes, proceeding away from the edges of the masking paper toward the other end of the area that you are shading (see Figure 11.3, sketch b). Cross the same area with other strokes and try circular strokes (Figure 11.3, sketch c). Variations and gradations in tone, previously determined in the charcoal study, should be carefully followed, and may be executed as shown in Figure 11.3, sketch d (gradations from light to dark), sketch e (gradations from dark to light), or sketch f, (diagonal gradation).

When this area has been shaded, lift the sheets of masking paper, move them to the other end of the area being shaded, and repeat the process, this time shading toward the opposite end, where you began. If necessary, this process may be repeated on the other sides of the area being shaded. When you lift the masking paper you may find a small ridge of charcoal which has seeped under the paper. To remove this, take a clean piece of cotton, about the same size as the one you have been using, and gently dust the charcoal ridge off your drawing.

Discard masking paper when it has become soiled, or when the edges become fuzzy. The ball of cotton should be discarded when it becomes lumpy or produces streaks.

Fig. 11.4 Use of Two Right-Angle Templates to Make a Rectangle in Smudge Charcoal.

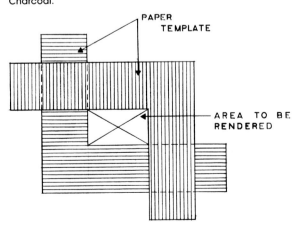

Fig. 11.5 Template for Curves made by Overlapping Several Sheets of Paper.

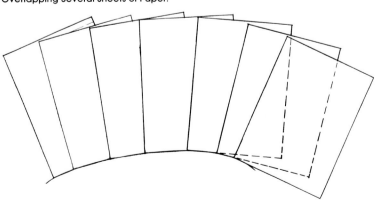

Proceed in a similar manner with shading all other areas of the perspective, such as the back wall and floor in Figure 11.1. The lightest background values of the screen, furniture, floor, and objects may also be put in during this step. Be careful to work around legs of furniture and other similar details so that you will not lose their locations before you are ready to render them.

Step 2. After you have put in the first set of washes, stand your drawing next to the freehand value study and look at it from a distance of 5 feet or more. How do your values compare with those you determined in the value study to be correct? Are any of the areas too light or too dark? If so, you may correct these mistakes when you repeat the process outlined in step 1. It is advisable from now on to work from the top toward the bottom of the rendering, so that you will not disturb charcoal that has previously been applied in adjoining areas. This second step is more than a reinforcement and correction of previous values. This is when you begin to apply general detail such as floor pattern and the differentiation of the sides of furniture, the shadows on the legs of a table and chairs, and the shadow side of the various members of the foreground. Small or narrow washes—such as those on members of a screen, the squares of the floor, and detail items—are all carried out in the same way as the large washes, with the pieces of masking paper held close together.

When step 2 has been finished, you may feel that your rendering has reached a hopeless stage. You may be tempted to use fixative on the charcoal that you have already applied to keep it from rubbing off your drawing. Resist this temptation, because if you apply fixative before the rendering is entirely finished, no further charcoal may be applied on the paper, nor will you be able to refine the rendering as you will want to do in step 3. Workable fixative can be used; however, it should be used sparingly.

Step 3. To complete the rendering, reassess it as in step 2, with an increasingly critical eye. It is now time to make your final value correction throughout the drawing. In order to obtain the darkest values, such as those in the furniture in Figure 11.1, mask around the areas to be darkened, dip your finger into the powdered charcoal, and gently but firmly rub the areas. The oil from your skin will combine with the charcoal to produce the desired effect. Remember, however, that once values have been darkened in this way, they cannot be easily lightened.

Detailed areas. Small details, such as vases, flowers, lighting fixtures, and pictures, may best be rendered with a stump. The stump is dipped in the powdered charcoal, the excess is removed, and then the stump is used to draw in the details. You will find that this produces a soft, but definite, result. Fine lines like those in Figure 11.1 may be applied with a sharp stick of charcoal and then softened with the stump. Definite patterns, such as figures etched in glass panels, may be inserted at this time by rubbing charcoal through the openings of a carefully cut stencil. If the lines of the pattern are to be lighter than the background, they may be erased with a kneaded eraser and the same stencil.

Textures. Various textures can be easily obtained by erasing parts of a charcoal wash with a pointed piece of kneaded eraser. Roll the eraser between your fingers for a short while until it becomes pliable and can be shaped to a point. The marble and wood-grain textures shown in Figure 11.6, sketches a and b, were drawn freehand with the eraser. The texture in sketch 3 was made by

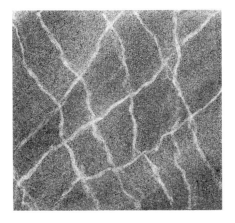

a

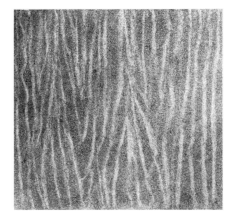

b

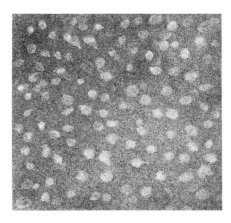

c

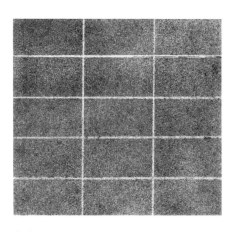

d

Fig. 11.6 Textures in Charcoal.

carefully dabbing with the point of an eraser. Each line in sketch *d* was made by erasing between two pieces of paper, held tightly and closely together.

To erase lights such as those on the back and side walls in Figure 11.1, use a clean piece of cotton and masking paper. Clean cotton will lighten the area but will not produce a highlight. In similar fashion, clean cotton may be used to lighten whole areas that have become too dark.

Highlights. To produce highlights such as those in the legs of the chairs and tables and on the edges of the picture frame, a kneaded eraser is used. Break off a small piece about the size of the first joint of your little finger and roll it between your fingers until it has become soft. Then, after masking the area to be lightened, gently rub the eraser several times in long strokes until the excess charcoal has been removed. If some of the areas will not lighten with the kneaded eraser, use a Ruby eraser in long strokes.

If you feel that you have completed your rendering, appraise it again from a distance of several feet. Any changes or corrections that you wish to make should be done at this time.

In order to fix a charcoal rendering, use a nongloss charcoal fixative spray such as Krylon or Spray-Fix from a distance of 4 or 5 feet. If the fixative is sprayed from too close a range, there is danger of large droplets striking the drawing and staining it.

After it is fixed, the drawing may be matted, as described in Chapter 6.

Pastels

When you wish to use color for rendering but do not have the time to use watercolor or tempera, a dry medium such as pastels can be used. Pastels have a number of advantages: they can be used alone or with other opaque media; they are fast, produce a delicate tone, are good for impressions rather than detailed renderings, and need relatively few accessories. In addition, pastel renderings can be made on various kinds of paper without the necessity of making a stretch.

Materials

Pastels are sold in sets or by the stick. There are two basic types: half-hard, usually available in square sticks, and soft, usually available in round sticks. Both half-hard and soft pastels are available in sets containing as few as 12 assorted colors and as many as, say, 360 assorted pure hues, tints, and shades. Half-hard pastels are also available in 8 graded grays.

Pastel papers. Like smudge charcoal, pastels require a rather rough surface for file action. Ordinary pastel papers, 19 × 25 inches, have already been described in Chapter 9 in the discussion of carbon-pencil rendering. In addition, pastel drawing books of similar paper are made in the following sizes: 9 × 12, 12 × 18, and 18 × 24 inches. They may be used for outdoor sketching or studies.

Besides the pastel papers described above, sand-surface pastel paper, velour pastel paper, and pastel board made with the same surfaces are also available. Generally speaking, these do not lend themselves very well to architectural work. On the other hand, ordinary white or colored charcoal paper, white rag tracing paper, buff detail paper, or even brown wrapping paper will do. Some watercolor papers give an interesting texture.

Pastel holders. Sticks of pastel (particularly in the soft grade) are easily broken, and holders are sold for small pieces.

Pastel fixative. Pastel fixative is the clearest type of fixative sold.

Shading devices

Tortillons. Although pastel is frequently smoothed with the finger, there are occasions when tortillons are required. They are small, round, paper stumps, pointed at one end and available in lengths of 2¾, 3, and 3¼ inches. Gray paper stumps, which are larger (¼ × 4¾, ⅜ × 5⅛, ½ × 5½, and ¹¹⁄₁₆ × 6 inches) are also helpful for smoothing pastel washes.

Powdering devices. Like smudge charcoal, pastels are often powdered for application. This is done by rubbing them on a sandpaper block or a metal pencil pointer.

Absorbent cotton. A box of absorbent cotton for applying pastel in a manner similar to that for smudge charcoal is required.

Masking paper. A number of 8½- × 11-inch sheets of thin white bond paper will be found helpful.

Powder mixing devices. It is often necessary to mix several powdered colors. This can best be done with a penknife or, even better, a palette knife.

Erasers. A kneaded eraser and a Pink Pearl eraser are useful.

Palette. As in all colored media, a palette must be selected from the many colors available before a rendering is begun. The same set of color principles is used for pastel as for any other color medium (see Chapter 6, Color — Fact and Theory). While the names may differ, a palette roughly comparable to that used for any color medium can be selected. Such a palette might consist of

1. Cadmium yellow deep
2. Light or deep ochre
3. Cadmium orange
4. Permanent red
5. Madder lake
6. Ultramarine blue deep
7. Indigo
8. Gray-blue
9. Permanent green deep
10. Moss green

Brands of pastel. Assortments of pastel can be found at all good art supply stores. Some of the more popular brands are Eberhard Faber's Nupastel and the Grumbacher, Rembrandt, and Patellos papers. Swan Carb-Othello manufactures colored charcoal and pastel pencils which are helpful when detailed work is required.

Practice Washes

Pastels are so simple to use that it is not necessary to make a carefully drawn sheet of exercises as for other media. Flat and graded washes may be practiced by powdering a small amount of any color, say blue, on a piece of white pad paper, dipping a small piece of absorbent cotton into it and rubbing this back and forth on a sheet of pastel paper. A smooth wash can easily be made by overlapping the strokes and crossing the first strokes with a second series of strokes. As with smudge charcoal, areas to be shaded must be masked. This is done with 8½- × 11-inch white bond paper.

Graded washes are easily made by the same process, but with the addition of more pastel powder and an additional number of strokes in the darker areas — thus building up layers of wash in areas where darker colors are required.

After the washes of powdered pastel have been made, textures, foliage, etc., are frequently created by using a sharp corner of half-hard pastel or a sharp piece of soft pastel broken off for the purpose. Because pastel is an opaque medium, tones can be built up by a series of powder washes, by a series of strokes, or by a combination of the two techniques. Two or more colors can be mixed directly on the paper.

Textures of building materials are made by first applying a base wash of powder pastel, then applying sticks or broken pieces of stick pastel over the washes to make various textures and shadows.

Each small wash, such as for blinds, curtains, furniture, carpets, or flooring, is made with a separate mask.

Entourage. Washes for bushes and trees can be applied in the same way as washes for buildings. Foliage can generally be made by using cotton and powdered pastel, and tree structures can be drawn directly with a stick of pastel. Detailed leaves in the foreground and trees in mid-distance can be applied directly with the stick.

Fig. 11.7 An Exhibition Building. (Renderer: Lawrence Braverman. Student project.)

Grass and roadways can be applied with flat washes, and later modified with stick strokes for shadows and tonal variations. This is where pastel pencils are helpful.

Skies. Flat, graded, or graded and clouded skies are usually applied with long horizontal strokes of powdered pastel. Clouds can be added with a light-colored stick of pastel applied directly over the undercoat. In addition, cloud streaks can be erased with a kneaded or Pink Pearl eraser in a manner similar to that used in pencil rendering.

Procedure

Because of the nature of pastels, the value study and the color study may be combined, using the sticks directly on a sheet of the same type of paper as will be used for the presentation. The linear perspective is transferred to the paper as described in Chapter 3, using a graphite pencil.

The entire rendering, in Figure 11.7, with the exception of scale figures, was accomplished by using paper masks and powdered pastel. The values of the light-blue sides of the building were made by mixing a great deal of white pastel with cobalt blue. The medium-blue shade sides, as well as the shadow cast by the sculpture, were a mixture of cobalt blue, white, and a small amount of orange. Streaks of light to relieve the monotony of the large shade areas were achieved with 45-degree strokes.

The sculpture was formed by carefully locating and drawing shade areas, then rendering them individually in shades of blue. The tan promenade around the pool was rendered by a mixture of red and white, with a small amount of yellow, and the foliage was rendered by using cotton, powder pastel, and paper cutouts. Some of the sharp top edges were then rubbed down with the finger. Joints in the stonework at the left and in the promenade were erased. Scale figures were drawn directly by using a broken piece of pastel.

The drawing was then lightly fixed with pastel fixative.

chapter 12

Watercolor Rendering

History of Watercolor

The medium that we now call "watercolor" is one of the oldest known. There are records of its use in China in the third century, and also of its use by Japanese and East Indian artists. Their brushes were of sable hair or pig bristles, and they were masters of the delicate and beautiful line in black ink, dark brown, or sepia. Early watercolors were painted on wood bark; later, silk was used, mounted on paper by a method similar to that used for making stretches today.

Few people realize that watercolor is centuries older than oil paint. It has always been highly regarded by artists because of its delicacy and great flexibility. Studies for many oil paintings have been made in watercolor because of the ease and speed with which it can be used, and some of the best-known masterpieces in oil were influenced by the brilliance of watercolor studies. This watercolor brilliance is still apparent in the decoration of the caves of Altamira and Perigord, painted 20,000 years ago. Egyptian wall paintings (see Chapter 1) were executed in a form of tempera, or opaque watercolor. The Greeks also used this medium, and the magnificent illuminated manuscripts of the Middle Ages were colored with watercolor or tempera.

The Eighteenth Century

For some reason, watercolor seems to have been forgotten between the Middle Ages and the beginning of the eighteenth century, when English artists began to use it again. It had been used only to tint pencil or pen sketches with black, brown, or sepia, but soon it was employed in monochrome, since full color had not yet reappeared. Paul Sandby (1725–1809) and Thomas Malton, whose work is illustrated in Chapter 1, were chiefly responsible for the use of this medium on landscapes and architectural subjects.

Painters who lived in the second half of the eighteenth century used a rich palette and sometimes brushed strong color on wet paper. The period they began lasted until the beginning of the twentieth century, when many additional colors and styles were developed.

The United States

Watercolor was slow to start in the United States, because in Paris, where most early American artists and architects studied, it was not considered a serious medium, and most students worked in oil; however, several late-nineteenth- and early-twentieth-century American artists, such as Winslow Homer, George Inness, and John Singer Sargent, realized the possibilities of watercolor and developed its use in this country.

Today's architectural delineators inherit their knowledge of watercolor from these few Americans, from the English school of watercolor painting and rendering of the same period, from delineators on the European continent who used simplified watercolor, and from a number of American architects and delineators who have helped develop it to its present state. It comes to us in three basic forms.

1. The technique in which watercolor and water are mixed and applied as a transparent medium to white paper made especially for this purpose.
2. Tempera (or showcard) colors, all of which are opaque.
3. A combination of transparent watercolors with opaque, or Chinese, white.

The term "watercolor" today usually means transparent watercolor, or transparent watercolor combined with a minimum of tempera. This chapter is devoted to these two categories. "Tempera rendering" usually means delineation in which all the paints used are opaque (as described in Chapter 13) or in which opaque temperas are sprayed upon the paper with an airbrush (Chapter 14).

There are a number of reasons why watercolor has survived for such a long time. To begin with, it is a clean, easily used medium, lacking the odorous quality of oil paints. It can be used on a small or a large scale, even in the same painting or rendering, always giving an accurate illusion of reality. There is no problem that it cannot solve, and it can be used as easily to portray a beach viewed through an ocean mist as a gloriously sunny scene. If necessary, several atmospheres can be created in the same painting, and several techniques can be combined. Some delineators make an entire rendering by building values with a series of light washes, but others use the wash method on the building or image itself and the direct method (that is, painting directly from the palette) for the entourage or surroundings. Because of the qualities that the various colors possess, the delineator is able to simulate practically any shade or texture desired with a minimum of effort. With practice, watercolor becomes a fast medium. In experienced hands, it produces results which appear to have been created by an effort much greater than that actually expended. A rendering in watercolor usually impresses a viewer favorably.

Materials Required

Pigments

Palettes and pigments were discussed in a general way in Chapter 6, and this discussion will now be expanded upon. As noted, Winsor & Newton's artists' colors are their strongest and most predictable line, while their student colors rank far below in quality. Many other companies supply colors that are good, but they are not always predictable. The foregoing are all sold in tubes. Watercolors also are available in cakes or pans, and because they are usually neatly packaged in a metal box, frequently attract the novice; however, such dried colors are extremely hard on expensive watercolor brushes, as it is necessary to keep dabbing and grinding in the cake or pan in order to obtain enough pigment for a wash of any size. A box of dried watercolors is helpful if held in reserve for mixing small washes, but it is wise to depend mainly on tube colors.

Tubes are sold in a number of sizes. For example, No. 2, which is called a "whole tube," is the standard size and measures $\frac{1}{2} \times 2$ inches. The No. 5 size measures $\frac{3}{4} \times 2\frac{1}{2}$ inches. Even the smaller tubes, however, contain enough watercolor for several renderings. Watercolors in tubes tend to dry out quickly, and unless constant use is anticipated, it may be better to purchase them in the smallest size possible.

The caps of watercolor tubes are often difficult to remove, particularly if the user has not cleaned all the paint from the threaded portion of the tube before replacing the cap. A stubborn cap can usually be removed by holding a match under it and rotating the tube until the cap is heated slightly, or by holding the cap under hot water for a few minutes. If the cap still refuses to budge, you have no recourse other than to unroll the bottom of the tube and make an opening through which to squeeze out the paint.

Generally, all watercolors fall into the following categories:

Those that make clear, transparent washes are cadmium yellow, cadmium orange, alizarin crimson, rose madder, cobalt blue, and Hooker's green.

Those that make "granulated" washes which give a mottled effect include yellow ochre, vermilion, French ultramarine blue, cerulean blue, and emerald green. Granulation occurs whether the color is applied in washes or by direct painting, and is not lessened by mixture with other pigments. This quality is advantageous in the painting of certain types of skies, trees, and building materials, and gives effects that can be obtained in no other way.

One final word about watercolors. The best available are Winsor & Newton's artists' colors. They are predictable; that is, they are always exactly the same, no matter when or where you purchase them. They are sold in whole tubes and half tubes. The author suggests using the half tubes, since whole tubes will sometimes dry out before they are used. Winsor & Newton's student colors are fair, but not nearly so true or predictable as the artists' colors. A number of other brands are also available but not always predictable — and predictability is a quality to be sought in pigments for rendering.

The best watercolors are expensive. They vary in price according to the color, but one tube of an expensive pigment will usually last as long as several tubes of a less expensive watercolor brand, because less is required for any specific job. The expensive pigments are stronger, and because they are predictable in both color and reaction, they will never surprise the artist unpleasantly. The less expensive colors simply do not possess these qualities. One other reason for using good pigments: they are relatively permanent. True, some colors are more permanent than others, even in Winsor & Newton's artists' line, but most of the less expensive paints fade and change color with time.

Brushes

The same brushes used for ink rendering (see Chapter 10) are employed for rendering in watercolor. Winsor & Newton's No. 4 and No. 12 red-sable "pencil'' brushes are recommended. You will also find a No. 2 and a No. 8 useful. In addition, some delineators use flat brushes for certain purposes. These should be the kind made for oil painting of either sable or camel's hair. The small flat brushes should be about ¼ or ³⁄₁₆ inch wide, and a large, springy, flat brush, ¾ inch wide, will also be found helpful for running skies and other large areas. A hog-bristle brush will be useful for "scrubbing" certain areas as the work progresses.

Although Winsor & Newton series 7 albata red-sable brushes are of the highest quality, the budget sometimes will not allow their purchase. In this case, a reasonably good brush, particularly in the smaller sizes, can be obtained in Winsor & Newton series 8, 9, and 33 or 133. Other fairly good brushes are made by other manufacturers in tiger's hair or camel's hair (which is actually made from the tail hair of Siberian squirrels). (Although the name "tiger's hair" is merely used to attract attention, some Japanese artists have actually used brushes bristled with shredded bamboo, bear hair, or mouse whiskers.

Care should be exercised in the purchase of brushes, as discussed in Chapter 10, and they should always be cleaned after use by swishing them in clean water before they are put away. They should never be allowed to stand in a container of water when they are not being used, since they will acquire a bend which you may never be able to correct. There are spring holders for brushes which suspend them so the bristles do not touch the bottom of the water container, and they may be found helpful, but the brushes may just as safely be placed flat on your table, or bristles up in a vase or other container, when not in use. Some delineators occasionally bathe their brushes in petroleum jelly, then wash them in soap and water.

Wash Dishes

The same white enamel or plastic wash dishes or pans used for ink rendering will be found most helpful in mixing watercolor washes. At all costs avoid wash dishes that are not white, as it is impossible to see the colors you are mixing in such pans. Some delineators prefer to use nests of china saucers, and these are useful for mixing small amounts of watercolors.

You will also require a container for clean water, and this should be large enough to hold a quart or more. A large china vase is excellent for large projects.

Palettes

An excellent, inexpensive palette that may be used for mixing colors in direct painting, is a 9-inch white dinner plate. Avoid using a plate with a colored pattern as this will be confusing. A small quantity of each pigment should be placed on the rim of the plate (Figure 12.1) with the colors in the same relationships as those in the chromatic circle (Plate II). If this is done you will automatically reach for each color in the same position every time you need it. If, on the other hand, the colors are placed haphazardly upon the palette, you will spend a great deal of time hunting for the colors as you require them. The center of the plate provides a splendid place for the actual mixing of the colors.

More expensive palettes are sold in art materials stores, but these are usually flat and have no concavity for mixing the colors. In addition, some have depressions for the watercolor pigments which actually limit the accessibility of the colors. These are to be avoided.

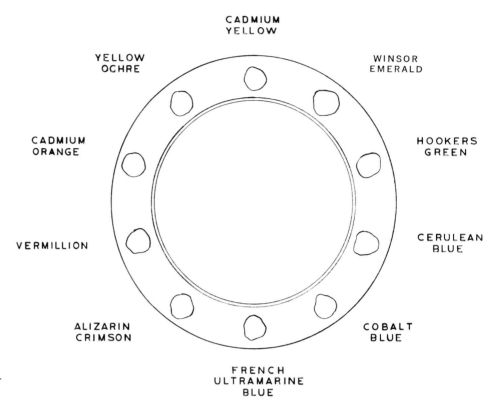

CADMIUM
YELLOW

YELLOW
OCHRE

WINSOR
EMERALD

CADMIUM
ORANGE

HOOKERS
GREEN

VERMILLION

CERULEAN
BLUE

ALIZARIN
CRIMSON

COBALT
BLUE

FRENCH
ULTRAMARINE
BLUE

Fig. 12.1 Placing Pigments on the Palette.

Paper or Illustration Board

The same qualities found in paper used for ink rendering (Chapter 10) are required for watercolor rendering. Be sure that the surface has a cold-pressed finish.

Miscellaneous Items

1. A dozen white blotters, for correcting errors and blotting mistakes
2. A silk or baby sponge, for sponging, lightening areas, applying pigment, and creating highlights
3. A sponge brush, for creating highlights in small areas
4. A piece of cheesecloth and a box of cleansing tissues for producing special textures
5. Ruby and Pink Pearl erasers, glass or steel erasers, and a razor blade, for correcting errors and creating special effects
6. A small bottle of liquid latex for masking such areas as tree structures while painting skies behind them

Getting Acquainted with Pigments

Colors in the Palette

As mentioned in Chapter 6 on the subject of color, the colors that you use will depend upon your own wishes; however, all exercises in this chapter will be conducted with the palette that the author prefers. This does not mean that other colors are not helpful; it merely means that experience has shown that colors normally required in rendering can be mixed from the pigments listed below. (See Figure 12.1.)

Cadmium yellow pale	French ultramarine blue
Yellow ochre	Cobalt blue

Cadmium orange   Cerulean blue
Vermilion   Hooker's green dark
Alizarin crimson (or rose madder)   Windsor emerald

Color Experimentation

After you have purchased these colors, you will want to determine their characteristics when used alone or mixed with other colors. Some of the pigments, such as cadmium yellow pale, cadmium orange, alizarin crimson, and cobalt blue are relatively clear; some are opaque, and still others have the quality of settling — that is, there are particles that settle out when the wash dries. These "sedimenting" colors include yellow ochre, vermilion, French ultramarine blue, cerulean blue, and emerald green. These are also colors which tend to resist mixture with other colors. You should experiment with your colors to discover the specifics of all these characteristics. The following exercises will assist you in determining the various qualities of your pigments.

On a piece of 140-pound inexpensive machine-made watercolor paper, about 15 × 20 inches, squeeze about ½ inch of each of the ten pigments along the long edge of the sheet, being careful to keep each color several inches away from the others. Wet your large brush and draw it across each color in turn, being careful to wash the brush completely after each pigment is touched. Note the relative differences between the various pigments, and their relative intensity.

Then use another sheet of the same paper for an experiment in color reaction. Mix a medium-intensity wash of each pigment, and using a large brush, run a horizontal wash of each directly across the sheet of paper, leaving a white space between each two washes so that they do not run together. When these washes are dry, run new washes vertically over the first washes, again being careful to leave sufficient space between them so that they do not run together. When the second washes are dry, analyze the results and you will see that some combinations blend to a new color, that others do not mix, and that still others create surprisingly beautiful textures by the settling out of one or both of the colors. This experimental sheet should be kept for future reference.

Practice Washes

The same methods are used for laying washes in watercolor as in ink. In order to attain a correct value, it must be built up of several light washes, each applied after the previous one has dried. Using a sheet of the same 15- × 20-inch paper as mentioned above, divide the upper portion into ten equal spaces with ¹⁄₁₆-inch spaces between. These will be used for practicing flat washes (Figure 12.2). The lower portion of the sheet should be laid out in the same manner and will be used for practicing graded washes (Figure 12.3).

Fig. 12.2 Flat Washes for Practice.

Fig. 12.3 Graded Washes for Practice.

Tilting the board at an angle of 10 or 15 degrees, and using a No. 12 brush, run each wash as described in Chapter 10, Ink Rendering. About ¼ inch of wash in a wash pan, with a sufficient amount of pigment to stain the water to medium intensity, will be sufficient for each flat wash.

Graded washes should be practiced in the spaces at the bottom of the sheet, again following the method described for ink rendering, using two wash dishes, one containing the medium-intensity wash and the other plain water, and two different brushes. These washes should be run from light at the top to dark at the bottom. On still another sheet of paper, the washes should be run from dark at the top to light at the bottom. Gradations by the French method should also be practiced.

Textures

Perhaps no other medium accepts modifications for the creation of textures as does watercolor. The surface of the paper may be sandpapered, sandpapered and glazed, scratched with a razor and glazed, sponged, scrubbed with a bristle brush, blotted, dabbed, spattered, or erased.

The indications of textures of building materials explained and shown here are basic and will, of course, not fit every case because of the possible difference of the materials involved. However, they will serve as guideposts and should be practiced until you have mastered the techniques described. These techniques should be practiced on the cold-pressed watercolor paper previously recommended, or on illustration board, ruling off rectangles with a pencil. (See Figure 12.4, sketches a to e.) The textures described below are for surfaces considered to be in sunlight. Color for similar textures in shade should be modified by the use of a richer, darker mixture of the same colors. The various textures should be drawn in with an H pencil at ¼-inch scale, making a careful line drawing.

Wood Siding and Clapboards

Make a pale mixture of a wash of yellow ochre and a small amount of alizarin crimson. Wash the surface of your practice square with this mixture, using your No. 4 brush. When this has dried, the joints may be introduced by using a darker mixture of the same colors and drawing the joints with the same brush held against the side of the tilted or raised straightedge (see Figure 12.4, sketch a). The same method may be used, with the modification described below.

After the base tone has been placed on the sheet, wood-grain texture can be introduced with a wiping motion, using a fairly dry brush (from which the moisture has been partially removed by touching it against a blotter or cheese-

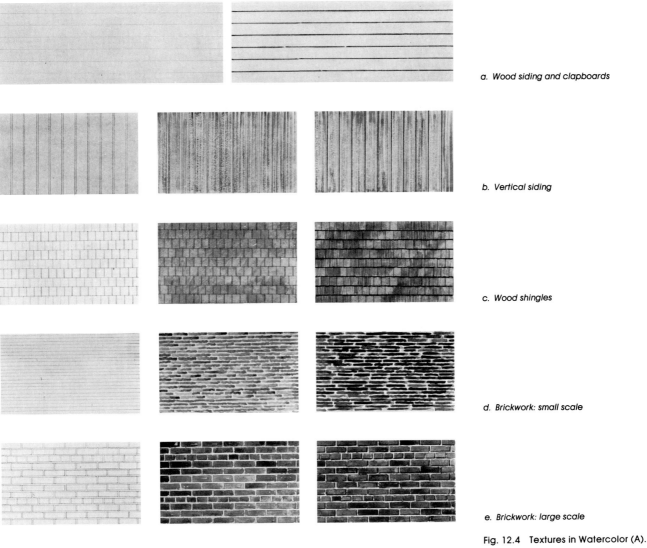

a. Wood siding and clapboards

b. Vertical siding

c. Wood shingles

d. Brickwork: small scale

e. Brickwork: large scale

Fig. 12.4　Textures in Watercolor (A).

cloth). If the drawing is at a scale large enough to clearly show the grain of the wood, your No. 4 brush can be used to introduce actual grain texture, working freehand over the base wash before the joint lines have been put in.

To render redwood siding in natural finish (Figure 12.4, sketch *b*), proceed as follows:

Step 1. Draw the siding and battens in pencil, and then place a pale wash of yellow ochre and vermilion over the entire area.

Step 2. Mix a slightly darker shade of the same color, dip a No. 4 brush into it, and draw the brush over a clean piece of paper, pressing down heavily enough to make the brush flat and relatively dry. Holding the ferrule of the brush against a tilted straightedge placed parallel with the vertical siding, draw the brush lightly over each board, leaving a wood-grain effect over the wash below.

Step 3. Using a still darker mixture of the same colors, holding the straightedge as in step 2, and working with a very small brush brought to a fine point, draw shade lines at the right side of each batten.

Wall and Roof Shingles

The actual color of the shingles, of course, will determine the mixture that is to be used. For instance, if a shade of brown is desired, it might be mixed with French ultramarine blue, alizarin crimson, cadmium orange, and yellow ochre. Since shingles vary in shade a great deal, particularly after they are stained, the base tones are best made by placing a number of washes one upon the other, being careful not to mix the colors thoroughly in the wash pan but merely drawing them together. After the base washes are dry, the shadow lines can be introduced with a slightly wavy freehand stroke (see Figure 12.4, sketch c).

Brickwork

The rendering of brick will vary according to the scale of the drawing, but no matter what the scale, the brick joints should first be drawn in with pencil. At a scale of ⅛ inch or less, a wash the color of the masonry between the bricks should first be passed over the paper. Another wash, the color of the brick and fairly intense in value, is then used to show the courses of brickwork. Using a small brush and small wavy lines, the various courses are painted over the base wash (Figure 12.4, sketch d). Finally, some of the bricks are darkened with additional washes.

At a larger scale, such as ¼ inch to 1 foot, the brickwork may be done as follows: A wash of the joint color is passed over the area and permitted to dry. The various courses of the brick are then drawn in a brick color applied with a ruling pen or small brush, guided by a straightedge. Where it is not desirable to show a great deal of texture, brickwork may be indicated by giving the surface one or more washes of the brick color, then drawing in the joint lines with a sharp 2H pencil, breaking the lines often to avoid monotony. At a very large scale, as in a rendered detail, each brick must be carefully drawn, the joint wash then introduced, and the various bricks rendered individually, care being taken to create variations in tone by introducing more washes over some bricks than others, in order to show the natural color differentiations of the bricks themselves (Figure 12.4, sketch e).

Stonework

Although there are dozens of different ways of laying stone, the delineator need only be interested in whether it is smooth or rough. The smooth, tooled stone, such as limestone, is rendered as follows:

Mix a warm gray from alizarin crimson, yellow ochre, and cobalt blue, and place one or more washes on the surface of a practice sheet. When these are dry, gently sponge the area, thereby introducing variations in tone. When the paper is again dry, simulate the natural differentiation of the various stones by introducing an additional wash or two over several of the stones. Then, using a fine brush, draw shadows on the underside and shade side of the stones (see Figure 12.5, sketch a). If the stones have beveled edges, this method must be modified as described below.

Paint a base tone on the sheet. When it is dry, paint each individual stone separately, leaving the light beveled edges the color of the first wash. Then darken the shade sides of the beveled edges by adding another wash (see Figure 12.5, sketch b).

Rubble walls, rough in texture, may be rendered by first painting the surface the color of the stone joints. Then, using a second sheet of white paper as a

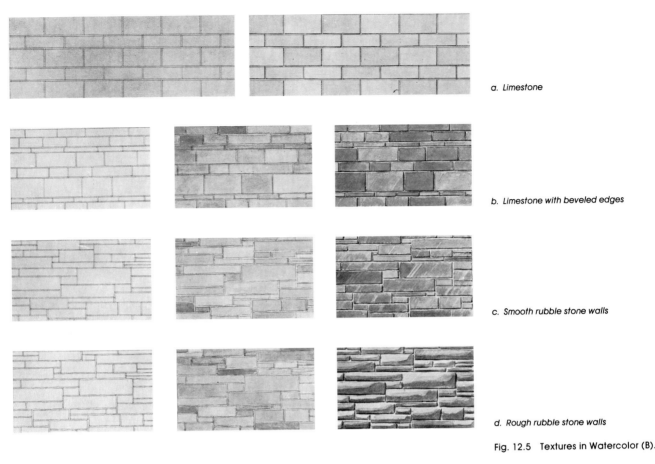

a. Limestone

b. Limestone with beveled edges

c. Smooth rubble stone walls

d. Rough rubble stone walls

Fig. 12.5 Textures in Watercolor (B).

palette, place a small amount of each of the pigments that you have used in the wash on this paper, several inches apart. Mix an average stone color by drawing the pigments together in a puddle with your brush, then apply this tone to about a half dozen widely dispersed stones. Now modify this average tone by adding more of the cool color, and paint several more widely dispersed stones. Modify it again by adding more of the warm color, and paint several more stones. Repeat this process until the entire surface has been covered. When you have completed the process, the drawing should look like a unified wall surface with subtle variations, and not a series of stones widely different in value or color.

Shadows beneath and next to a number of stones may be painted with a fine brush, merely using a dark shade of the colors that you have been working with. Care must be taken to break these shadows (see Figure 12.5, sketch c), or monotony will result. If it is desired to show the roughness of the stones, a number of them may be "shaped" by introducing shade areas on the underside and on the shade side, using a slightly darker tone than the general tone of the stone itself, and working with a fairly dry brush (see Figure 12.5, sketch d).

Metal

An increasing amount of metal is being used in contemporary architecture. The color, of course, depends upon the composition of the metal but, generally speaking, is rather light. Since, for the most part, metal is flat and lacking in texture, interest is best obtained by grading the washes, or by placing the washes, letting them dry, and then scrubbing with a sponge to create differentiations in value.

Glass Openings

Small openings. First, working in pencil, completely draw the window that you plan to render, being careful at the same time to draw the curtains, shades, blinds, or other window treatment being considered. Using a paper palette (as described above) and a small amount of each of the colors of your rendering, paint the opening left between or below the window treatment; create variation in tone throughout the small wash. When this is dry, paint the shades or blinds their proper colors. Then put in shade and shadow areas such as the shadow cast by the window frame on the curtains and blinds. Finally, with a fine brush or ruling pen, and a fairly dark, grayish color, draw the shadows cast by the various members of the windows on the glass, etc. (see Figure 12.6, sketch a).

Large glass openings. Glass openings that are large enough to allow one to see inside are painted in detail. If one is looking directly into the window, all the

Fig. 12.6 Glass Openings. (Advertisement for Polyloom Corporation of America, Inc. Renderer: William C. Wilkinson.)

a. Small openings

b. Large openings

interior furnishings, floor, walls, pictures, etc., must be painted, being careful to allow for the depth of values created by shadows in various parts of the room. Shadows cast on the glass by jamb and head, mullions and muntins, are then painted to indicate the glass (Figure 12.6, sketch b). If the glass opening is being seen so that it reflects light and other objects in it, the objects reflected must be first drawn in pencil (see Chapter 8, "Water and Reflections") and then painted in tones that are usually darker than those of the objects being reflected. The upper portions of such glass areas sometimes reflect the color of the sky and should be painted a tone slightly deeper than that of the sky (Figure 12.6, sketch b).

Entourage

Foreground trees and bushes by the built-up method. Foreground trees and bushes must be accurately drawn, sometimes down to the last detail, with a soft pencil before the rendering is begun. Each leaf may be actually drawn in some cases. Whether the individual leaves or tree masses are drawn in detail or generalized, they must be located before the rendering is started so that the tree structure itself is not painted over these areas. The light color — the color on the side of the tree receiving sunlight — can then be painted over the entire wood structure of the tree as a flat wash. When this is dry, a light wash the approximate color of the foliage masses is mixed and washed over these areas. After these areas dry, the modeling of the tree structure itself is begun by using short but rather definite strokes to indicate the various shades of bark tonality. These small, dark areas will, of course, be for the most part on the shade side of each member, with the

Fig. 12.7 Foreground Trees.

(1)　　　　　(2)　　　　　(3)

a. Built-up method

(1)　　　　　(2)　　　　　(3)

b. Direct method

Fig. 12.8   Mid-Distance Trees.

a   b   c

darkest tones on the extreme shade side. The individual leaves of foliage masses are then modeled one by one, care being taken to differentiate color and value throughout. Finally, shadows cast by foliage masses and branches on branches and trunk must be carefully plotted and painted (Figure 12.7, sketch *a*).

Foreground trees by the direct method.   There are, of course, many different ways of painting trees by the direct method, but the easiest of these is as described here. Make an accurate drawing of the tree structure and, using a flat, dry brush, draw the entire tree structure in an appropriate color. Draw from the ground up, just as the tree grows. The shade side of the tree can be darkened by using the same brush. The foliage can be introduced upon the tree structure with either a large "pencil" brush (Figure 12.7, sketch *b*1), a flat brush (Figure 12.7, sketch *b*2), or a small bit of sponge torn away from the silk sponge, held in the fingers, dipped in the paint and dabbed on the various areas (Figure 12.7, sketch *b*3).

Trees in the mid-distance.   These also can be rendered by either the built-up method or the direct method. The same process as for the foreground trees and brushes should be followed in the direct method, but the foliage masses may be applied in a generalized way by the use of small washes or stippling (Figure 12.7)

In the direct method, the tree structure is usually drawn as for the foreground trees, and the foliage is painted by the use of a smaller (No. 4) brush in individual strokes (see Figure 12.8*b*).

Fig. 12.9   Background Trees.

a   b

a   b   Fig. 12.10   Foreground Foliage.

Background trees. An interesting method of painting background trees consists of drawing the trees in the distance and then painting them with a pale flat wash. While this wash is still damp, and with the board lying in a flat (not tilted) position, dip the brush into a strong (almost pure) pigment mixture of the same color and lightly drop it at the baseline of the trees in the distance. This strong pigment will bleed into the damp surrounding areas and give the illusion of darker-based trees (see Figure 12.9).

Bushes. Foreground bushes as well as mid-distance ones are built up in much the same manner as foreground trees. That is, they are first given a light general wash, then modeled with a dabbing motion to add texture and form (see Figure 12.10). Bushes in the distance can be shown with practically a flat wash.

Grass. Perhaps the most important thing to remember in painting grass is that there is a great differentiation in value and color throughout grass areas. A flat, even wash gives an unsatisfactory appearance. A lawn made of a series of different tones and values to show the actual variation in the grass is much more interesting. Additional interest can also be given to grass areas that appear to be too plain by the use of short, vertical (or nearly vertical) strokes placed close together to simulate grass blades. In building up the tones of grass areas, a great deal of interest can be obtained by failing to cover the undertones entirely in overpainting (Figure 12.9).

Skies. The four basic ways to render skies are described below.

1. A graded wash, usually light at the horizon and dark at the top of the rendering, is made with no attempt to indicate clouds (Figure 12.11, sketch a).
2. The same type of sky is painted, and then clouds are erased with a Ruby eraser (Figure 12.11, sketch b).
3. The entire sky area is dampened with a wash of clear water, and colors are dropped or stroked in to create the illusion of a broken, cloudy sky (Figure 12.11, sketch c). In this method the board must be flat (not tilted) and the colors dropped in must be of a fairly deep intensity; otherwise they will dissipate into the damp sky, and the cloudy textures will disappear. In this method it is also frequently necessary to raise the board and tilt it first one way and then the other in order to coax the color to run into the areas desired.

a

b

c

d

Fig. 12.11 Skies.

a. and b. By graded washes
c. By dropped-in pigments
d. By airbrush

4. Excellent skies, of course, can be painted in watercolor with an airbrush (Figure 12.11, sketch *d*), an atomizer (Figure 12.12, sketch *a*), or toothbrush spatter (Figure 12.12, sketch *b*). Additional techniques for painting skies are discussed in various chapters of this book.

Professional Techniques and Shortcuts

Renderers known for their ability with watercolor use a number of short cuts and tricks that are worth mentioning, since the end results are most helpful to the final rendering. To begin with, Whatman rough-finish illustration board gives interesting pigment-settling effects to flat and graded washes. Also, masking all borders with drafting tape before starting will give the rendering sharp borderlines — thus making a mat unnecessary.

Detailed leaves may be drawn with black chalk and "fixed" by washing them with clear water. Another shortcut is to do sky areas by first masking tree trunks and branches with Maskoid liquid frisket, then wetting the entire sky area thoroughly with a 2-inch-wide housepainting brush and permitting it to soak for 15 or 20 minutes. The colors for sky are mixed (with a base of Antwerp blue or cobalt blue); the sky area is blotted; and rendering begins on a moist, but not wet, surface. By this time a sufficient and controlled amount of water should have been absorbed by the paper so that no streaks or uneven dry edges will occur. While still wet, the sky areas and clouds that are to be light in tone are wiped out

a

b

Fig. 12.12 Skies.
a. By fixative atomizer
b. By toothbrush spatter

with a bristle brush, cellulose sponge, or blotter (see Figure 12.12). If necessary, clouds are erased after the sky washes have dried and for this it is best to use a Blaisdell New-Way eraser (covered with twisted paper).

Many renderers use casein paint (which is similar to tempera) for scale figures or street objects, which is applied after all transparent watercolor work is finished. Generally, the foreground figures are painted drab colors and those in the mid-distance warm colors, while objects near the building are painted yellow or white. Red is avoided because it shows as black in a black-and-white photograph.

Each renderer will use techniques developed from experience. One cannot fail to notice that each problem is handled in an individual way (see Plate V). There is no pat method for handling all renderings. Usually the buildings are left quite light, as compared with surrounding areas (Plate V). Plates VIII and IX illustrate various techniques, as well as use of mixed media to solve specific problems.

Watercolor Variations

The watercolor methods described in this chapter are those used by the purist. The purist will never countenence the use, for example, of opaque color in watercolor work. Yet, from a practical standpoint, as indicated above, many of the most successful professional renderers develop their own methods. Some combine white ink with watercolors for portions of their renderings. As delineators gain experience, they sometimes find it expedient and more to their personal liking to render in a manner slightly different from that which was taught. This is a natural phenomenon. As we mentioned in Chapter 2, one must develop one's own style, and as long as satisfactory results can be obtained, departure from the usual methods can be justified and even considered desirable. The medium must be molded to the individual, and until this has been done the delineator may not achieve maximum success.

chapter 13

Tempera Rendering

Characteristics of Tempera

Tempera is a water-soluble paint that becomes sufficiently insoluble when dry to allow overpainting with more tempera. Imperfect washes and errors can be eliminated by sponging, or they can be repaired by merely covering them with more paint. Tempera can be used on white or colored paper or illustration board, and is excellent for night as well as day renderings. Almost any project can be rendered with this medium, as shown in the illustrations presented in this chapter.

Tempera is available in shades of gray for use in renderings that are to be reproduced in black and white, as well as in most of the colors of transparent watercolors, plus a few more. Tempera shows up in a precise, sculptural way in either black-and-white or color photographs. It gives such a realistic appearance that a photograph of a tempera rendering is often mistaken for a photograph of a finished building. The colors themselves are strong and brilliant and must be mixed with a great deal of white (and sometimes a small amount of black) before they can be used.

Since tempera colors are mixed with a white base, the hues that result can be duplicated in actual job finishes, and the final color scheme for a project can be determined during the rendering project.

The more subtle hues, tints, and shades can be mixed with tempera, but because the colors obtainable are subtle, they are difficult for the novice to duplicate. Therefore it is advisable to mix more of each color than one intends to use, and to save the excess for repairing damages, or for use on other parts of the rendering, until it has been completed.

Materials

Paper

Tempera can be used on cold-pressed or hot-pressed handmade paper that has been stretched, on illustration boards with the same finishes, or on stretched colored charcoal paper. The better grades of boards are recommended because they have hard, tough surfaces that withstand such hazards as sponging and drafting tape, which frequently destroy the surfaces of less expensive boards.

Pigments

Tempera is available in ready-mixed sets of grays, either warm or cool. The numbers of the shades in sets vary according to brand. Some, for instance, are numbered 0, 1, 2, 3; others 1, 2, 3, 4 and 5. The lightest shade usually bears the lowest number, the darkest the highest number. The author recommends warm grays for architectural work.

Tempera pigments, whether gray or colored, are produced in tubes, jars, and cakes. The tube colors have more body; those sold in jars usually contain a large amount of water. The tube colors are slightly more expensive than those in jars. It is not advisable to use cake temperas for rendering. All tempera dries if not used within a reasonable time; therefore, as with watercolor, it is advisable to buy the smaller sizes of tubes or jars. Jars of color can be kept moist by adding water and a little glycerin periodically before they have dried.

A thin line indeed separates the various kinds of opaque paints. Some are sold as temperas, others as designer's watercolors, poster colors, or showcard colors. Winsor & Newton's designers' opaque watercolors, while they are especially made for gouache painting, are excellent for opaque renderings, as are Grumbacher's designers' colors, Weber Malfa, Shiva "Nu-Tempera," and Rich Art poster colors.

Like transparent watercolors (Chapter 12), opaque watercolors are made in a great many hues and usually vary in price according to pigment. Nearly all the colors recommended for transparent watercolor are available, but in addition such colors as the following can be obtained in tempera, designer, or showcard paints:

Marigold yellow	Brilliant green
Mistletoe green	Magenta
Burgundy lake	Cadmium primrose
Rose malmaison	Permanent orange
Peacock blue	Permanent green
Persian orange	Flame red
Forest green	

Buying such colors can be very confusing if one depends entirely upon their names, particularly in purchasing tube colors. The author recommends limiting the palette and dabbling only occasionally in the unknown. In any case, before purchasing a tube of an unfamiliar color, it is advisable to take off the cap and examine the contents.

The following palette of tube colors is recommended.

Cadmium yellow pale	Cobalt blue
Yellow ochre	Cerulean blue
Cadmium orange	Viridian
Vermilion	Windsor emerald

Flame red	Ivory black
Alizarin crimson	Permanent white (or any opaque white, commonly
Ultramarine blue	known as Chinese white)

If jar colors are used, the palette listed below is recommended. (This list was selected from Rich Art colors.)

Yellow (spectrum)	Light blue
Dark yellow	Blue (spectrum)
Yellow ochre	Ultramarine blue
Orange (spectrum)	Emerald green
Vermilion	Green (spectrum)
Red (spectrum)	Poster white
Dark red	Poster black

In addition to the above palettes, whether they are purchased as tube or jar colors, it is recommended that small jars or cakes of gold and silver be obtained.

Since tempera colors dry hard, removing tube caps and jar covers frequently becomes a problem, particularly if excess paint was not cleaned off before they were replaced. It is, of course, advisable to wipe any such excess paint away before the covers or caps are replaced. A tube cap that is stuck can usually be removed by holding a lighted match under the cap while rotating the tube (be careful not to burn your fingers), and a jar cover may be loosened by holding it under warm or hot water.

Brushes

Expensive watercolor brushes purchased for use with transparent watercolors or inks will quickly be ruined by tempera. In general, four types of brushes are used for tempera painting:

1. *Red sable, bright-shape.* Like watercolor brushes, tempera brushes are made by different manufacturers and thus vary greatly in number and size. Winsor & Newton's bright-shape series 52, No. 3, No. 4, and No. 6, or series 807, No. 1, No. 2, No. 4, and No. 6, are excellent, as are Grumbacher's series 320, No. 3, No. 6, and No. 14. Tempera brushes should be examined carefully when purchased (using the procedure described in Chapter 10) to make certain that there are no loose ferrules or hairs. Like watercolor brushes, tempera brushes should immediately spring back into a straight position after being bent, as for use. (Note: Be sure that you purchase short-hair, thin "brights" with square, straight edges—not "longs.")

2. *Round "pencil" brushes.* Purchase some of these watercolor-type brushes and reserve them for tempera work. No. 1, No. 4, and No. 6 in sable or camel's hair will be found useful.

3. *Flat bristle oil-painting brushes.* Because tempera is a thick paint, rendering brushes should never be used for mixing. Bristle brushes are excellent for mixing and are available in many brands, all quite inexpensive. A No. 4 is about the right size, and a No. 7 will also be helpful.

4. *Stipple (stencil) brushes.* Flat-ended stipple brushes, Winsor & Newton or equal, No. 0 and No. 1, are helpful for texturing.

Every brush should be washed in clean water immediately after use. Brushes which are permitted to dry with paint in the bristles quickly becomes useless. As suggested in Chapter 10, they should be stored dry in boxes with mothballs.

Mixing and Storing Equipment

Because tempera is an opaque paint (unlike transparent watercolor), it can be mixed in metallic (unpainted) containers. Wash dishes of enamel, iron, or plastic of course, may be used, but since it is necessary to preserve a small quantity of each color until the rendering has been completed, it is advisable to obtain an aluminum muffin tin with as many large cups as possible — preferably at least a dozen.

Palette

Excellent for use as a large-size palette is a flat, white enamel tray (one with slightly turned-up edges) similar to those used in butcher shops. Opaque white pad paper and white illustration board also make good tempera palettes.

Water Container

The same type of water container recommended for watercolor rendering can be used for tempera work. It should hold at least a quart of water, preferably more.

Miscellaneous Items

Additional equipment needed for tempera rendering includes

1. A dozen white blotters
2. A silk or "baby" sponge
3. A dozen or more wooden spoons or wooden tongue depressors, for removing paint from jars
4. A ruling pen
5. A straightedge or T square
6. Masking or drafting tape

Color Experimentation

You should become familiar with tempera colors before you try rendering with them. Place a small amount of each pigment on an inexpensive illustration board or a piece of watercolor paper. Look at each color, and compare it with its neighbors. Now mix each color with an increasing amount of white and notice the changes that this produces. You will observe that the addition of white sometimes changes the color instead of merely lightening it, while the addition of black frequently produces a surprising new color. Black added to yellow, for instance, produces a kind of green, because there is a great deal of blue in the black. For the same reason, black tempera added to red or orange produces a purplish color. All these factors must be taken into consideration in mixing tempera.

Practice Washes

In general, a building is usually rendered in a series of flat base washes which are modified by lines or textures placed over them. Therefore, before proceeding further it is advisable to practice making tempera washes. To begin with, tempera should be mixed with just enough water to produce a mixture of a creamy consistency. It is meant to be opaque and should, if the wash is applied correctly, completely cover the surface, so that none of the paper will show through. Washes are best applied with flat brushes.

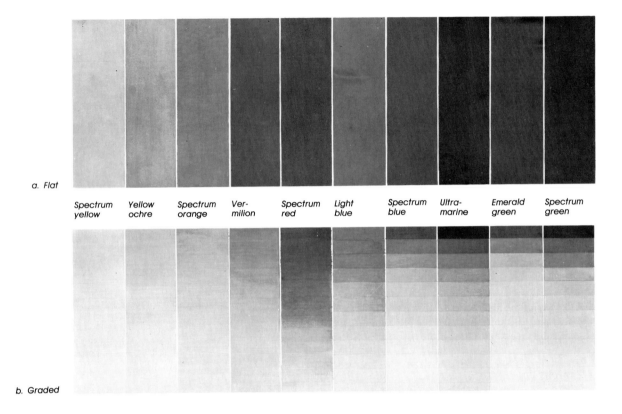

a. Flat

Spectrum yellow | Yellow ochre | Spectrum orange | Ver-milion | Spectrum red | Light blue | Spectrum blue | Ultra-marine | Emerald green | Spectrum green

b. Graded

Fig. 13.1 Practice Washes in Tempera

Using a sheet of 15- × 20-inch illustration board, draw a ½-inch border around the outside edge in pencil, and divide the resulting space into an upper and a lower portion, with a 2-inch space between them. Then divide each of these portions into ten equal spaces with ⅟₁₆ inch between them (as shown in Figure 13.1). Label each rectangle with the name of a color. The top rectangles will receive flat washes in full intensity (sketch *a*); the lower rectangles will receive graded washes (sketch *b*).

Beginning with spectrum yellow, for instance, proceed as follows: Place the desired amount of Chinese white in one cup of your muffin tin and add the color to it drop by drop, mixing with the bristle brush as you add each drop, until you have achieved the shade that you want. Because tempera colors are very strong, only a few drops, or a small bit from a tube, will stain a large amount of white to a desirable value. If you were to begin with the color and add white, it might be necessary to use an entire jar of white to obtain a desirable color.

Using the raised edge of a straightedge and a small conical brush or a ruling pen, surround each area with a fine line in its proper color, to assure that your edges will be straight. Then dip flat brush into the tempera, remove the excess on the edge of the cup, and begin to paint at the top with short (¼- to ½-inch) vertical overlapping brush strokes, brushing the thick paint out as you do so. Brush hard, as if this were your last bit of paint. Work from left to right, and when you have covered the entire upper edge, add more paint to your brush and repeat the procedure, overlapping the bottom of the first strokes with the second row. Repeat this process until you reach the bottom of the first rectangle.

Then go on to the second rectangle. Leave no white spaces within the rectangles, but also refrain from touching surfaces that have been painted before they dry, since this will result in a scarred surface. It will take a few minutes for each rectangle to dry. Ideally, all the rectangles should dry completely opaque and smooth. Do not be surprised if some of the washes are not completely opaque;

this takes some practice and experience. Any faults may be corrected by placing a second wash over the first, identical except for the addition of a little more water.

The building-up process can be repeated to produce an opaque quality or to correct mistakes in rendering until about three coats have been placed upon the sheet. After that the paint will probably begin to crack and flake off the painted surface. If such a problem occurs, mask around the area which drafting or masking tape and paper, making sure that the tape is securely fastened, and then sponge the tempera off the surface with a damp sponge. It may be necessary to wash the sponge several times, but almost all the tempera can be removed in this way. When the area has dried it may be rendered upon as before.

By this time you will probably have noticed that tempera is darker when dry than in the liquid state. This can be quite a problem, since the success of a rendering depends heavily upon obtaining the right shade for each portion. It is advisable, before using any tempera paint, to brush a small amount of it on a piece of white paper and to dry it quickly. One way to do this is to light a match and pass it back and forth under the paint, being careful not to let the flame ignite the paper. Using a hair dryer is a safer method. The edges of the paint usually dry first, allowing the true color to be seen. Be careful not to burn the paint and change its color, when using a hair dryer.

Graded Washes

For the most part, tempera is not meant to be graded when used to render a building. It can, however, be used in this way, perhaps not so successfully as transparent watercolor, by the wet-into-wet method and the French method. The first five rectangles at the bottom of Figure 13.1 should be used for practicing the wet-into-wet method, the second five for the French method. For the wet-into-wet method, follow the instructions given below.

Surround a rectangle with drafting tape and paper, making sure that the tape is firmly in place (Figure 13.2). Place an amount of color, say spectrum yellow for the first rectangle, in a cup. Place a similar amount of white in another cup, using a wooden spoon to handle the color if jar color is being used. Using a bristle brush, mix a sufficient amount of water with the pure yellow to give it a creamy consistency. Take a brushful of the yellow and, using a horizontal stroke, cover about ¾ inch at the top of the rectangle. Using a mixing brush, add a small amount of white to the yellow in the cup, and mix it thoroughly. Then add a brushful to the first wash and, again using horizontal strokes, brush it gently into the bottom edge of the first wash. Repeat this process about every ¾ inch until you reach the bottom of the rectangle. Then follow the same procedure for each of the remaining four colors.

Note: Be sure that the paint is dry before you remove the drafting tape. Remove each piece gently and slowly by pulling it downward and to the side at the same time, so that you will not scar the surface of the board.

The French Method

To make graded washes by the French method, follow the procedure described below.

Prepare a creamy mixture of a color — say light blue — in one cup, and place an equal amount of Chinese white in another. Divide each rectangle into ½-inch increments, and draw lines at these points with a pencil and straightedge (Figure 13.3). To grade from dark to light, introduce a small amount of blue into the

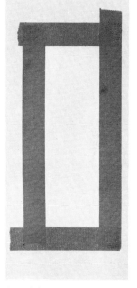

Fig. 13.2 Masking the Wash.

Fig. 13.3 Washes by the French Method.

white and stir with a bristle mixing brush until it has been mixed thoroughly. Draw around the upper increment with this color by resting a small conical brush on the edge of a straightedge as a guide, and then fill in the space with the same color. When the first increment is dry, add another small amount of blue to the mixture, stir it thoroughly, and repeat the process, this time covering the second increment. Repeat the process for the entire height of the rectangle, and you will achieve an excellent gradation. Go through the same process for each of the remaining four colors.

After this exercise is completed, clean your brushes immediately. Otherwise the paint will dry so hard that it will be almost impossible to remove. Take the muffin tin and brushes to a sink and dump out all the liquid paint, then run clean cold water into each cup in turn, scrubbing with the largest bristle brush that you have. (Note: Do not use warm water, it does not soften the pigment so well as cold water.) Clean each brush in turn, swishing it around in clean water and then squeezing out the excess gently with your fingers.

As mentioned earlier, it is advisable to preserve some of each color for damage repair until the rendering has been completed. Tempera dries quickly and becomes a hard, cracked substance in the bottom of the container. It cannot easily be returned to a liquid state by adding water to it. Therefore, after each work session, add a few drops of water (no more) to each color and mix it in with a clean bristle brush. Then wet the area around the top of each cup with some of the paint. Finally, press a piece of heavy tracing paper over the top of the entire muffin tin. The paint will dry between the muffin tin and the tracing paper, forming a seal. This procedure will keep the color for about one day. When you are ready to use it again, merely puncture the tracing paper and tear it away from each cup.

Textures

The textures described herein are for surfaces in sunlight. Generally speaking, the color that is used for a surface in sunlight is darkened for shade and shadow by adding more of each pigment, and in particular, more of the darker colors in the palette being used.

Using a 20- × 30-inch piece of white illustration board, draw a ½-inch border around the outside edge in pencil and divide the remaining 29-inch width into 11 equal spaces, with ⅛-inch space between each two. Then draw a line 8½ inches down from the top border. This will produce 11 equal rectangles in which textures can be practiced (see Figure 13.4). Beneath each rectangle, letter one of the following labels:

1. Wood siding made with ruling pen
2. Wood siding made with small brush
3. Wall shingles
4. Stucco and concrete
5. Brick at small scale
6. Brick at large scale
7. Brick at very large scale
8. Cut stone
9. Rubble coursed
10. Rubble uncoursed
11. Metal

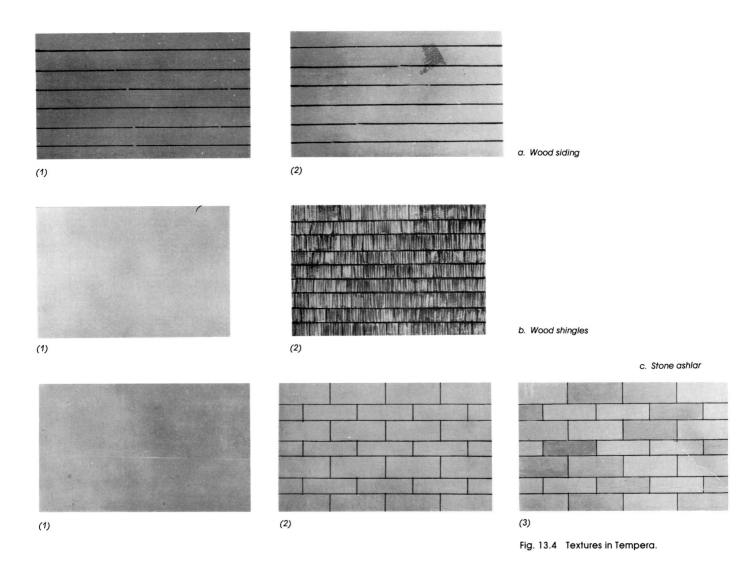

(1)   *(2)*   *a. Wood siding*

(1)   *(2)*   *b. Wood shingles*

c. Stone ashlar

(1)   *(2)*   *(3)*

Fig. 13.4   Textures in Tempera.

Wood Siding

The color of the wood, of course, will vary with its finish, but for a natural-finish wood, make a pale mixture of white, yellow, green, and a small amount of alizarin crimson. Lay a flat, opaque wash to this color in the first rectangle. When it is dry, using a ¼-inch scale and a graphite pencil, draw the siding across the wash at 8 inches to weather (8-inch exposure of each board). Then mix a darker wash using the same pigment with perhaps a small amount of cobalt blue. With a ruling pen, draw the shadows under the butts in the upper half of the rectangle (see Figure 13.4, sketch a1). For practice, draw the shades in the second rectangle with your smallest conical brush, guided by the raised edge of your straightedge (Figure 13.4, sketch a2).

Clapboards can be indicated in the same manner as siding, but should be drawn to indicate 5 inches of exposure.

Wall Shingles

While the actual colors of the shingles to be rendered will vary, an adequate base color for this exercise can be made by mixing ultramarine blue, alizarin crimson, cadmium orange, and yellow ochre with white. Place a base tone upon the paper as described above; then draw the wood shingles at a ¼-inch scale with a sharp HB pencil. Using a small brush and a darker mixture of the same paint used for the base tone, draw the butts of the shingles with short, broken, wavy lines (Figure 13.4, sketch *b*). Then draw occasional vertical spaces between the shingles with straight freehand lines, or draw the straight lines with the aid of the raised edge of a straightedge. If additional variation in color and value seems desirable, it may be introduced by mixing small amounts of the same colors used in the base tone of a paper palette, picking out a few shingles in lighter and darker tones.

Stucco, Concrete, and Dressed Stone Ashlar

An excellent color for stucco, concrete, or cut stone in sunlight can be made by mixing a small amount of white with No. 2 gray. If this gray is unavailable, it can easily be mixed by adding yellow ochre, cobalt blue, and alizarin crimson to white. A flat tone of this color will suffice for stucco or concrete. For cut stone, the joints should either be (1) lined in, using a graphite pencil, straightedge, and triangle, and then covered with an off-white tempera in a ruling pen, or (2) drawn with a small brush, using the raised edge of the straightedge as a guide (Figure 13.4, sketch *c*).

Brickwork

The type of indication for brickwork will depend upon the scale of the drawing. At small scale (⅛ inch or less; Figure 13.5, sketch *a*), a wash of the brick color is first applied to the area, and the joints are ruled over it in pencil at 4 courses of 11 inches. Brick, of course, varies in color, but for this exercise make a pale terra-cotta mixture using white, yellow ochre, vermilion, and cobalt blue. The joint color will be a pale gray mixed with white and a small amount of the same colors.

At a larger scale (¼ inch = 1 foot), place a wash of light, warm gray over the entire rectangle. Then with a straightedge and pencil draw all the courses at 4 courses to 11 inches. Now, using a ruling pen or fine brush, and with a straightedge as a guide, brush or rule in each course of brick, breaking the lines of each course fairly even and leaving the width of a joint between them (Figure 13.5, sketch *b*).

For very large scale brickwork (½ inch or larger), give the area a wash in the joint color, draw the individual bricks in pencil, and then mix an average color for the brick and paint most of them individually. Modify this color by adding more pigment or more white, painting in the remaining bricks in varying tones (Figure 13.5, sketch *c*).

Rubble (Coursed and Uncoursed)

Place a wash of pale gray (the joint color) over the entire surface. Then carefully draw every stone in pencil, using horizontal pencil lines as a general guide. Place a small amount of each color you are using — in this case, those used for cut stone — on a piece of white illustration board, and, with a medium-sized conical brush, draw the several colors and white together to form an average stone color. Paint this color upon half a dozen widely dispersed stones. Then modify the average color by adding more of one pigment than the other so that the next wash is warmer than the first, and paint another half-dozen stones. Vary the color again and repeat the process. Continue until every stone has been covered. Then mix a darker tone than any that you have used, and with the smallest conical brush, draw an occasional shadow under and next to a number of stones (Figure 13.5, sketches *d* and *e*).

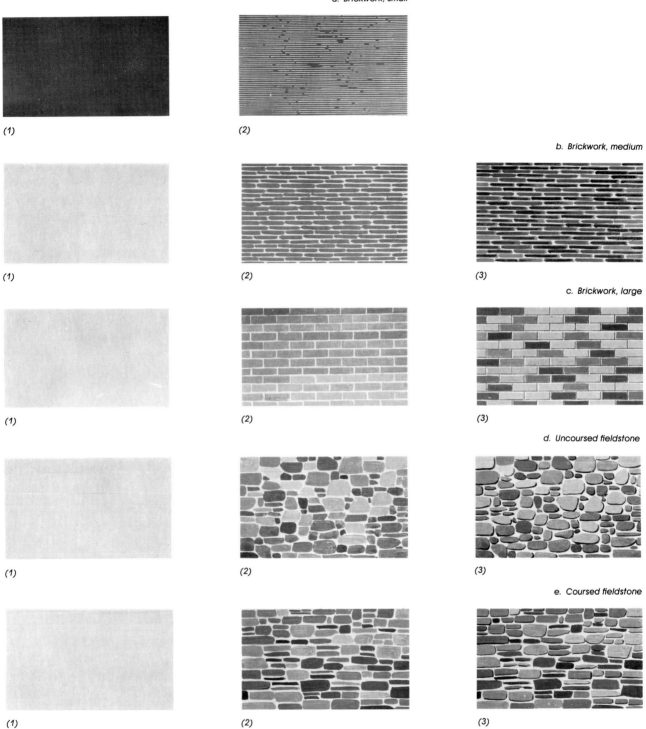

a. Brickwork, small

(1)   (2)

b. Brickwork, medium

(1)   (2)   (3)

c. Brickwork, large

(1)   (2)   (3)

d. Uncoursed fieldstone

(1)   (2)   (3)

e. Coursed fieldstone

(1)   (2)   (3)

Fig. 13.5 Other Textures in Tempera.

Metal

Like all building materials, metals vary in color. Aluminum usually has a warm gray tone, stainless steel a tone that is more bluish. For this exercise mix a small amount of cobalt blue with some white and water and place a base tone upon the rectangle. Then make another mixture of white, blue, and a small amount of black, and apply the joints with a fine brush or ruling pen, using a straightedge as a guide.

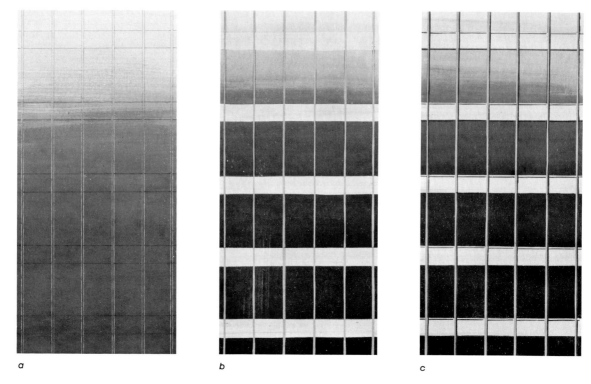

a   b   c

Fig. 13.6 Multiple Glass Openings.

Multiple Glass Openings

Small glass openings are painted exactly as described in Chapter 12 for water-color. Larger openings are painted as for watercolor, except that when there are large banks of windows the entire glass area is first painted a general tone, or for skyscrapers, a graded tone. When this is dry, the mullions, muntins, and span-drels are superimposed upon it (Figure 13.6).

Entourage

Whereas in transparent watercolor it is necessary to leave white spaces wher-ever trees and bushes are to be placed, tempera trees and bushes may be painted over areas that have previously been painted. All trees and bushes are painted from a palette. Small amounts of each of the several colors being used are placed near one another on the palette, so that they may be pulled together with a wet brush, and this thick color is then applied directly to previously penciled trees and bushes. The opaque quality of the paint allows for a building-up process.

Background trees are generally painted in light, flat, pale washes with soft edges to suggest leaves (Figure 13.7, sketch a). These are always painted in first. The tops of the background trees should be of irregular shape. Mid-distance trees are next applied. These are detailed in structure, darker in value, and darker in hue (Figure 13.7, sketch b). The foliage masses are carefully drawn, then painted with flat washes, again with soft edges. Some delineators prefer to stipple this color on with a flat brush.

As in transparent watercolor rendering, the foreground trees and bushes are painted quite completely in detail (Figure 13.7, sketch c). The structure and bark texture are shown in considerable detail; branches and twigs are shown completely and as realistically as possible to help create the illusion of reality. As in all media, it is important not to hide the design of the building with foliage

(1) Wet-into-wet   *(2) Separate planes*

b. Mid-distance trees

(1) Foliage dabbed with ³⁄₁₆"   *(2) Flat wash*   *(3) Foliage painted on damp*
flat dry brush   *paper with ½-inch flat charged brush*

c. Foreground trees

(1) Overhanging branches   *(2) Framing foreground trees*

Fig. 13.7   Trees in Tempera.

masses, but rather to arrange them so that the building is either framed by them or seen through them.

The trunks of large trees can be rounded by working wet into wet. First paint the light side of the tree its proper pale color, and then add darker color on the opposite side and blend it into the light color. For reasons of composition, it is sometimes desirable to paint several tree branches as if the tree were located behind the spectator. These are usually painted quite dark and help to push the building back into the mid-distance. For all trees in tempera, several different shades of the same color should be used in foliage masses so as to prevent monotony and to create the illusion of light, local color, shade, and shadow.

Grass

Grass is generally given a sunny quality. It may be painted wet into wet by starting at the horizon and painting forward, changing the color now and then in

MEDIUM: Full casein rendering.

Fig. 13.8 Pacwest Center. (Owner: Russell Development Company, Inc. Architect: The Stubbins Associates, Inc., and Skidmore, Owings & Merrill Associates, Architects. Renderer: Howard Associates, Inc.)

order to relieve the monotony and to create the illusion of perspective (refer to Figure 13.9). The spaces between these variations should be graduated so that they are smallest near the horizon and largest near the spectator. Usually grass is darkest in the foreground and lightest in the distance. Tree shadows upon the grass will add to the illusion of reality, and describe the rise and fall of the ground. These should be relatively pale in value, except in the immediate foreground, where they should be quite dark.

Skies

In tempera work, as in casein, skies are used only when they enhance the design being studied. There are many occasions when a sky is not necessary, or when it is insignificant in its plainness. Basically there are four different types of skies.

1. *Flat skies.* These are made with a wash of a single tone or color. (See Figure 13.8 and Plate VII.)
2. *Flat skies with clouds.* (See Figure 13.9.)
3. *Graded or domed skies.* (See Plate IX.) Graded skies can be painted in the same way as described for wet-into-wet graded washes, or by a series of rough-edged flat washes as in Plate IX, which the lightest flat wash at the horizon and the darkest at the top of the picture. It is advisable, when painting any sky other than a flat wash, to mask the top edge of the building with drafting tape and paper to assure a clean line.
4. *Airbrush skies.* By masking in the same way as described above and covering the entire building as described in Chapter 14, skies may easily be sprayed with an airbrush.

Making a Tempera Rendering

A perspective line drawing is first applied to the paper or illustration board by the method described in Chapter 3. A value study and a color study must be made for each project, and an exploration of the color scheme selected should be made before the rendering is begun, as described in Chapter 12. With the exception of renderings on colored paper, it is advisable to cover all portions of the paper with tempera, even areas that must be painted white, since any portions not covered in such drawings would have a different appearance from the tempera.

Generally speaking, to do a tempera rendering, proceed as follows:

Fig. 13.9 Suthlo Industrial Park, Branchburg Plaza. (Architect: Rotwein & Blake. Renderer: William C. Wilkinson.)

1. Give the sunny walls of the building their main wash.
2. Give the shade side of each building its main wash.
3. Apply shadow areas.
4. Paint the interior furniture and wall and ceiling colors in glass areas. Paint the general tone of curtains as a flat wash, and then shape the curtains.
5. Paint mullions and muntins over glass areas.
6. Paint doors, louvers, and grilles.
7. Apply wall textures with brush or ruling pen.
8. Correct and straighten crooked edges.
9. Paint the sky.
10. Indicate the grass areas.
11. Paint the background trees.
12. Add trees and foliage in the mid-distance.
13. Paint foreground trees, bushes, and shadows, and add tree and building shadows on the ground.
14. Indicate scale figures and automobiles last.

Comparative Renderings

The renderings discussed below illustrate various techniques for tempera rendering.

It is sometimes necessary to prepare a number of comparative renderings to illustrate variations in a basic design. See Plates V and IX. These renderings are particularly meritorious in that the buildings are all shown in rich, colorful settings. It is interesting to note that clients are attracted to buildings that are bathed in bright sunlight. All the foregrounds in Plates V and IX are dark yet somewhat transparent. The grass surrounding the buildings seems full of sunlight; the trees vary from dark green through red-orange and autumn yellow. Where skies are shown, they are a clear blue. Note that as a result of careful planning, the colors of the trees near the house, in each case, vary in order to complement the building. For example, in Plate IX, top, the cool gray roof is complemented by a reddish-brown base and by dark blues immediately in back of the building. In Plate VIII, bottom, where the second story of the building is of a dark material, it is complemented by the use of brilliant trees around and behind it. Invariably light is used against dark and dark against light, for contrast.

Casein Paints

Similar to tempera in many ways, casein paints, which are made from skimmed milk, are often used for rendering. They are water-soluble and remain moist and pliable while they are being used, but dry quickly and soon become water-resistant. They can be used as gouache, tempera, or transparent watercolor and are available in sets of as many as 40 different colors and white. Generally speaking, they can be used in the same manner as tempera colors.

A meticulous quality that is obtained by superb draftsmanship is illustrated by Figures 13.8 and 13.9. After first carefully constructing his perspective, the renderer selected the direction of the sun and, as may be seen here, thus provided a minimum amount of shade area so that the majority of the buildings are bathed in sunlight. The renderer was most faithful in the representation of textures and used pencil, washes, opaque paint, and dry-brushed paint to achieve this.

Once the building was completely rendered, the sky, entourage, foreground, and background were painted directly, using "japan"-edged brushes and a straightedge. For long vertical lines the renderer used colored paint in a ruling pen. Whenever possible, casein painting is done from dark to light.

Both Figure 13.8 and Figure 13.9 were rendered on Crescent gray illustration board.

This delineator prefers to use a limited palette because of the necessity of matching colors when revisions are called for. The palette includes the following Shiva casein paints:

Cadmium red extra scarlet	Yellow ochre
Cadmium orange	Naples yellow
Cadmium yellow medium	Cerulean blue
Cadmium yellow light	Shiva (Thalo) blue

Figure 13.9 illustrates the importance of selecting a correct light source. The structural members on the light side are the color of building material in sunlight, while the shade side is a much deeper tone of the same color. Trees, hedges, and lawns are relatively grayed in tone and seem to support the building in its setting. A brilliant blue sky completes the rendering, which was done on colored illustration board.

chapter 14

Airbrush Rendering

History and Properties of the Airbrush

The airbrush was developed about 1882 by the Airbrush Manufacturing Company of Rockford, Illinois. It is an instrument roughly resembling a fountain pen, through which may be sprayed a mixture of air and paint. The air source can be either a compressor or a tank of carbonic gas. The earliest mechanical compressors were hand pumps. Later hand pumps resembled those for bicycles, while early electric pumps were similar to those used for dispensing beer.

The chief advantage of the airbrush is that rounded forms which are difficult to render by the wash method may be easily represented. Another advantage is that the paint dries almost immediately upon application. Properly applied, airbrush washes are transparent, and excellent atmospheric effects can be obtained. Airbrush is particularly suitable for the rendering of projects which are architecturally very smooth or glassy in appearance.

Masking

In order to localize an area that is to be sprayed, it is necessary to mask all other portions of the rendering. The airbrush is equally effective on very small or very large areas, and once the process of masking is mastered, airbrush becomes a quick medium. Simple gradations can be made with one quick spray, and even the most difficult gradations call for little investment in time. Reflected light in shade and shadow, as well as curved and rounded planes, are rendered almost as easily as flat planes. As mentioned in Chapter 13, the airbrush is often used for spraying skies in brush tempera work, and it may also be used to soften or modify renderings in transparent watercolor or brush tempera.

Of course, because the masking sometimes prevents the renderer from seeing more than the one small area being worked on, a rather thorough knowledge of the rendering and the ability to imagine what the whole rendering will look like when it is finished are necessary. The delineator also needs a good memory, in order to remember each portion that has already been rendered and to imagine what earlier portions will look like in conjunction with the area being sprayed at the moment. As in all other techniques, a charcoal study and a color study are necessary before an airbrush rendering can be started.

Airbrushes

There are a number of airbrushes on the market, but the best results in rendering can be obtained by using a Thayer & Chandler model A, C, or E, or a Paasche model F-1 or V — all of which are relatively small.

The above brushes are made with either single or double action. The single-action brush, usually used by beginners and students, sprays a mixture of paint and air when a trigger is pressed downward. The double-action brush, on the other hand, permits control of the amount of air and paint, so that a very small amount or a large amount of either can be sprayed by manipulation of the trigger. When pressed down, the trigger sprays air alone; as it is pulled back, it sprays paint in increasing amounts along with the air. This, of course, is the better brush. The buyer must take care to select the kind of brush that is needed. Paasche model F-1 is a single-action brush, while model V is a double-action brush comparable to Thayer & Chandler double-action models. If an airbrush is kept clean and not dropped, and if it is serviced regularly, it should last for many years.

Air Sources

One of two basic air sources is used: a compressor or a tank of carbonic gas. For a single airbrush, the simplest compressor is a Paasche (D ¼ horsepower) oilless single-diaphragm air compressor which is light, portable, and quiet in operation. It delivers up to 30 pounds of pressure and provides approximately 500 hours of service before the diaphragm must be replaced. A larger compressor for general use, requiring air pressure to 2 cubic feet per minute at a uniform, continuous flow, is also available. The pump in this unit operates automatically. When it is connected to electricity, the unit will pump up to 60 pounds of pressure. A regulator may be set at the desired air pressure. When the air pressure is reduced to 40 pounds by use, the unit starts again automatically and pumps up to 60 pounds into the storage tank.

If for some reason you do not wish to purchase a compressor, tanks of compressed carbonic gas may be rented in 20- and 50-pound sizes. In order to control the release of the carbonic gas pressure, it is necessary to purchase a regulator and gauge, which are fastened to each new tank in turn. The 20-pound tank is quite small in diameter, while the 50-pound tank is much bulkier. The renting of a tank of gas usually entails payment for the gas itself plus a daily rental for the tank. Because this can be quite an expense, many delineators purchase a "stubbie" 10-pound tank, which is about 22 inches high and lasts about 30 working hours. This is sold with a regulator gauge and petcock. When the carbonic acid is used up, the stubbie tank can be refilled by any carbonic gas company.

Spray cans. A spray can of air may be purchased for small, simple renderings. Each can of air lasts about half an hour and is relatively expensive. In addition, a valve and hose must be purchased, which, of course, are used on the can of air. One disadvantage of this type of air source is that its flow is not controllable; it may be turned off and on only. The pressure varies between 25 and 30 pounds.

Air Hose

The air hose of fabric-covered rubber, which connects the tank or compressor to the airbrush, should be about 10 feet long. Be sure that you obtain the proper fittings for your particular air source and airbrush since these fittings vary according to the airbrush and air source used.

Airbrush Hanger

Most airbrushes are sold complete with a hanger that can be fastened to the edge of a drawing board. When not in use, the airbrush is hooked into the hanger, where it is relatively safe from harm.

Frisket Paper

The pressure of air emitted by an airbrush is sufficiently strong so that all areas except that being sprayed must be firmly masked. There are two basic types of frisket paper: (1) gumless, transparent, relatively waterproof paper, which may be fastened down with rubber cement thinned to half consistency with rubber cement thinner, and (2) gummed, transparent paper such as E-Z Frisket, which is made with a removable backing. This is available in rolls 24 inches × 15 feet or 24 inches × 60 feet, or in sheets 18 × 24 inches or 19 × 12 inches. Many art materials stores sell this paper by the yard.

No gummed paper can be stored for any length of time, because the gum undergoes a change in consistency which sometimes makes it useless. In addition, gummed frisket paper should never be stored near heat, which will dry it out. Therefore, it is advisable to purchase only enough for the job at hand.

The gumless frisket paper sold in art materials stores is quite transparent, and so the drawing can be seen beneath it. Any substitute that you can find, such as Saran Wrap, will also do. Before these items appeared on the market, tracing paper was employed, but this had two grave disadvantages: it was neither transparent nor waterproof.

Frisket Knives

When an area is to be sprayed, first the entire drawing is covered with frisket paper, and then that portion over the area to be sprayed is meticulously and accurately cut out and removed. Gummed frisket paper may or may not leave a small residue, which can be removed by rubbing with a clean finger. If rubber cement is used, with the gumless type of frisket paper, it can be removed by rubbing with a finger after it is dry.

Since only the thickness of the frisket paper is to be cut, and it is important not to cut the rendering paper, great care must be taken in cutting each mask. For this purpose, special frisket knives are sold. They have metal holders, usually of aluminum, which resemble penholders and hold small, replaceable, razor-sharp blades. The least expensive type holds the blade in a fixed position, which is excellent for cutting straight lines. For cutting curves, however, pivoting frisket knives are best. Both types are made so that the blades may be replaced when necessary.

Paper or Illustration Board

The same papers or illustration boards suggested for use in brush tempera rendering (Chapter 13) are also suitable for airbrush rendering.

Paint

Although transparent watercolor can be sprayed through an airbrush, tempera is most often used because of its fast-drying quality.

Note: Do not use a small airbrush for spraying fixative, lacquer, oil paint, waterproof ink, glue, liquid plastic, or metallic paint, since it will clog the brush. If you wish to spray any of the above substances, you should use a large airbrush such as Paasche model H or V1, Thayer & Chandler model C, or Wold model W-9. It will be necessary, of course, to clean any of these large airbrushes with the solvent of the material you have sprayed.

Other Materials

Drafting tape. It is frequently necessary to use 1-inch drafting tape for holding pieces of frisket paper or other masking paper in place.

Pins. On occasion, the frisket paper, even though it has been carefully applied, will start to curl from the moisture of the paint. These curling spots can be help in place temporarily by the use of a pin stuck through the frisket paper and into the drawing itself. A handful of coins will also be found helpful for holding the frisket in place.

Silk sponge. Corrections in airbrush cannot be made by spraying colors over areas which have been damaged or which are wrong in color. Since airbrush is a transparent medium, the damaged area, or any color below, will only be emphasized by attempts to cover it.

Therefore, carefully and tightly mask around such areas with drafting tape and paper, and sponge them gently with a damp sponge. If the tape and paper mask are fastened tightly enough, no water will get under them to damage surrounding areas, and the same mask may be left in place for the spraying of the new tone. The paper must be entirely dry before the next tone is sprayed.

Newspapers. A quantity of newspapers should be kept at hand for covering areas outside the edge of the frisket mask. The newspaper should be fastened to the edge of the frisket paper with drafting tape.

Brushes. Tempera brushes are often used to supplement airbrush work (see Chapter 13).

Mixing and storing equipment. Mixing and storing equipment for airbrush is similar to the equipment for brush tempera (Chapter 13). A water container like that described in Chapter 13 — or larger, if possible — will be required.

Miscellaneous equipment.

One dozen white blotters

Tools for paint handling: wooden spoons or tongue depressors

Palette, as described in Chapter 13

Cleaning the Airbrush

Like the pen, the airbrush is a means for applying a medium. Also like the pen, it must be kept clean if it is to produce good results. The passages through which paint and air pass are so small that they easily become clogged, and therefore the airbrush should be cleaned after every spray. Dip a clean watercolor brush into clean water and drop the water from the brush into the cup of the airbrush. Then, while pressing the lever of the airbrush, hold your fingers over the nozzle so that the water that is sprayed must pass between your slightly constricted fingers. The back pressure will cause the water to force its way under pressure into the passages of the airbrush and break any crusts that have dried therein. This process should be repeated several times until the brush sprays clean water, smoothly and evenly. Be careful to perform this chore at some distance from your rendering, so that droplets of water cannot damage sprayed areas of your rendering.

Consistency of Paint

Tempera sprayed through an airbrush should be about the consistency of milk. If it is thicker it will clog the brush; if it is thinner, it will spray droplets.

Practice Washes

Before making practice washes, fill the cup of your airbrush with clean water and spray it into the air so that you can watch the spray. By adjusting the nozzle at the tip of the brush with your thumb and forefinger, you can control the width of the spray. Wide sprays are used for large areas, narrow sprays for small areas. The airbrush should be adjusted so that it produces a medium-wide fine spray for general use. Do this several times so that you become familiar with the method for adjusting your brush. If you are using a double-action brush, fill it again with water, press the lever down, and pull it back slightly so that you may see the potential of your brush. Now you are ready to practice with tempera.

Mix a small quantity of any three colors, say dark green, spectrum orange, and spectrum red, in wash dishes. Tack a 20- × 30-inch illustration board or sheet of machine-made watercolor paper on a drawing board. Draw several rectangles, each about 2½ × 5 inches, on the upper portion of the sheet. These rectangles will receive flat washes. Three similar rectangles on the lower portion of the sheet will receive graded washes (Figure 14.1).

Flat Washes

Before beginning, letter the names of the colors under the rectangles. Each color should be mixed with white so that it is about half intensity. If you are using plain (ungummed) frisket paper and rubber cement, lift the brush out of the container and paint over the lines surrounding the first rectangle. The brush strokes should be at least ½ inch wide. When this is slightly dry, press a piece of frisket paper firmly in place on the first rectangle. It should cover the rest of your drawing; if it does not, complete the masking by fastening newspaper with drafting tape to the edges of the frisket paper so that the entire drawing is covered.

After a few moments the rubber cement will be sufficiently dry so that you can cut along the borderlines of the first rectangle with a frisket knife. Press gently but firmly so as not to cut into the paper or illustration board below. When you have cut all four sides with the point of the frisket knife, gently raise a corner of the frisket that you have cut out and lift it slowly from the drawing. Then rub a clean finger gently back and forth over the rubber cement that is left in the masked area until every trace of cement has been removed.

| a. Flat Washes | (1) Dark green | (2) Spectrum orange | (3) Spectrum red |

| b. Graded Washes | (1) Light to dark | (2) Dark to light | (3) Dark to light to dark |

Fig. 14.1 Practice Washes in Airbrush.

If you are using gummed frisket paper, first remove it from its backing by prying one corner loose. Gently pull it free while holding the backing flat on the desk or drawing board. When the backing has been removed, drop the frisket paper in place, gummed side down, over the area to be masked, making sure that no air bubbles form during the process. Then fasten it as tightly as possible by rubbing the frisket paper with a clean triangle, working from the center toward the edge to remove air bubbles. The corners of gummed frisket paper often begin to curl. You should fasten them down with pins or tape; otherwise the entire frisket mask may lift itself from the paper below. The gummed paper is cut from the area to be sprayed in the same manner as described above. Both the gummed and the ungummed papers are sufficiently transparent to allow the cutting lines below to be seen.

Now that the mask is in place, you are ready to spray your first flat wash. Mix a small amount of dark green paint in a wash dish. Make sure that it is of a fairly thin consistency. Fill the cup of the airbrush with the paint, using a large bristle brush. Before applying the paint, press the trigger and watch the paint spray into the air. If it is spraying smoothly, go on to the next step, described below.

If you are right-handed, hold the hose in your left hand about 2 feet from the airbrush, so that the brush may be manipulated without the weight of the hose upon it. Moving your hand constantly from right to left and back again, press the lever of the brush down and back so that it begins to spray. Starting at the top of the first rectangle, move your hand back and forth slowly downward, holding the airbrush about 12 inches away from the paper. Keep the airbrush moving at all times, or dark spots will occur. When you have reached the bottom of the rectangle, if you have moved your hand at an even pace throughout the process, you should have a flat wash. If any areas seem to have been slighted, you may, *after the first wash is dry*, repeat the process, giving the light areas a little more paint.

Perform this entire process, two more times, using a different color for each of the three upper rectangles. Make sure that each rectangle in turn is dry before removing the old mask and applying the new one. Also be careful to clean the airbrush thoroughly before applying each new color.

After you finish, take a good look at the rectangles. If they are even in tone, you have been successful. If they are streaked, perhaps you should practice again. Chances are that they will be quite beautiful, but perhaps one or two will have too much paint on them. Every beginner makes this error. Because the paint is sprayed upon the drawing and the frisket paper mask at the same time, the beginner has no basis for comparison and sprays on much paint before realizing it. The beauty of airbrush work lies in its transparency and delicacy, and the artist should not forget that a relatively thin layer of paint is required. The exact amount of paint to be sprayed will, of course, vary with the value required, and proficiency will develop with practice. However, it is safe to advise that, when you are just beginning, you should spray less rather than more paint upon any given surface. You can always repeat the process and darken a wash, but you cannot lighten it by spraying white over it, because this would change the wash to another color entirely. For the same reason, all the rest of the drawing must be masked while each single area is being sprayed. One cannot, for instance, spray a wall color on a sash area, hoping to cover the wall color when spraying the sash. The wall color will always show through.

Graded Washes

Label the rectangles on the lower half of the sheet, which has been reserved for graded washes, with the proper colors, as you did on the upper half. Mask the first rectangle, as described above. Now you are ready to discover how easily gradations may be made with an airbrush. Using the same left-to-right movement of your hand, begin at the top and move downward with decreasing speed; this way, the wash will be lightest at the top and darkest at the bottom. By gradually decreasing the speed with which you move your hand, you can leave more paint on the lower part than on the upper. While it is slightly more difficult to repair unevenness in a graded wash, this may be done by beginning again at the top of the wash and giving overly light areas of slightly larger amount of paint in order to correct the unevenness. With a small amount of practice, washes can be beautifully graded.

For practice, grade the first color from light at the top to dark at the bottom, the second from dark at the top to light at the bottom, and the third from dark at the top to light in the center to dark at the bottom. Immediately clean the airbrush by running water through it several times, and place it in its hanger. Then remove the frisket paper and look at your practice sheet. You will notice that the washes you have sprayed have a fine, transparent, and atmospheric quality which reminds you of the results obtained with an ink wash. The same lightness and delicacy is present, but the brilliance of the color gives it a new dimension.

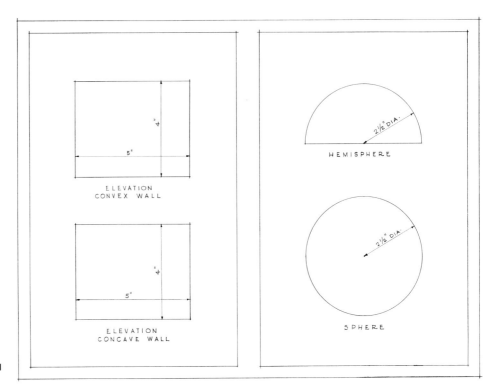

ELEVATION
CONVEX WALL

ELEVATION
CONCAVE WALL

HEMISPHERE

2½" DIA.

SPHERE

2½" DIA.

Fig. 14.2 Rendering Curved or Spherical
Shapes.

Rendering Curved and Spherical Shapes

Using another piece of watercolor paper or illustration board (this one 15 × 20 inches) in a horizontal position, prepare it as follows (see Figure 14.2): Draw a ½-inch border around the outside, and divide the width into two halves with a 1-inch space between. This gives you two rectangles 14 inches high and 9 inches wide. Subdivide the left rectangle into two smaller rectangles, which will be rendered as a concave and a convex wall in elevation. Make this subdivision as follows: Using a scale vertically, mark off 2 inches from the lower border, 4 inches more for the height of the lower wall, 2 inches for the space between the walls, and another 4 inches for the height of the upper wall. That will leave 2 inches for the upper border. Measuring horizontally, mark off 2 inches from the left border to the left edge of the bottom wall, and 5 inches more for its width. The upper wall should be located in the same way.

Divide the right-hand portion of the sheet as follows: At a point 4⅝ inches from the bottom border place a dot; then draw a light horizontal line which will be located on the horizontal axis of a sphere. Repeat the process from the top border. The center of the sphere at the bottom of the sheet and the center of the hemisphere at the top may be located along these axes by placing a dot 4½ inches from the right border on each axis. Using a large compass, draw a circle 5 inches in diameter at the bottom, and a half circle at the top, using the points that you have just located as centers (Figure 14.2).

Mix a quantity of a color, perhaps dark green with Chinese white, for these exercises, and proceed as follows: Assuming that the upper wall in the left-hand portion of the sheet is convex, draw above it, or on a piece of tracing paper placed over it, a plan of the wall which will, of course, be a half circle 2½ inches in diameter. Rest a 45-degree triangle on the horizontal T square and draw the point of tangency on the right side of the half circle. Reverse the 45-degree triangle and find the point of tangency on the opposite side. Assuming that the light is coming from the left, at a 45-degree angle, the highlight of the curve will be at the left point of tangency. The darkest dark will be at the right point of

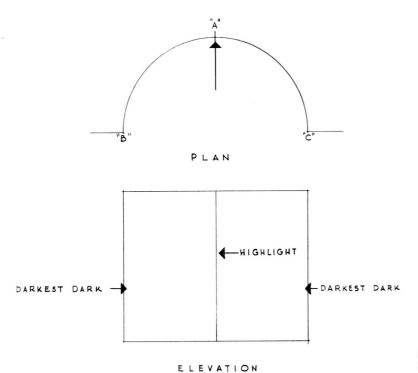

Fig. 14.3*a* Locating Highlight and Darkest Dark on a Concave Wall.

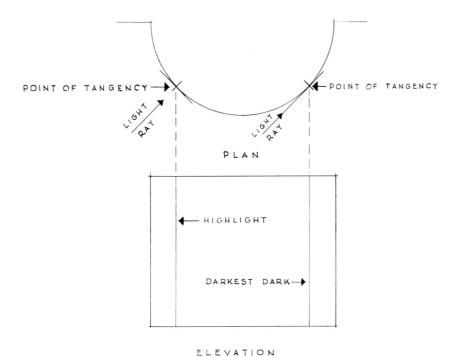

Fig. 14.3*b* Locating Highlight and Darkest Dark on a Convex Wall.

tangency. Locate the highlight and the darkest dark by projecting them vertically upon the top rectangle, then mask as previously described (see Figure 14.3*a* and *b*).

Double-Graded Washes (Convex and Concave Walls)

Turn the board so that its short dimension is toward you, and fill the cup of your airbrush with paint. Begin spraying at the top of the rectangle, moving rather quickly until you are in the neighborhood of the darkest dark. There move the

Fig. 14.4   Elevation: Convex Wall.

Fig. 14.5   Elevation: Concave Wall.

brush more slowly; then proceed downward at an increasingly rapid rate until the highlight area is reached. Then slowly proceed toward the bottom of the rectangle (Figure 14.4). After you finish, look at the gradation and see if it is smooth; if not, repeat the process, being sure to get the darkest dark in its proper place, grading toward the highlight at an accelerated rate.

The concave wall in elevation at the lower portion of the sheet may be rendered by spraying according to a plan similar to that used above, but this time spraying it so that it is concave. If the light source is assumed to be perpendicular to point A in the plan (for the sake of simplicity), the highlight will be at A. The darkest darks will be at the extreme front edges of the wall at A and C, and the values between these points and the highlight will grade gradually.

Again turn the drawing board so that the narrow edge of the board is toward you, and placing the mask in position, fill the cup of your airbrush. Moving it left and right, begin at the top of the rectangle and make a quick gradation from quite dark at the top to a highlight at the previously located point. Then, without interruption, proceed downward at a gradually decreasing rate, so that the lower portion of the rectangle is darkest. Repeat the process until a smooth gradation of sufficient value results (Figure 14.5).

Rendering the Sphere

The sphere at the right side of the paper may be rendered as follows: Fasten a sheet of frisket paper so that it covers the sphere and the surrounding area. Cut an opening in the frisket the exact shape of the sphere. The darkest dark of the sphere, which can be accurately determined by the rules of shades and shadows, will be located on the underside and to the right of the sphere, slightly above the bottom, so that light will seem to be reflected there. Fill the airbrush cup with paint, and with a circular motion proceed to spray a small amount of paint around the circumference of the sphere. Then, with a rocking, curved motion along the lower-right and upper-right portions of the sphere, spray more paint on the lower-right portion of the dark side, and less on the left side and the upper-right side. Moving at an increasingly rapid rate toward the center of the sphere, smooth the wash from the darkest portion to the light face, where the wash will disappear entirely (Figure 14.6).

Spraying the Hemisphere

To spray the hemisphere, proceed as follows: Fasten a sheet of frisket paper over the area, cut the exact shape of the hemisphere, and lift that portion of the frisket

Fig. 14.6 Rendering the Sphere.

Fig. 14.7 Rendering the Hemisphere.

paper which will expose the hemisphere for painting. Assuming that the light is coming from the left and above at 45 degrees, the highlight and the darkest dark can easily be determined in plan, as in Figure 14.3a. Fill the airbrush cup with paint, and with a continuous back-and-forth motion, spray a small amount of paint to the right, decreasing the amount of paint as you do so, so that the right side of the hemisphere receives a small amount of paint. Now repeat the process, starting at the darkest dark, and move to the left until the highlight is reached. This will receive no paint at all. Finally, spray the left side, from dark at the left edge to the white of the paper at the highlight (Figure 14.7).

Textures

The textures described here are for surfaces in sunlight. Generally speaking, the color used for such surfaces is darkened for shade and shadow by adding more of each pigment, particularly of the dark colors of the palette being used. Form is easily obtained by the use of airbrush; textures are not. They are indicated as conventions rather than as realistic imitations of actual textures.

Preparing the Practice Sheet for Textures

Using a 10- × 15-inch piece of white illustration board or machine-made water-color paper, draw a ½-inch border around the outside in pencil. Now lightly draw a 1-inch space inside the border on all four sides. This will produce a rectangle 12 inches wide and 7 inches high. Divide the 12-inch width into six equal parts with ⅛-inch spaces between them. Now turn the board so that the narrow end is toward you, and you will have six rectangles approximately 2 inches high × 6 inches wide. Label these as follows, in the ⅛-inch spaces:

1. Wood siding or clapboards
2. Marble
3. Stucco or concrete
4. Cut stone
5. Brickwork
6. Metal

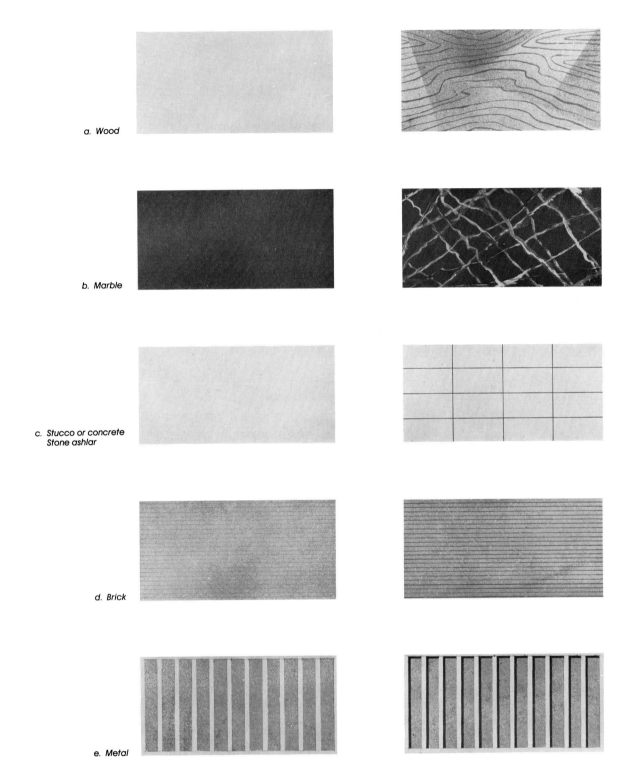

a. Wood

b. Marble

c. Stucco or concrete
Stone ashlar

d. Brick

e. Metal

Fig. 14.8 Textures in Airbrush.

Next draw the various textures in pencil in the rectangles at ¼-inch scale. (Figure 14.8 shows some textures that may be used as guides.)

Natural-finished wood. Mask the entire sheet and cut out the mask in the area for the first rectangle. Make a mixture of yellow ochre, white, and alizarin crimson, and spray a flat or graded base tone over the entire area. Graining may be painted freehand over the base tone with a small pencil brush and fairly thick paint. Light reflections are made by spraying a small amount of white on the background color before the graining is applied, using the edge of a piece of stiff paper as mask.

Marble. To give the effect of marble, spray the background color first. Then place some of the same color and some Chinese white on a paper palette. Mixing these together in various shades, from quite dark to almost white, apply the graining with a small, fairly dry brush.

Stucco or Concrete. Mask the area to be sprayed and cut the frisket paper for this rectangle. The color of this material may vary, but for this exercise make a mixture of white, yellow ochre, alizarin crimson, and cobalt blue. The base tone is usually sufficient to indicate these materials.

Cut Stone. Cut stone or architectural terra-cotta may be indicated by using the same colors as for stucco or concrete. The base tone is sprayed, and then the lines are drawn with a fine brush or ruling pen and straightedge. For light stone use dark joints; for dark terra-cotta use light joints.

Brickwork. After masking, spray the base tone with a light mixture of white, yellow ochre, vermilion, and a small amount of cobalt blue. The joint lines can then be drawn with a 3H pencil, a brush, or a ruling pen, using a slightly darker tone of the same paint.

Metal. Spray the base tone with a color like that described under ''Metal'' in Chapter 13, and rule in the joints with a ruling pen or small brush.

Glass Openings

Glass openings are rendered as described for tempera rendering in Chapter 13. Each small area, such as the blinds, curtains, and furnishings, must be separately masked and sprayed. No attempt should be made to give the glass area a film of paint to simulate glass. If the glass area is large enough so that the spectator can see into it, the only indication that glass is present is made by casting shadows from mullions or overhang upon the glass.

Entourage

Although it is possible to airbrush foliage masses for trees and bushes, it is most usual to paint them directly from a palette, as described for brush tempera in Chapter 13. Grass is usually shown by masking the areas, then spraying graded washes, dark at the front and light at the rear. Then variations in tone, as well as tree and building shadows, are painted over the general spray. Large ground shadows are sprayed, but small shadows are usually painted directly with a brush and thin tempera. Scale figures are best painted directly from the palette, as in brush tempera.

Skies

The airbrush excels in the rendering of skies. They can easily be domed, clouded, or mottled. Before you spray the sky, however, the entire rendering, including the building and ground areas, must be carefully masked so that the sky color will not seep under the masking paper onto any other portion of the drawing. Because the sky sometimes receives a lot of paint, the edges of frisket paper are inclined to lift; therefore, wherever possible it is more satisfactory to

a. Domed sky

b. Domed sky with light clouds

Fig. 14.9 Skies in Airbrush.

use drafting tape and paper for masking around sky areas. In addition to the building and ground areas, the borders of the drawing should also be masked so that the drawing will have sharp edges.

Domed sky. The simplest kind of sky is, of course, the domed sky, which is darkest at the top and lightest at the horizon (see Figure 14.9, sketch *a*). This is sprayed with the same horizontal left-to-right stroke as described for the practice washes. The sky area is usually quite large, and the wash may take quite a lot of time to spray. Great care must be taken to simulate accurately the values predetermined in the value study, since there is no way to judge how the sky will look against the rest of the rendering when it is covered with frisket paper. It is wise to spray less paint rather than more, since a flat, opaque sky is not at all handsome.

Domed sky with clouds. It is quite usual to show light clouds in a domed sky, and this is done by sprinkling bird gravel over the cloud areas, then spraying as for a domed sky (see Figure 14.9, sketch *b*). When the paint is dry, brush the gravel off the sky and into a wastebasket, and you will find clouds that look quite atmospheric. Dark clouds can be made in this medium by narrowing the spray and

Fig. 14.10 Interior Lobby. (Architect: Iglehart & Struhs, Architects. Renderer: Lewis Iglehart, Architect.)

MEDIA: Ink, Prismacolor, pencil, and ink with airbrush on matte Mylar.

passing the airbrush back and forth, moving from the top of the sky down, painting a dark cloud now and again. Spaces should be left between the clouds, which should become smaller toward the horizon (see Plate IX).

Making an Airbrush Rendering

Preparation for an airbrush rendering is similar to that for brush tempera. The perspective line drawing is applied to the sheet or illustration board with a clean

Fig. 14.11 Entrance to Continental Center. (Architect: Swanke Hayden Connell, Ltd. Renderer: Lewis Iglehart, Architect.)

MEDIA: Watercolor and ink with airbrush

pencil line, making certain that the drawing is entirely clean before any work is begun. If any dirt — such as a fingerprint — is present, it will show through the airbrush washes. As mentioned before, the value study and color study are both of the utmost importance and must be relied upon heavily in the course of working with this medium.

You may ask, "What do I render first?" Of course, there are many ways to proceed. The author prefers to render the entire building first, then the sky, and finally the ground, trees and bushes, scale figures, and automobiles. Since in airbrush work only a small portion of the rendering can be seen at a time, one may just as well complete the building before proceeding with the sky and foreground. If any difficulty is going to be encountered, it will probably be in working on the building, and if the difficulty is going to develop into a catastrophe, one has not wasted a lot of time on the foreground and sky. Also, sometimes a client needs the rendering before it is completed; if the building, at least, has been rendered, the presentation is of some value.

Before beginning any airbrush rendering, you should first carefully plan the order of masks and washes so that trouble can be foreseen before it is met (Figure 14.10). Careful planning can result, of course, in less masking than if the problem is attacked in a haphazard way (Figure 14.11).

chapter **15**

Mixed Media and Unique Media

While the purist will use one medium in a rendering, many experienced delineators will combine various media for reasons such as specific techniques required, economy of rendering time, or particular results.

In recent years, the illustrator has been exposed to newly developed products which are compatible with the products and tools of media described in the preceding chapters. Armed with the knowledge of basic delineation, the renderer can experiment with these modern products using the established exercises for grading, shading, color mixing, and rendering.

New developments in the computer graphic, photographic, and reprographic industries have provided the delineator with such products as Mylar drawing film, clear film polymers, Mylar drawing pencils, and Mylar plotter pens and ink.

Felt-Tipped Pens

For occasions when a broader penlike instrument may be required, a number of felt-tip pens are available.

The Flo-Master felt-tip pens are made in several sizes, such as standard, advanced, and king size. Essentially, this type of instrument has a refillable metal fountain-pen-like body. The felt tips come in various sizes and shapes—conical, rectangular, and round. Flo-Master ink is made in eight colors—black, red, blue, green, purple, orange, yellow, and brown—and is sold in metal cans. It dries instantly, is waterproof, and is available either transparent or opaque. Solvent and thinner for Flo-Master inks are also available for use in softening and rejuvenating the felt tips.

While the Flo-Master is a refillable instrument, a number of similar pens which are not refillable are also available. Among these is the Berol magic marker, which comes in red, yellow, orange, black, blue, brown, purple, and green. It is available in standard and king size. Studio sets of magic markers are available in twelve basic and twelve complementary colors. Special sets of twelve assorted warm grays, plus nine cool grays, two blacks, and one white, are also available, as are studio sets. For those who specialize, colors in various sets are available, such as fundamental colors, wood colors, stone and masonry colors, landscape colors. Fine-point studio magic markers are available in twelve colors which have been prematched and color-coordinated to the studio colors. These nonpenetrating watercolors dry instantly.

The Pentel sign-pen marker is nylon-tipped and produces a fine line. It can be used on every kind of paper or board. The water-soluble ink does not show through. It is available in seven colors: black, red, blue, yellow, green, orange, and brown. It is nonrefillable.

Dri-Mark felt-tip markers are waterproof and smearproof, and are available in numerous colors as well as grays.

Pantone color markers are available in various color sets of six pens per set and two types of points, the broad nib (120 colors) and the fine-line nib (48 colors). Also helpful when using Pantone markers is the Pantone "color tint overlay selector" set which comes in a complete range of over 200 solid colors and 58 screen tints, all printed on heavy nonadhesive film.

For delineation on clear film or plastic, a Flo-Master pen will be permanent and cannot be altered or erased. Schwan-Stabilo is recommended for use on plastic film when a workable marker is needed, and it can also be erased. Color selections in sets of fine, medium, and wide nibs are available. The Stabilo markers are most often used for overhead projector (OHP) illustrations.

Illustration Materials

Papers. Newsprint paper pads are the most economical illustration material for felt-tip marker sketches and studies. These pads are available in sizes of 9×12 inches, 12×18 inches, 14×17 inches, 18×24 inches, and 24×36 inches. However, the delineator should be cautioned that bleeding is a serious problem with this type of paper.

Media that may be mixed with markers on newsprint include charcoal, pencil, Conté crayon and pastel. Thus, value studies and color studies with mixed media may be produced before the final rendering is attempted. Other economical papers for felt-tip markers are standard office copy-machine paper, which is available in sheets and on rolls, and colored construction paper, which is available in sizes ranging from 9×12 inches to 24×36 inches, packaged in assorted colors.

For the final rendering the delineator should use a more expensive paper, such as Strathmore marker pads, series 500, which is a 16-pound paper made of 100 percent cotton fiber. This paper provides excellent color saturation without the bleeding or streaking which is a problem with less expensive papers. Strathmore pads are available in sizes 9×14 inches, 11×14 inches, 14×17 inches, and 19×24 inches.

Boards. Illustration boards are excellent for presentation purposes using the felt-tip marker and can be used with mixed media.

Cold-pressed boards (80- to 100-pound) by Superior, Bainbridge, Strathmore, and Whatman provide the best surface texture for markers, pen and ink, watercolor, and pastels. It is advisable to use heavy-weight or double-thickness illustration board. The standard sizes are 20 × 30 inches, 22 × 30 inches, 30 × 40 inches, and 40 × 60 inches.

Tracing paper. Felt-tip markers are economical, easy to use, and require little or no preparation; therefore, they are popular with architects and delineators. Sketches on tracing paper can be easily reproduced with a diazo copy machine, as well as photographically reproduced for presentation or record retention.

The most popular tracing papers used for felt-tip marker drawings are K & E Albanene 100 percent rag paper and Bienfang No. 360. Both are available in pad sizes ranging from 8½ × 11 inches to 18 × 24 inches, and in 20-yard rolls of 30-, 36-, and 42-inch widths. The major advantages of these high-quality tracing papers are their abilities to absorb the marker fluid with no bleeding or streaking and to preserve the brightness of the marker color tones.

A mixed-media technique possible on the two above-mentioned tracing papers would involve use of ink and pencil combined with felt-tip markers.

The delineator should be cautioned when reproducing color drawings with ultra-violet (UV) light to avoid the blue and green areas of the color wheel in the rendering, for the UV light will lighten or wash out these colors. If the renderer works more with the red, violet, and yellow areas of the spectrum, the reproduction quality will be more successful.

Film

Architects and engineers have been using Mylar, which is a trade name for the film produced by the DuPont Company. Mylar is popular because it has a dimensionally stable base. This means it will not change size because of changes in relative humidity and will not yellow with age. Listed below is information about pencils and erasers the renderer may be interested in using when working on Mylar.

A. Acceptable plastic pencil brands
   1. Ruwe No. 205, No. 3S, No. 4S, and No. 5S
   2. Berol Turquoise Filmograph
   3. A. W. Faber-Castell Dri-Line No. 1915
   4. Staedtler Mars Dynagraph
   5. Eberhard Faber Microlar
   6. Koh-I-Noor 1500 M
   7. Dixon-Crucible FTR, FTR Matte
   8. Duro-O-Lite Film King
   9. Pentel
B. Pencil line removal
   1. Rubber, vinyl, or plastic erasers are most desirable.
   2. Abrasive erasers can damage the Mylar tooth.
   3. Electric erasers are to be used with caution. If an electric eraser is used and a shiny area develops which will not take redrawing, the eraser has melted because of friction — thus filling the voids between the tooth of the Mylar surface. A Pink Pearl eraser used over the shiny area will remove the melted plastic eraser from the voids between the tooth of the Mylar, thus restoring the drawing surface of the Mylar.
   4. Vinyl erasers
      a. A. W. Faber-Castell Magic-Rub No. 1954 and No. 1962
      b. A. W. Faber-Castell Filmer No. 1956
      c. Eberhard-Faber Filmer Race Kleen No. 521
      d. Best Tad

e. Koh-I-Nor 286
f. Dur-O-Lite Film King
g. Berol Turquoise
5. Plastic erasers
a. Pelikan PT 20 (9600)
b. Staedler Mars Techniplast
c. Faber-Castell TGK 7092
6. Rubber erasers
a. Eberhard-Faber Pink Pearl No. 100 and No. 101
b. Eberhard-Faber Ruby No. 212
c. A. W. Faber-Castell Parapink No. 7021

Plastic or Mylar pencils work best with Mylar film because they are compatible media, as illustrated in Figure 15.1. Graphite pencils (H, F, and B leads) can

Fig. 15.1 Administration and Chapel Building, Arneytown Veterans' Cemetery. (Architect: Frank C. Marcellino, A.I.A., of Clarke & Rapuano, Inc. Renderer: Frank C. Marcellino, A.I.A.)

MEDIUM: Mar-Dynagraph Mylar pencils on Mylar.

Fig. 15.2 Lobby Renovation. (Architect: Iglehart & Struhs, Architects. Renderer: Lewis Iglehart, Architect.)

MEDIA: Prismacolor pencil and ink with airbrush.

be used, but the delineator should be careful not to smear the image while working with this medium. Ink is an outstanding medium on Mylar and can be applied by pen, brush, and airbrush, as shown in Figure 15.2. Ink can be a problem in that it may flake from the surface of the drawing when dry. For color renderings it is possible to paint or airbrush large areas with Easter-egg or food-coloring dyes mixed with vinegar. This technique will not damage the Mylar surface, and later detailing can be done with plastic pencil, graphite pencil, and ink. The Easter-egg and food-coloring dyes can be removed with Mylar erasers for changes at any time. To remove these dyes from Mylar, the delineator should first moisten the area to be changed with a small amount of water on a Q-tip, and then carefully erase, using a Mylar eraser.

Wash-Off Film and Positive Film

Wash-off film, commonly known as "wash-off Mylar," is basically the same material as noted earlier. However, the image is created by a photographic reproduction made from the illustrator's original. This silver image can then be added to or altered as previously described when working on the original Mylar with ink. To avoid damaging the wash-off Mylar surface when making changes on a specific area of the drawing, it is advisable to mask off the area with tape. Then moisten a Q-tip with household Clorox, and slowly rub the image to be removed. After the image is removed with Clorox, a blotter is used to remove the excess Clorox. With a fresh Q-tip, wash the area with clear water and blot off all excess water. Once the masking tape is removed and the washed area is completely dry, it is possible to continue drawing on the Mylar. The delineator is cautioned that this process will also remove Mylar plastic lead.

A direct positive film is made by means of a positive-to-positive silver-type emulsion. This process does not include the negative intermediate step. The direct positive is a polyester film like Mylar, but it does not have a matte surface to draw on. It is possible to use some felt markers on it, as described earlier, but pencil and ink cannot be used on clear film. It is possible to render on clear film in color by using the following formula:

Mix: ⅓ water plus ⅓ ammonia plus ⅓ alcohol.
Add Rit dye of the colors desired.

The delineator is warned that this solution should be used in a well-ventilated area. The solution may be used for drawing with quill pen, inexpensive water-color brush, ruling pen, or airbrush. Changes are not possible when using this mixture; therefore, it is important that a very careful value and color study be developed before the final rendering is started.

Mylar and clear film are available in the following sizes (given in inches):

8½ × 11
11 × 17
17 × 22
24 × 36
30 × 42
36 × 48

Rolls of 50-yard lengths in 24-inch, 30-inch, 36-inch, and 42-inch widths are also available.

Diazo Process and Film

A discussion of film, film products, and film development must include the availability of the diazo process. The diazo machine, commonly found in the architect's office, is frequently known as the "office blueprint machine." Simply stated, the diazo process is a reproduction method that uses material (paper, film, Mylar, etc.) coated with a light-sensitive (UV) diazo compound. After exposure, the material is processed through ammonia vapor to produce a positive azo dye image. Products are available to produce Mylar film and transparent positive clears, which are called "slicks" or "throwaways."

An importance piece of office equipment is the vacuum frame, which is used in conjunction with the office diazo machine. The vacuum frame is generally used to produce the exposure for overlay registered film. The air is removed from the enclosed compartment which contains the original artwork (or artworks) and the diazo light-sensitive material. Once the air is removed, the resulting vacuum draws all the materials tightly together. At this point the ultraviolet light is used to expose the illustrator's image to the diazo film or paper. After the vacuum-frame exposure is made, the diazo-sensitive film is passed through the ammonia process portion of the diazo print machine and, if the time of exposure is correct, the developed copy is complete.

There are several advantages for the architect or renderer in using this repro-graphic technique, as follows:

1. Less expensive equipment and material are required than in photographic methods.

2. The delineator can produce composites of overlay copies of several pieces of artwork, and the copies can be screened.

3. Copies of cut-and-tape artwork can be produced.

4. The architect achieves time-saving independence of the commercial printer for small projects.

There are, however, also some disadvantages to using an in-house diazo process, as follows:

1. The commercial photographic process is the best method to use when a high-quality final product is needed.

2. Diazo material has a short shelf life.

3. The in-house process is slower and usually lacks the quality control of the professional reproduction house.

4. Additional space is required in the architect's office for equipment, layout, and material storage.

Should the delineator want to make changes on diazo film, it is possible to do so using a Q-tip and isopropyl alcohol. If a high-quality fixed molecular image material is used, then the image must be removed by scratching it off with a single-edged razor blade or matte knife. It is important to take the necessary safety precautions when removing errors from the film.

Computer Graphic Rendering

Computer graphic technology is a subject beyond the scope of this book; however, it is worth mentioning because this electronic technology has made its presence felt in all areas of architectural design, engineering, and planning. The computer, once a luxury of the large corporate architectural firm, is now available in the form of the inexpensive personal computer (PC) system for use in both the home office and the small architectural firm. Computers enable architects to produce plans, elevations, sections, and details. This information can provide secondary benefits for the architect, such as three-dimensional perspectives, program analysis, cost estimating, and management data, just to mention a few. More important, the delineator may present various perspectives on a screen, enabling the architect to choose the view to be illustrated. This approach can save the delineator valuable drawing time by ensuring the architect's approval of the chosen view. A plot of the selected perspective is produced, and the renderer can begin immediately to do the necessary value and color studies.

Computer-Aided Design

Computer-aided design (CAD) is important to understand, for its basic procedures are similar to those used in overlay drawing, as discussed earlier in this chapter. The delineator should approach CAD in the same way as any other medium, that is, from the standpoint of basic tests and exercises, as shown in Figure 15.3a–c. Procedures for a simple line drawing of a building are prepared, and details are then added in various separated segments of the drawing as desired.

For example, a level (overlay) can be used for the building; another level for shades and shadows; another level for entourage; and yet another level for people, cars, and street furniture. Planning a rendering by such a method is known as "preplanning." Preplanning enables the delineator to add, delete, and move objects on a particular level without disturbing other levels of the rendering.

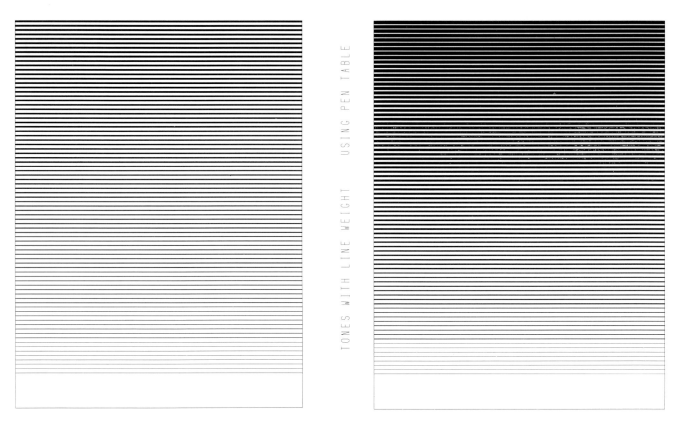

a. and b. Tones with line weight, using pen table.

c. Tones with multidirectional lines.

Fig. 15.3 Computer-Generated Line-Drawing Exercises.

MEDIUM: Ink plot on Mylar.

Fig. 15.4 Computer Rendering; Demonstration Drawing. (Source: California Computer Products, Inc.)

This concept is illustrated in Figure 15.4, which shows the various levels and then the final composited ink-line rendering. The computer adds certain capabilities: speed for changes, recall of drawings, flexibility of many vantage points, and multiple levels for complex composited images. Delineators using CAD have the advantage of a time-saving production tool never before available to their art. When the hardware (equipment) is coupled with compatible software (system program or language), a drawing is digitized on a cathode ray tube (CRT) screen. The delineator may communicate with or command the computer by using a light pen, keyboard, or crosshair cursor from a previously developed menu (legend). Images assembled on the CRT screen are sent to the memory or central processing unit (CPU) to be stored. Once a drawing is stored in the CPU, the renderer may choose to return the drawing to the CRT for review, or the image can be directed to the plotter, where an actual drawing is produced in the designated scale on paper, film Mylar, or tracing paper, using ink, ballpoint pen, felt-tip pen, or electrostatic print, or a combination of these media.

Another effective technique is to combine CAD graphics with a delineated overlay, as illustrated in Figure 15.5a–c. First, the delineator develops a perspective on a CAD or PC graphic system. Once the view to be rendered has been selected, it is plotted and value studies are prepared. The original plotted drawing is then transferred to a watercolor board, as described in Chapter 12, or it is overlaid with tracing or Mylar film for a final rendering in ink or pencil. This overlay is used to show shadows, building materials, sky, and entourage, according to procedures described in earlier chapters; thus, the illustrator can produce a quality drawing without the mechanical appearance of a computer drawing.

Fig. 15.5 (Renderer: Ronald Lubman, R.A.)

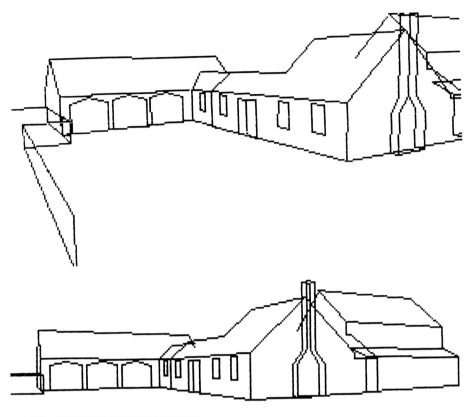

a. and b. Line drawings on personal computer.

c. Ink and pencil overlay of drawing b on tracing paper.

MEDIUM: Felt marker on diazo sepia paper print.

Fig. 15.6 Waiting Room. (Architect: Port Authority of New Jersey and New York. Renderer: David Stiles.)

Fig. 15.7 Arden Heights Wood Park Community Building. (Architect: Frank C. Marcellino, A.I.A., of Clarke & Rapuano, Inc. Renderer: Frank C. Marcellino, A.I.A.)

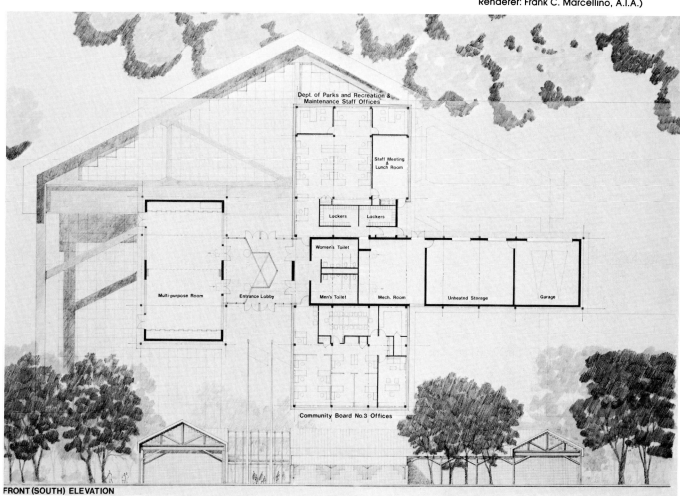

FRONT (SOUTH) ELEVATION

MEDIA: Chartpack and Pantone markers, Berol Prismacolor pencils, and Staedler Mars Lumograph pencils on tracing paper.

MEDIA: Ink and watercolor.

Fig. 15.8 Aerial View of Citicorp Center. (Renderer: Carlos Alvarado. Student project. Instructor: Albert Lorenz.)

The delineator should be aware that these new approaches to drawing are available, but costly. However, with each new development in hardware and software, it is possible to achieve greater technical sophistication as new drawing possibilities unfold. Each year CAD graphic systems are more powerful, less costly, and easier to use, and each year more delineators are using them, but the basic rules of value and color studies, preplanning a rendering, and presentation remain paramount.

The Impact of Computers

Discussions with professional renderers nationwide have revealed some very interesting opinions about the impact of computer technology. Generally, renderers are extremely interested in the computer as a drawing tool. However, most delineators interviewed stated that they earn their living by drawing and feel they lose artistic touch when using a machine. Large rendering studios have undertaken practical analyses of the economic return of using a computer. Such studios can well afford CAD systems, but the studies indicated that the studios would not be compensated for the time required to input the architect's plans and elevations in order to arrive at the desired third-dimension capability. This did not prevent some of these larger studios from investigating the possible future use of CAD graphic systems.

Architectural staff renderers were found to be enthusiastic about in-house computer capabilities. The CAD system enabled them to become directly involved with the project team during the design process. These staff delineators were extremely excited about the latest computer innovations, such as solid modeling, projecting through space, and the multitude of color capabilities. One staff renderer admitted that available computer capabilities by far surpass the stock of any graphic art supply store.

Architects who provide both architectural and rendering services were found to be the most active users of computer-aided design. This group of professionals advised that computer graphic shows, conventions, and user groups had enabled them to become more CAD-efficient, more aware of new products, and more willing to experiment with in-place systems.

chapter 16

Rendering Plans

The rendering of plans presents different problems for the delineator which must be overcome for a successful presentation. The major problem in plan delineation is that the plan is essentially a two-dimensional concept. Perspective, shadows, cloud formations, entourage, and textures are limited tools when creating this type of drawing.

Plans are primarily used by the architect to define the size and shape of space, to describe circulation patterns, and to clarify the major structural elements. The plan is one of the most important drawings used in the presentation of a project to a client. Thus, it would be inappropriate to present a simple line drawing of a plan along with an elaborately delineated perspective or elevations, for these would distract attention from the plan. Therefore, the renderer should clarify and enhance the entire presentation by using the same media and similar techniques for plans as for the other drawings in the presentation.

Ink and Watercolor Plans

Excellent results may be obtained by rendering plot plans in pen and ink and watercolor. Such drawings may be applied to cold-pressed stretches or to illustration boards with the same surface. The plan of the building is first placed upon the sheet in graphite pencil. Each contour is drawn with a clean pencil line, and textures such as those for the terrace and tile are laid out. Trees and other details such as rock outcroppings are first drawn in pencil. Shadows are applied upon the ground as if the plan were cut 4 feet above floor level. The entire grass area is rendered first, with the same number of light washes as there are contours. The first pale wash of this color is applied to the highest contour, then (after the first wash is dry), to the second highest contour, then to the third highest, fourth highest, etc., until the lowest contour has been given one wash.

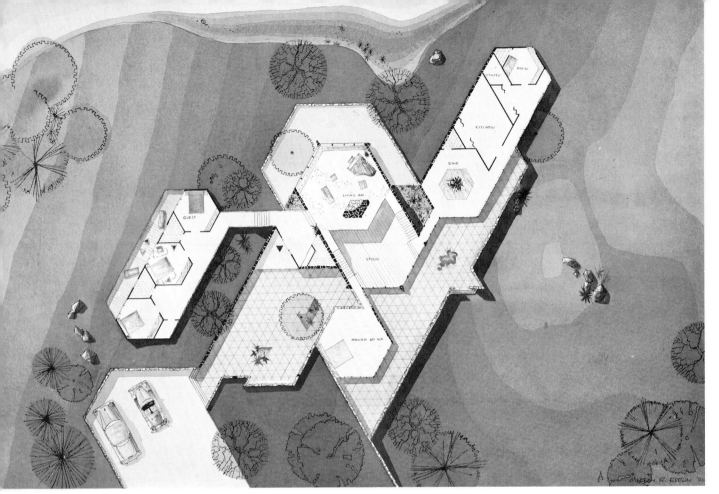

Fig. 16.1   Plan of a Residence. (Renderer:
Milton R. Edelin. Student project.)

Fig. 16.2   Plan of a Residence. (Renderer:
Leslie Feder. Student project.)

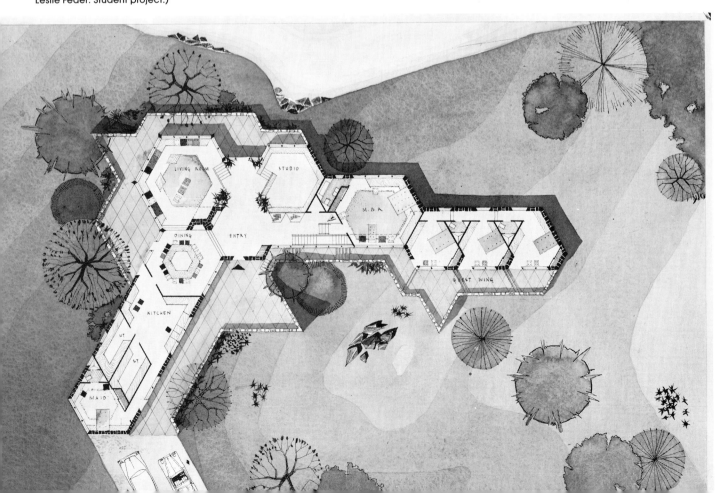

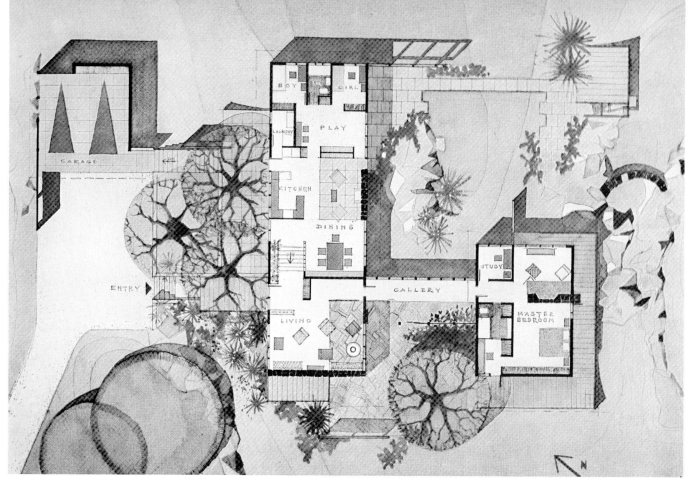

Fig. 16.3 Plan of a Country House. (Renderer: Heino Kart. Student project.)

Fig. 16.4 Plan of Park. (Renderer: Spencer L. George. Student project. Instructor: Robert F. Lindsay.)

MEDIUM: Watercolor.

In this way the rise and fall of the ground is shown. Bodies of water are rendered in the same way, but the lowest contour is given the most washes, the highest contour a single wash.

After the ground area has been rendered, the walls, partitions, and furniture are carefully delineated in waterproof black ink. The shadow of the building is then cast upon the ground in a darker tone of the color used for the ground washes. Shadows cast upon the road areas will, of course, be a darker tone of the road color.

Flagstones and concrete textures are next applied with pen and diluted ink. The trees are rendered with a small brush by working directly from the palette, first giving each wooden member of the tree a flat wash, then modeling each member with a darker wash on the shade side. The foliage of the tree is usually given a transparent wash so that the architecture may be seen through it. Low planting is painted directly from the palette, as are the various plant forms.

Often several kinds of tree indications are used on the same plan. Deciduous trees are given a different indication from conifers, large conifers a different indication from small ones. The structure of trees is sometimes shown and at other times omitted. Variation adds charm and interest to the rendered plan.

As in all rendering, it is all too easy to fall into the realistic color scheme of bright green grass, blue water, etc., but sophisticated color schemes have a much greater appeal to the client. The grass areas, for instance, in Figures 16.1 and 16.2 are blue-green, yellow-green, and gray-green. Water is shown in each, but it is gray-blue rather than brilliant blue. Furniture in Figure 16.1 is blue and grayed orange, while that in Figure 16.2 is brown and black. The terraces in Figure 16.2 are pale blue, those in Figure 16.2 grayed orange. In other words, the colors used in all parts of each rendering are obtained from a previously determined color scheme, as in Chapter 12. These are all mixed together for each hue, the shade desired determining the exact amount of each color that is to be included in the mixture.

The illustrations of rendered plans in Figures 16.3 and 16.4 were executed in various media.

Plate V

Trump Tower
ARCHITECT: Swanke Hayden
Connell Ltd.
RENDERER: Richard Baehr, A.I.A.
MEDIUM: Tempera

Plate VI

Interior of the Circle Theater
ARCHITECT: Dalton, Van Dijk,
Johnson & Partners
RENDERER: Howard Associates, Inc.
MEDIUM: Ink on vellum with color
added to photocopy

Plate VII

Florence Composition
RENDERER: Robert Zaccone, A.I.A.
MEDIUM: Acrylic on watercolor board

Plate VIII

Office Building
ARCHITECT: John Graham and
Company — Architects, Planners,
Engineers
RENDERER: Earl Duff
MEDIUM: Acrylic

Plate IX

Seaport Plaza
ARCHITECT: Swanke Hayden Connell Ltd.
RENDERER: Lewis Iglehart, Architect
MEDIA: Ink and watercolor with airbrush

chapter 17

A Gallery of
Professional Renderings

Fig. 17.1   Nassau Community College
ARCHITECT: The Eggers Groups, P.C., Architects and Planners
RENDERER: Octavio Figueroa   MEDIUM: Pencil

Fig. 17.2 Interior Walkway
Washington University
ARCHITECT: The Eggers Group, P.C.,
Architects and Planners
RENDERER: Octavio Figueroa
MEDIUM: Pencil

Fig. 17.3 Proposed Residence
ARCHITECT AND RENDERER: Robert
Zaccone, A.I. A.
MEDIUM: Colored pencil on tracing paper

Fig. 17.4 Proposed Office Building
ARCHITECT: Berkus-Group Architects
RENDERER: David Haskin
MEDIUM: Pen and ink

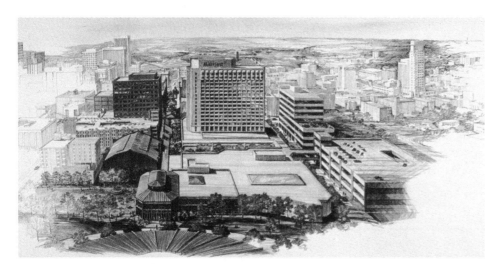

Fig. 17.5 Sixth Street Festival Market-
place
ARCHITECT: Marcellus Wright Cox & Smith,
Architects
RENDERER: Howard Associates, Inc.
MEDIUM: Ink and color on vellum

Fig. 17.6 AT&T Headquarters
ARCHITECT: Johnson/Burgee, Architects
RENDERER: Mark de Nalovy Rozvadovski
MEDIUM: Pen and ink

A Gallery of Professional Renderings / 213

Fig. 17.7 AT&T Headquarters
ARCHITECT: Johnson/Burgee, Architects
RENDERER: Mark de Nalovy Rozvadovski
MEDIUM: Pen and ink

Fig. 17.8 AT&T Headquarters
ARCHITECT: Johnson/Burgee, Architects
RENDERER: Mark de Nolovy Rozvadovski
MEDIUM: Pen and ink

Fig. 17.9 TRW New Headquarters
ARCHITECT: FCL Associates
RENDERER: Howard Associates, Inc.
MEDIUM: Ink on vellum with color added
to photocopy

Fig. 17.10 St. Joseph's Church
ARCHITECT: Berkus-Group Architects
RENDERER: Richard Yaco
MEDIUM: Pen and ink on vellum

Fig. 17.11 Interior of St. Joseph's Church
ARCHITECT: Berkus-Group Architects
RENDERER: Richard Yaco
MEDIUM: Pen and ink on vellum

Fig. 17.12 Demonstration Rendering
COMPLIMENTS: Calcomp Sanders
Computer Co.
MEDIUM: Pen and ink plotted on Mylar

Fig. 17.13 Office Building
ARCHITECT: John Graham and Company,
Architects, Planners, Engineers
RENDERER: Dale Jorgensen
MEDIA: Pen and ink and color wash on
diazo sepia print

Fig. 17.14 New Jersey Bell C.D.C. II
ARCHITECT: The Grad Partnership
RENDERER: Licht/Levine
MEDIA: Computer-generated perspec-
tive, rendered with opaque watercolor
and designer's gouache

Fig. 17.15 Rochester Riverfront
ARCHITECT: Davis Brody
RENDERER: Richard Baehr, A.I.A.
MEDIUM: Tempera

Fig. 17.17   Pacwest Center
ARCHITECT: The Stubbins Associates, Inc.,
Architects; Skidmore, Owings & Merrill,
Associate Architects
OWNER: Russell Development Company,
Inc.
RENDERER: Howard Associates, Inc.
MEDIUM: Casein

Fig. 17.18   Student Project
RENDERER: Anthony Szekalski
MEDIUM: Acrylic on illustration board

Fig. 17.19 Student Project
RENDERER: Anthony Szekakski
MEDIUM: Acrylic on illustration board

Fig. 17.20 Interior Atrium
Trump Tower
ARCHITECT: Swanke Hayden Connell Ltd.
RENDERER: Lewis Iglehart, A.I.A.
MEDIUM: Ink and watercolor with airbrush

Fig. 17.21 Seaport Plaza
ARCHITECT: Swanke Hayden Connell Ltd.
RENDERER: Lewis Iglehart, A.I.A.
MEDIUM: Ink and watercolor with airbrush

Fig. 17.22   South Street Seaport
DESIGN CONSULTANT: Imero Fiorentino,
Associates
RENDERER: David Stiles
MEDIUM: Tempera with blackline on
brown wrapping paper

Fig. 17.23   Office Interior
ARCHITECT: Zeph Ginsberg, Architect
RENDERER: Robert Zaccone, A.I.A.
MEDIA: Pen and ink, watercolor, airbrush,
and colored pencil on Bainbridge board

Fig. 17.24 "V.I.P. Apartment"
Bedroom for the State of Kuwait
ARCHITECT: Swanke Hayden Connell Ltd.
RENDERER: Robert Zaccone, A.I.A.
MEDIA: Pen and ink, airbrush, watercolor,
and colored pencil on Bainbridge board

Fig. 17.25 "V.I.P. Apartment"
Living Room for the State of Kuwait
ARCHITECT: Swanke Hayden Connell Ltd.
RENDERER: Robert Zaccone, A.I.A.
MEDIA: Pen and ink, airbrush, watercolor,
and colored pencil on Bainbridge board

Bibliography

Adams, Maurice, B.: "Architectural Drawing," *Royal Institute of British Architects Transactions,* vol. I, new series, 1885.

Architekturzeichnungen, Verlag Ernst Wasmuth, Berlin, 1912.

Atkin, William Wilson: *Architectural Presentation Techniques,* Van Nostrand Reinhold, New York, 1976.

Birren, Faber: *New Horizons in Color,* Reinhold Publishing Corp., New York, 1955.

————: *The Story of Color: From Ancient Mysticism to Modern Science,* The Crimson Press, Westport, Conn., 1941.

Bishop, A. Thornton: *Composition and Rendering,* John Wiley & Sons, New York, and Chapman & Hall, London, 1933.

Blomfield, Reginald: *Architectural Drawing and Draughtsmen,* Cassell, London, 1912.

Brisebach, August: *Carl Friedrich Schinkel,* Insel-Verlag, Leipzig, 1924.

Burden, Ernest E.: *Architectural Delineation: A Photographic Approach to Presentation,* 2d ed., McGraw-Hill, New York, 1982.

Burford, James: "The Historical Development of Architectural Drawing to the End of the Eighteenth Century," *The Architectural Review,* August 1923.

Capart, Jean: *Egyptian Art,* George Allen & Unwin, London, 1923.

Carter, H., and A. H. Gardiner: "The Tomb of Rameses IV and the Turin Plan of a Royal Tomb," *Journal of Egyptian Archaeology,* vol. IV, 1917.

Cole, Rex Vicat: *Perspective. The Practice and Theory of Perspective as Applied to Pictures, with a Section Dealing with its Application to Architecture,* Lippincott, Philadelphia, 1927.

Color as Seen and Photographed: A Kodak Color Data Handbook, Eastman Kodak, Rochester, N.Y., 1950.

Columbia Encyclopedia, 2d ed., William Bridgewater and Elizabeth J. Sherwood (eds.), Columbia University Press, New York, 1950.

Cullen, Gordon: *Townscape,* Reinhold Publishing Corp., New York, 1964.

Current, William R., and Karen Current: *Green & Green, Architects in the Residential Style,* Amon Carter Museum of Western Art, Fort Worth, 1974.

Davies, N. de Garis: *The Rock Tombs of El Amarna,* Archeological Survey of Egypt, XIII, part I, Egypt Exploration Fund, London, 1903.

de Cerceau, Jacques Androuet: *Les Plus Excellents Bastiments de France*, new ed., A. Levy, Paris, 1868. Original ed., 1607.

The Encyclopedia Britannica, Encyclopedia Britannica, New York, 1933, vol. V, p. 992; vol. XIV, p. 1006; vol. XVII, p. 1006; vol. XXIII, p. 999.

Falda, Giovanni Battista: *Le chiesa di Roma*, Giovanni Giacomo Rossi, Rome, 1680.

Ferriss, Hugh: *Power in Buildings*, Columbia University Press, New York, 1953.

Fouche, Maurice: *Percier et Fontaine, Biographie Critique*, H. Laurens, Paris, 1904.

Frey, Dagobert: *Bramantes St. Peter entwurf und seine apokryphen*, Schroll, Vienna, 1915.

Gandy, Joseph: *Designs for Cottages, Cottage Farms and Other Rural Buildings, Including Entrance Gates and Lodges*, John Harding, London, 1805.

Gardner, Helen: *Art through the Ages*, 3d ed., Harcourt, Brace, New York, 1948.

Giedion, Siegfried: *Space, Time, and Architecture*, Harvard University Press, Cambridge, Mass., 1941. Rev. ed., 1962.

Goodspeed, George S.: *A History of the Babylonians and Assyrians*, C. Scribner's Sons, New York, 1927.

Guptill, Arthur L.: *Color in Sketching and Rendering*, Reinhold Publishing Corp., New York, 1945.

——: *Drawing with Pen and Ink*, Pencil Points Press, New York, 1930.

——: *Sketching and Rendering in Pencil*, Reinhold Publishing Corp., New York, 1944.

Harbeson, John F.: *The Study of Architectural Design*, Pencil Points Press, New York, 1927.

Hunter, Dard: *Papermaking: The History and Technique of an Ancient Craft*, Alfred A. Knopf, New York, 1943.

Jacobson, Egbert: *Basic Color: An Interpretation of the Ostwald Color System*, Paul Theobald, Chicago, 1948.

Jacoby, Helmut: *Architectural Drawings 1968–1976*, Architectural Book Publishing Co., New York, 1977.

——: *New Architectural Drawings*, Frederick A. Praeger, New York, 1969.

Jordan, Henricus: *Forma Urbis Romae, Regionum XIII*, A.M.D., Berlin, A.D. 374.

Kautzky, Theodore: *Painting Trees and Landscapes in Watercolor*, Reinhold Publishing Corp., New York, 1952.

——: *Pencil Broadsides: A Manual of Broad Stroke Technique*, Reinhold Publishing Corp., New York, 1940; Van Nostrand Reinhold, New York, 1960.

——: *Pencil Pictures*, Reinhold Publishing Corp., New York, 1947.

——: *Ways with Watercolor*, Van Nostrand Reinhold, New York, 1963.

Kip, Johannes: *Britannia Illustrata: Views of All the King's Palaces, Several Seats of the Nobility and Gentry; All the Cathedrals of England and Wales*, Overton, London, 1727.

le Pautre, Anthoine: *Les Oeuvres d'Architecture d'Anthoine le Pautre*, Chez Iombert, Paris, 1751. Text by Augustin Charles d'Aviler. (First edition published in 1652, without text.)

Limbach, Russell T.: *American Trees*, Random House, New York, 1942.

Luckiesh, Mathew: *Color and Colors*, D. Van Nostrand, New York, 1938.

Magonigle, Harold Van Buren: *Architectural Rendering in Wash*, Charles Scribner's Sons, New York, 1929.

Malton, James: *An Essay on British Cottage Architecture*, Malton, London, 1804.

Mariani, Valerio: *La Facciata Di San Pietro Secondo Michelangelo*, Fratelli Palombi, Rome, 1943.

Martin, James: *Security, Accuracy, and Privacy in Computer Systems*, Prentice-Hall, Englewood Cliffs, N.J., 1973.

McGoodwin, Henry: *Architectural Shades and Shadows*, Bates & Guild, Boston, for William Helburn, New York, 1922.

Mitchell, William J.: *Computer-Aided Architectural Design*, Petrocelli/Charter, New York, 1977.

Moller, Georg: *Bemerkungen über die aufgefundene originalzeichnung des domes zu Koeln*, Heyer und Leske, Darmstadt, Germany, 1818.

Munsell, Albert H.: *A Color Notation: A Measured Color System, Based on the Three Qualities, Hue, Value, and Chroma, with Illustrative Models, Charts, and a Course of Study Arranged for Teachers*, 2d ed., George H. Ellis, Boston, 1907.

——: *A Grammar of Color*, Strathmore Paper Co., Mittineague, Mass., 1921.

——: *On a Scale of Color-Values and a New Photometer*, 1904.

Munsell Book of Color, Munsell Color Co., Baltimore, Md.

Munsell, Joel: *Chronology of the Origin and Progress of Paper and Paper Making,* 5th ed., J. Munsell, Albany, 1876.

Nevins, Deborah, and Robert A. M. Stern: *The Architect's Eye, American Architectural Drawings from 1799–1978,* Pantheon Books, New York, 1979.

Norwich, John Julius (general ed.): *Great Architecture of the World,* Mitchell Beazley Publishers, London, 1974.

Piranesi, Giovanni Battista: *Roman Architecture, Sculpture and Ornament,* selected examples from Piranesi's monumental work first published in Rome, 1756, E. & F. N. Spon, London, 1900.

Pitz, Henry C.: *Drawing Trees,* Watson Guptill Publications, New York, 1956.

Sargent, Walter: *The Enjoyment and Use of Color,* Charles Scribner's Sons, New York, 1923.

Schmitz, Hermann: *Baumeisterzeichnungen des 17 and 18 jahrhunderts,* Ehemals Staatliche Museen Berlin, Kunstbibliothek, Berlin, 1937.

Stitt, Fred A.: *Systems Drafting,* McGraw-Hill, New York, 1980.

Szabo, Marc: *Drawing File for Architects, Illustrators and Designers,* Van Nostrand Reinhold, New York, 1976.

"Techniques and Tradition in British Architecture," *Country Life,* vol. 81, Jan. 16, 1937.

Uffizi: *Disegni di Architettura (Civile e Militaire)* (Texte) 1885, Presso I, Principali Lebrai, Rome, 1885. Reprinted: Florence, 1904.

Vincent, Jean Anne: *History of Art: A Survey of Painting, Sculpture and Architecture in the Western World,* Barnes & Noble, New York, 1955.

Viollet-le-Duc, Eugene Emmanuel: *Compositions et Dessins de Viollet-le-Duc,* Libraire Centrale d'Architecture, Paris, 1884.

Ware, William R.: *The American Vignola, Part I, The Five Orders,* 5th ed., International Text Book Company, Scranton, Pa., 1904.

Index

About the Author

ALBERT O. HALSE was a professor of architecture at Columbia University and a registered practicing architect specializing in interior design and color consultation. His degrees included Bachelor of Architecture, Master of Arts, and Doctor of Education from New York University.

For many years the author taught architectural rendering at the School of Architecture, Columbia University. During this time, he was able to further develop, test, and prove the theories and principles set forth in this book.

Dr. Halse was a member of the American Institute of Architects and the American Institute of Interior Designers and held various offices in local chapters of these organizations.

Spencer L. George, a practicing architect with a Master of Architecture degree from Cranbrook Academy of Art, and **Helen A. Halse,** office administrator for Albert O. Halse, were the editors for this new edition. They have made every effort to continue Dr. Halse's work in the spirit he intended, with an emphasis on preparing users to draw confidently with any medium.